Advance praise for *Mommy Guilt:*

"I was hooked from the very first page! The writing style of *Mommy Guilt* is so friendly and supportive that I felt like I was sitting in my kitchen having a chat with the authors over a cup of tea. Practical and positive exercises, stories, and tested wisdom will help any mother find relief from the too-common experience of feeling guilty."

—Jeanne Elium, coauthor, *Raising a Son* and *Raising a Daughter*

"A practical how-to guide for every mom, no matter her mothering experience. Using simple, helpful tips and easy-to-understand examples of healthy behavior, *Mommy Guilt* helps us moms find and stay on the narrow path of happy moms raising happy children. *Mommy Guilt* is a 'must read' for every mom."

—Susan Lavelle, Founder of Moxie Moms

"Do you get Biff and Muffy holiday letters? I do. You know, the ones where your friends brag about their perfect children. Well, they used to bother me, but not anymore. *Mommy Guilt* helped me put it all in perspective. My kid is happy and healthy. OK, so maybe he isn't perfect. (But then, I'll bet Biff and Muffy aren't either.)"

—Susan E. Dubuque, author, *A Parent's Survival Guide to Childhood Depression* and mother of not-so-perfect, but still wonderful, son Nicholas

MOMMY GUILT

Learn to Worry Less,
Focus on What Matters Most,
and Raise Happier Kids

Julie Bort • Aviva Pflock • Devra Renner

AMACOM AMERICAN MANAGEMENT ASSOCIATION
NEW YORK • ATLANTA • BRUSSELS • CHICAGO • MEXICO CITY • SAN FRANCISCO
SHANGHAI • TOKYO • TORONTO • WASHINGTON, D.C.

Special discounts on bulk quantities of AMACOM books are available to corporations, professional associations, and other organizations. For details, contact Special Sales Department, AMACOM, a division of American Management Association, 1601 Broadway, New York, NY 10019. Tel.: 212-903-8316. Fax: 212-903-8083. Web site: www.amacombooks.org

This publication is designed to provide accurate and authoritative information in regard to the subject matter covered. It is sold with the understanding that the publisher is not engaged in rendering legal, accounting, or other professional service. If legal advice or other expert assistance is required, the services of a competent professional person should be sought.

Library of Congress Cataloging-in-Publication Data

Bort, Julie, 1964–
    Mommy guilt : learn to worry less, focus on what matters most, and raise happier kids / Julie Bort, Aviva Pflock, Devra Renner.
        p.   cm.
    Includes bibliographical references and index.
    ISBN 0-8144-0870-2 (pbk.)
    1. Mothers—United States—Psychology.   2. Motherhood—United States.
3. Parenting—United States.   4. Guilt.   I. Pflock, Aviva, 1967–   II.
Renner, Devra, 1967–   III. Title.

HQ759.B657   2005
306.874'3—dc22

                                                            2004030415

Printing number

10   9   8   7   6   5   4   3   2   1

CONTENTS

Foreword   vii

PART 1
Introducing Mommy Guilt

CHAPTER 1. The Pitter-Patter of Guilt   3

CHAPTER 2. When You Hear the Mommy Guilt—Tune It In or Turn It Off   8

CHAPTER 3. The Seven Principles of the Mommy Guilt-Free Philosophy   17

CHAPTER 4. Giving Birth to Guilt   30

CHAPTER 5. The Start of First-Rate Parenting Choices (and the End of Second-Rate Childhood Habits)   45

PART 2
The Stuff of Guilt

CHAPTER 6. Yippee! Guilt-Free Yelling   59

CHAPTER 7. Throttle Down That Tone of Voice, Part Two   67

CHAPTER 8. A Parent's Guide to (Almost) Stress-Free Housekeeping   77

CHAPTER 9. The Guilty Gourmet   87

CHAPTER 10. Family Time and the Fair-Fight Zone   97

CHAPTER 11. Husbands as Fathers   111

CHAPTER 12. School-Yard Guilt   120

CHAPTER 13. Working on Guilt   136

CHAPTER 14. A Sporting Case of Mommy Guilt—Or Stage
    Fright?   147

CHAPTER 15. An Extraordinary Guilt   157

CHAPTER 16. Other Issues That Cause Guilt   163

PART 3
Building on Your Mommy Guilt-Free Foundation

CHAPTER 17. Time: How to Make It, How to Take It, and How
    to Spend It, Guilt-Free   179

CHAPTER 18. Guilt-Free Pleasure—Time with Your Spouse   191

PART 4
Appendices

APPENDIX A. Take the *Mommy Guilt* Survey   201

APPENDIX B. Food Staples to Keep in Your House   233

APPENDIX C. Emergency Guilt-Relief Guide   237

APPENDIX D. Additional Reading   247

Index   249

About the Authors   257

FOREWORD

Books on parenting are a dime a dozen, but this book is worth its weight in gold! As a mom, grandma, and child therapist, I agree with the authors that it is important to stop stressing and start enjoying your children. Whether you are a mom or a dad, when you read this book you will feel like you have found wise counselors and advocates who are willing to sit down with you and work through the distressing everyday issues that nearly all families must deal with. In this book, though, the authors often ask you to do more than just sit down with them; you will be asked to pick up a pen and paper, think about your current strengths and strategies, and then decide how you may need to change some of them. This is a book you can read cover-to-cover at one sitting or conquer a chapter a week. You may also choose to dive sporadically into sections as issues arise. This book, as well as the authors' Web site, will offer you the tools and resources you need at that very moment to deal with your struggles. Wherever you start, you will find that you can refer to this book again and again as you and your children grow.

The Seven Principles of the Mommy Guilt-Free Philosophy make sense psychologically and developmentally for moms and their families and have potential for application beyond parenting. It was refreshing and encouraging to see the principles of the Mommy Guilt-Free Philosophy applied to the relationship between spouses and, by extension, I expect they could be fruitfully applied to relationships with coworkers as well. The authors introduce each of the principles clearly, and then illustrate them again and again by weaving them through issues as diverse as the supermarket tantrum, choosing a school for your child, setting priorities, and guilt-free yelling. Throughout the book, I found the issues had the ring of truth. They sounded like reports from real life and, in fact, they were drawn from the lives of more than 1,300 families, including the authors' own. Especially useful was the way the authors paired scenarios of situations gone amok with a second, more informed, guilt-freeing strategy. So true-to-life were the authors' chosen scenarios that I recognized some of them from my own mommy days—when I held a young child perched on my left hip or disentangled one hanging from my legs—and my kids will tell you that I did better in the kitchen than in the cleaning-up department.

A great strength of this book is that the authors give you language—actual words to say to a child or spouse. Many times, as parents, we actually do understand the concepts, we just don't know how to communicate these concepts to a 2-year-old, or a 5-year-old, or 12-year-old (or in the case of a spouse, to a 27- or 39-year-old!). My recommendation is that when you find an issue that speaks to you right now, you read the recommendations, maybe even write down some of the responses on a 3-by-5-inch card, and tape it to your fridge. It takes practice to get it right, to claim those words as yours and speak them to your family with the love and authority you intend.

Another strength of this book is that the examples, exercises, and charts are presented across the childhood years so you can hone in on the expectations for children the age of your own, and you can see what the expectations and possibilities are for children in the next age/stage. It is clear that the authors understand that kids grow and change, and the more subtle message is that parents must grow and change as well. The discussion of discipline in the chapter "Yippee! Guilt-Free Yelling" is a good example of the need to keep both child and parent development in mind. The authors are right that there is no better way to keep good behavior going than to offer contingent, positive reinforcement; no better way to stop bad behavior than swift, clear negative reinforcement; while to encourage a shift or to encourage your child to try a new behavior, a reward/bribe can be very effective (note their cautions about bribes—how true!). To make this system of behavior modification work best, you need to include your kids as they grow in decisions about what rewards and punishments are age appropriate. At one memorable point in our daughter's life, I looked over the jumble of stuff that was in her room and offered her a quarter to clean it all up. She too, looked over the room and finally said, "No. You just better keep the money, Mom, and clean it yourself!" If I had had this book on the shelf, I could have consulted it and learned how to update my offer on what it would take to get the room clean! The best reward for a child is often time spent with a parent—better than money any day. After my young grandson had done a really fine job of picking up, I asked, "So what would you like as a reward?" He looked up with a sparkle in his eye and said, "Let's go in the kitchen and crack eggs!" And so we did.

I especially enjoyed the chapters "The Guilty Gourmet" and "Family Time and the Fair-Fight Zone." Our family loves to cook and eat, and looking back over the years it is clear that some of our best times together have been in the kitchen. Both as a parent and as a therapist, I have always believed that kids and food go together. Kids can help to buy and prepare food, share in the eating and even in the cleanup (although in our family, if you helped cook the meal, the other guys had to clean up). There are, of course, unexpected adventures and problems to be solved if you let kids into the kitchen. Our son, aged three, sitting on the kitchen counter so he could watch me make a cake, helpfully added a full cup of water to the cake batter when I turned to reach for the cake pan. A little more flour and sugar and another egg and we were ready for the oven (again!). Our son was delighted with his cake and so were we. Food buying and prep also offer great opportunities for real-world application of math (doubling or halving a recipe), science (how many grams of fat in that can of tuna?), and for modeling the generosity of spirit when gifts of food are prepared for family and friends.

I confess that I really enjoyed reading this book. As a clinician I am impressed with the breadth of issues raised: stressors specific to solo parenting, working moms, stay-at-home moms, parenting the child with special needs. As a parent and grandparent, I enjoyed puzzling over my choices on each of the quizzes, zipping down the exercises, remembering my children's skills and abilities at different ages, walking through competing scenarios, even mentally checking my kitchen cupboard for the recommended stockpile of foods for making quick, low-hassle meals. I believe that you will enjoy it too!

Margaret S. Steward, Ph.D.
Professor Emeritus, Department of Psychiatry
School of Medicine
University of California, Davis

Margaret S. Steward is Professor Emeritus in the Department of Psychiatry and a past Associate Dean of the School of Medicine at the University of California, Davis. She holds a diplomate in clinical psychology from the American Board of Professional Psychology. Her research, teaching, and clinical interests focus on children and families at risk as a result of prematurity, illness, divorce, and/ or abuse. As an academic administrator, she focused on recruitment, hiring, and career development of junior faculty. She has served as a consultant and conducted workshops on children's cognitive, linguistic, and emotional development in the United States and Australia for staff from health, mental health, social welfare, and law enforcement agencies and from the judiciary. For the past decade she has been a reviewer for the Australian Research Council.

MOMMY GUILT

➤ PART 1 ◄

Introducing Mommy Guilt

CHAPTER 1

THE PITTER-PATTER OF GUILT

Before the twinkle in your eye becomes an expansion in your waist, the conversation about starting a family takes place. It usually goes something like this:

"What do you think about a baby?"

"I think we're ready."

"Good. Me, too."

Well, maybe you say a little more, toss around the financial responsibilities, check out the space in the house, or generate a quick list of names. One thing you rarely do is have a conversation like this one:

"Do you want to be the cook, maid, nanny, chauffeur, chaperone, or banker? I think I'd like to be the disciplinarian and dictator."

"All right, I'll take on nanny, cook, and chauffeur, but we have to toss a coin for the others."

Of course, if the initial conversation covered all these important details, far fewer people would have children. These details, though, often leave mothers frustrated, stressed, guilty, depressed, and experiencing moments when they wonder why anyone would ever embark on the journey through parenthood.

With this book, we hope to show you how parenting can become more enjoyable for you, your spouse, and your children. Remember, we didn't say *fun,* we said *enjoyable.* As parents ourselves, with more than 450,000 hours of parenting to our credit (and counting!), we are living with the daily struggles that all moms face and have retained valuable knowledge certain to be of value to you, too.

Within these pages, we discuss some of the most common parenting issues—the kind that can easily max out your guilt-o-meter. We offer practical solutions while introducing an underlying philosophy: We believe that your parenting experience is a gift, and you have the right to open it up and enjoy it! We hope you will read Chapter 1 through Chapter 3 in their entirety. Beyond that, the book may be used as a reference guide when situations arise that stress you out and you need to bring sanity back into your family life. Not every area in this book will apply to every reader, since we know that most moms are basically happy and experience countless hours of enjoyment with their children. Yet, we all appreciate a bit of support and encouragement to help us over the rough spots in taking care of our families. And that's why we are here. Think of us as a brigade of your closest friends sitting on your bookshelf, ready 24/7 to help you with life's most stressful parenting issues—from the mundane "how to get dinner on the table every night" to the major leaguer "how to stop yelling."

Whether you choose to read our book from cover to cover and absorb the entire Mommy Guilt-Free Philosophy in one trip (minus the guilt!) or you pick our book up whenever the need presents itself, we hope you will feel encouraged that you are not imagining your Mommy Guilt. Indeed, according to 1,306 parents surveyed for this book, 95 percent said they experience feelings of guilt associated with parenting. It is our goal to help you overcome the pangs—and sometimes downright agony—of Mommy Guilt. When you come to terms with your Mommy Guilt and learn techniques to reduce it, you are free to focus on the truly important things in life, like the happiness of your family and the joy it brings you. In turn, you will experience increased feelings of confidence in how you handle your roles as parent and spouse.

The tiny bundle of guilt

And so it begins, before we go through pregnancy, labor, and delivery or adoption. We feel a deluge of emotions. For some couples, this is enough to leave them wondering, "What did we just do?" For others, it is such a wonderful experience that they can hardly wait to do it all over again. In any case, everyone goes home to start the honeymoon with a new, expanded family. This honeymoon tends to be much shorter than the one immediately following a wedding. After a few days and nights without sleep, everyone feels like crying. (If this is the stage you are at now, don't panic! Babies won't know, or care, if you feel like you don't know what you are doing! They also don't care if you go without a shower until 3 P.M., leave dirty dishes in the sink, or forget to brush your teeth.)

For most folks, the decision to have a child wasn't made to impress everyone by being a supermom or superdad. If yours was, it's time to remove that cape and change your plans. Most of us decide to be parents so we can have a special bond with a little life that we will love, take care of, and nurture into a wonderful human being.

So if your baby is two weeks, two years, or twelve years old, forget all those things that are going wrong and spend a few minutes just holding your "baby." Ignore the telephone, delay the dishes, or turn off the TV. Close your eyes and enjoy the moment. Now, take the memory of how good you feel after that brief time of pure happiness with your child and put it in an easily accessible place in your brain. This is what we mean by enjoyable. The moment won't make all the other things go away, but it will remind you why you wanted to have children and of what's really important.

What's next? We can tell you that some things will have to slide, and we will help you to prioritize. We will continue to remind you that almost all moms experience this feeling of Mommy Guilt—and once Mommy Guilt gets a hold of you, it may never let go, even through years of parenting or raising multiple children. In fact, a whopping 70 percent of *Mommy Guilt* survey respondents said that parenting more than one child caused them to feel an increase in guilt. For 40 percent, their guilt has increased as their children grow older.

The joy we derive from being parents is in our ability to appreciate and embrace the existence of our children. Enjoying children is not the same as spoiling them—nor will too much enjoyment of parental life spoil a parent. Indeed, the temperament of a household is strongly influenced by the emotions and attitude of the mother. When a mother is happy, the whole family is happier.

Spoil a parent, now there's an interesting concept. As you are reading this book, you are probably feeling anything but spoiled. We want you to take a few steps toward the idea of spoiling yourself. The first step is to escape guilt. In order to escape guilt, we must first know what guilt is. Guilt is defined by Webster as: "1. The state of one who, by violation of law, has made himself liable to or deserving of punishment; culpability. 2. Wrongdoing; wickedness. See synonyms under *sin*."[1] When did it become against the law to not feed your child enough vegetables? Leave clothes in the dryer overnight? Fall asleep in the middle of the day? Serve a bowl of cereal for dinner or (gasp!) dessert before dinner? Is it really a sin to work outside your home? Alter your career path to stay home with your children? Not have a home-cooked dinner on the table at 6 P.M. every evening? You see, according to Webster, we are not doing anything criminal that defines us as guilty. We're giving you a "Get Out of Guilt Free" card to help you have more fun with your family—and your family to have more fun with you. The next step is to actually release any guilt or unpleasant feelings associated with the idea.

I remember the precise time when the guilt-free epiphany came to me. I had just given birth to my first son. It's funny about that new mother period—everyone imagines it will be this tranquil time of oohing and aahing over the new baby, the blissful homecoming as you sweep back into your former life with this little bundle of joy. Hardly anyone talks about the fights. There are fights. In talking with other moms and dads, it is a truth that people somehow don't readily remember, or maybe they just don't readily admit to it. But I remember and admit it.

So here we are with our lovely little baby. I am making every attempt to nurse this child, with limited success, and my husband is being a jerk about it. (At least, in my hormonally infused brain, I felt like he was being a jerk, thinking to myself, "Hell, it's not like he could do this at all, but there he is accusing me of doing it wrong!") I became so upset about it that I couldn't nurse at all. And being unable to nurse made me even more upset. What a lovely cyclical event it turned into! Lucky for me, my oldest and dearest friend had come out to help that week. She and I had a long talk about how bottles were invented to feed children, not to make moms feel inadequate or guilty. She reminded me that my husband probably felt a bit helpless and his jerky-ness was a result.

After that talk, I nursed as best as I could and began to supplement feedings as necessary. While I wanted to be the perfect mom, I realized then that the definition of perfection is fluid from person to person and situation to situation. I promised myself that I would simply focus on being a fantastic parent within the scope of my own abilities.

Supermom meets super guilt

Lucky is the mom who dispenses with guilt when it first hits in those new baby days. Lucky and rare. While we are fairly certain that generations of moms have suffered from some form of Mommy Guilt, it appears that today's moms have been harder hit. Is it the supermom image, the feminist movement, technology, or geographically dispersed family units? It is a combination of these things and more. We cannot deny that we are expected to do it all. The question is, who has that expectation? The answer is us. Women have fought a long, hard battle toward equality with men. We can fill the same jobs and do the same work, but it isn't complete quid pro quo. Men are unable to get pregnant, they don't give birth, and although they have nipples, they cannot nurse. We enter motherhood through the things that only we can do and quickly expand our self-images. We see ourselves as supermoms—doing it all ourselves forever, with grace and style!

Does a father suffer from feelings of guilt? Don't assume, ask him. Some men have instances where their behavior falls so short of their own standards that they feel guilty about it. But walk into a room full of dads, ask them if they feel guilty over parenting and they'll probably give you a funny look and wonder what you are talking about. Men are twice as likely to experience absolutely no feelings of guilt associated with parenting than women are, according to our *Mommy Guilt* survey. Of course, these men suffer negative feelings about parenting, but "frustration" and "anger" are often the names given to those feelings.

So why do moms name it guilt? Could it be that we also feel frustrated, upset, and angry but, since we are mothers, think we should not feel these emotions? Could it be that we worry that a carefree attitude is somehow equivalent to not caring enough? The authors of this book believe this reason to be at the root of it. We believe Mommy Guilt is actually all of our negative emotions about parenting lumped together, including feelings of inadequacy.

Anger, frustration, confusion, denial, and desperation are all actually part of the process of parenting. Parents who tell you that they never have these feelings are not coming clean. Parenting will test everything you've got, and in solving problems and helping your child through new experiences (wonderful and painful), you will know a kind of joy that simply can't be found any other way. Parenting will be the ultimate life-experience gift you give to yourself. It is better than graduating high school or finishing a two-year quilting project, better than bungee jumping, and better than being promoted at work. But, to get there, you've got to turn your energies toward enjoying the experience of being a parent. You've got to empower yourself by recognizing that you're going to experience those negative feelings, and by ditching the guilt associated with them. Once this happens, you can give yourself permission to feel good about what you are doing as a parent. And your kids will feel good about having you as *their* parent!

As mentioned earlier, if we thought about all that parenting entails before we signed up for the experience, our population would be in decline. Since we can't return the children, we must figure out how to enjoy being parents. Enjoyment of the parenting process is not only an obtainable goal, it is one that, once reached, will promote happier children. We are going to show you how to cast aside the Mommy Guilt and turn, instead, to the Mommy Guilt-Free Philosophy.

Note

1. *Webster Comprehensive Dictionary*, (Chicago: J.G. Ferguson Publishing Company, 1986), vol. 1, p. 562.

CHAPTER 2

WHEN YOU HEAR THE MOMMY GUILT—TUNE IT IN OR TURN IT OFF

Okay, it's not that easy to simply stop feeling guilty. People don't have emotional on/off switches. When the guilt strikes, there you are, and Webster be damned.

Guilt is a valid emotion, just as all emotions are. The trick is to identify whether it is a help or a hindrance. Guilt helps when it motivates people to stop harmful behaviors and spurs them on to make amends. Guilt hinders when it leads to a negative outlook that spurs nothing but more negative feelings and behaviors. (See the quiz at the end of the chapter called What's Your Guilt Station Identification?)

I should start by saying I was abused and abandoned. Now that I'm married and have a ten-month-old, I watch everything I do and say to her to make sure I do not make any of the mistakes with her that my parents made with me. For example, it was my five-year wedding anniversary and my husband's aunt had agreed to baby-sit. My daughter had a slight cold so I cancelled everything. I knew I would not be able to have fun knowing that my daughter was not feeling well. My husband's aunt picked her up anyway and my husband insisted we go out as planned. The guilt I felt the whole night ruined our evening. My husband was very unhappy. He blamed me and we ended up in a big fight.

I immediately went to his aunt's house to get my daughter and since then I will not leave her for anything. I feel so guilty because when I just walk out the door to another room she cries and it hurts me to see her upset. What I'm saying is, good or bad, our own experience is what we learn from. I realize I am doing too much to make sure my daughter never feels unloved or abandoned. I am afraid she will become so dependant on me it will be impossible for her to start school and feel confident in herself.

Leaving a very ill infant? No way! However, leaving a baby with the sniffles in the care of a loving aunt for an evening is definitely feasible. But wait! Do you hear that? The guilt is so loud it is practically deafening. This woman's Mommy Guilt is screaming at her to overcompensate and stay with that child every minute. She can't even move from one room to another without the child. In this situation, the healthy response is to tell that guilt to pipe down.

Still, guilt might not always be shouting out an inappropriate message. Tuning in to what your guilt is trying to tell you is one way to figure out when you need to listen to it and when you need to change emotional channels.

We were new to the neighborhood and had spent the past week trapped inside while we unpacked and got organized. The kids had an understandable case of cabin fever but I found myself on edge and snapping at them anyway. I wasn't proud of my behavior but didn't see an alternative. A neighbor stopped by and invited my kids to her house to meet her children. When I saw them all outside playing together, I realized that if I had stopped yelling long enough to listen to my own emotions, I would have suggested they go outside hours before.

And the guilty beat goes on

Most parents find guilt to be one of those familiar tunes that gets stuck in their heads, playing over and over again. While the particular areas parents feel the most guilt over depend on the ages of their children, once an area makes it to the list, it stays there, according to the *Mommy Guilt* survey. See if you can recognize any of these golden oldies:

Parents of infants

- ➤ The No. 1 area of Mommy Guilt is finding enough time, after taking care of the children, to spend with their spouses.
- ➤ No. 2 is keeping up with housework and/or living in a messy house.

Parents of toddlers

> ➤ The No. 1 area is keeping up with housework and/or living in a messy house.
> ➤ No. 2 is finding enough time, after taking care of the children, to spend with their spouses.
> ➤ No. 3 is yelling at the kids.

Parents of preschoolers

> ➤ No. 1 is yelling at the kids.
> ➤ No. 2 is keeping up with housework and/or living in a messy house.
> ➤ No. 3 is finding enough time, after taking care of the children, to spend with their spouses.
> ➤ No. 4 is the kids' eating habits (allowing junk food for dinner, lack of veggies in the diet, eating too much or not enough, and so forth).
> ➤ No. 5 is fairly dividing time, chores, financial resources, and so forth among the children.

Parents of school-age kids

> ➤ No. 1 is yelling at the kids.
> ➤ No. 2 is keeping up with housework and/or living in a messy house.
> ➤ No. 3 is finding enough time, after taking care of the children, to spend with their spouses.
> ➤ No. 4 is fairly dividing time, chores, financial resources, and so forth among their children.
> ➤ No. 5 is the kids' eating habits.

Parents of middle-school-age kids

> ➤ No. 1 is keeping up with housework and/or living in a messy house.
> ➤ No. 2 is yelling at the kids.
> ➤ No. 3 is finding enough time, after taking care of the children, to spend with their spouses.
> ➤ No. 4 is the kids' eating habits.
> ➤ No. 5 is fairly dividing time, chores, financial resources, and so forth among their children.
> ➤ No. 6 is school-related issues (selecting a school, selecting academic programs, finding time to volunteer, and so forth).
> ➤ No. 7 is spending too much time at work. (Note: when adjusting the results to screen out respondents who did not work full-time outside the house, this area ranked No. 1 for all age groups.)

As these results from the survey show, the number of "all-guilt, all-the-time" broadcasting stations increases over time. The results also show that moms feel guilty about decisions they make every day.

The next time you find yourself listening to one of these guilt tunes, try paying closer attention to the lyrics of the song. Maybe you need to turn it up, so you can hear its message more clearly. Maybe the station is so loud about so many things that you simply need to turn it down—or off. If you need to change the station, do it! Your family will benefit from your selective listening. In Chapter 3, we'll teach you how to hum a new tune: the Mommy Guilt-Free Philosophy.

EXERCISE: What's Your Guilt Station Identification?

Achieving balance between a positive outlook and healthy skepticism can be a matter of turning a few knobs. The following quiz is designed to help you analyze the emotional radio stations you tend to listen to. Read the scenarios listed below and select the choice that best represents your likely reaction.

1. Your child wakes up in the morning complaining of pain in her ankle. After physically examining the ankle and not finding any obvious problems, your first thoughts are:
   A. Doesn't look serious. I'll distract her with some homemade pancakes.
   B. Dang! Maybe she fractured it. I better make a doctor's appointment and get it checked out right away.
   C. She's probably angling for some extra attention. I'll snuggle her for a few extra minutes.
   D. I'll give her some children's pain reliever and then see if the pain returns.

2. You get a call from a local nonprofit group—a pet project of someone you know and one you feel is a worthy cause. The members want you to join their board and help them with a major event. You:
   A. Are excited about a cool, new challenge but tell them you will only do it if they assemble a team to help you out.
   B. Accept the assignment but warily, doing it only because you know it is important to your friend.

    C. Wonder why they are calling you out of the blue and are suspicious as to why they have no one internally to lead the project.

    D. Feel flattered to be particularly sought out and tell them you are glad to help.

3. You tell a friend about a great sports/arts/childcare program that you plan to enroll your child in. She calls the next day and leaves a message to let you know she has enrolled her child in the last available spot. Your initial reaction is to:

    A. Do nothing, and not return her call until you can stop feeling upset over the situation.

    B. Call her back and tell her, "Great choice!" and continue looking for another program that you are equally excited about.

    C. Tell her, "That's great," the next time you speak with her but feel secretly disappointed.

    D. Call to tell her, "We considered doing that program, but then I decided to spend that time together with my children, rather than drop them off to be in the care of strangers."

4. For your child's next birthday, your child wants to have the party at the local park. You respond in one of the following ways:

    A. "Great idea!" and since the venue is free, decide to spend the saved money on a surprise gift: pony rides!

    B. "Great idea!" and immediately get to work on the invite list.

    C. Tell the child that because the season offers unpredictable weather, it would be better to have the party at home.

    D. Seek out another park with a great play area, a veranda, and just in case a big storm hits that morning, develop a backup plan of converting to an indoor party at the last minute.

5. Your child is invited to a birthday party for a friend your child really likes. The parents extend the invitation to you, too, saying they want to get to know the parents of their child's friends better. You like your child's friend, but from your interactions with the parents so far, you have found them to be bores. You:

    A. Go to the event. You are polite but slightly standoffish so that the parents don't mistake your attendance for an outreach of friendship.

    B. Go, taking your spouse or a friend with you. By bringing your own company, you can graciously accept their invitation and not be stuck bored to tears.

    C. Accept on your child's behalf, but as politely as possible, refuse the invitation extended to you.

    D. Go, deciding if they want to be friends with you, you should make a better effort to like them.

6. When your children come home with problems, you can always be counted on to:

    A. Make them feel better by giving them a life lesson on how much worse it could be.

    B. Provide a friendly shoulder and commiserate—being their "company" for their misery.

    C. Try your hardest to find ways to fix their problem, and if not, you can distract them so that they forget about it.

    D. Listen and act supportive, until they are calm and can figure out ways to fix their problem on their own.

7. Reading the local newspaper makes you feel:

    A. Anxious about all the terrible things that go on in the world and resolved to be a person who behaves in a positive way and doesn't contribute to the world's problems.

    B. Charged up and ready to go out and make a difference in the world.

    C. You don't typically read the newspaper because you find it pointlessly depressing.

    D. Worried that you or your children could wind up victims.

8. When thinking about last week, how many of your days would you describe as bad?

    A. Three or four

    B. Five or six

    C. None

    D. One or two

Scoring chart for box 2.1

Key. Use the chart below to find your points to each question. Add up your points to find your score.

Question No.	A	B	C	D
1	1	4	2	3
2	2	3	4	1

Question No.	A	B	C	D
3	2	1	3	4
4	1	2	4	3
5	4	2	3	1
6	3	4	1	2
7	2	1	3	4
8	3	4	1	2

Your score:

8–12 points = overly optimistic. You better turn up the volume! Your cheery outlook is your strength, but it needs to be balanced by a realistic view of the world. If not, your insistence on seeing only the bright side can wear you out and lead to frequent feelings of disappointment. As a parent, you may be aiming for perfection in your child's life. You might believe that all will be well if you work harder at things and make sure your children's problems are quickly solved (often by you). You may feel that it is your role to not let your children dwell on the downside. You may try hard to distract your children from negative feelings. While you pride yourself on how much you accomplish each day, you may rarely have time to experience some of the quiet joys of parenthood. Have faith in your child's abilities! Rather than dashing in to patch up their latest scrape, try holding yourself back and watching how your children right themselves on their own.

13–20 points = practical, but optimistic. You are willing to change stations but prefer your favorite style of music. This serves you well. You are open to new ideas and new people, yet you don't feel obligated to take on more than you think you can handle. When disappointment occurs, you allow for it, but don't let it derail you. As a parent, you try to maintain a sense of balance. You are understanding when your children face problems, and may be too quick to intervene on their behalf, but you realize that they are going to have good days and bad days like the rest of us. You view your job as helping them experience more good than bad. You make a conscious effort to enjoy your children and try to enjoy the "administrative" part of the job as well, saying yes only to projects that excite you. You may have a tendency to "wing it" a little too often, having faith that things will turn out well (and the positive attitude to enjoy lemonade when life hands you lemons). You may benefit from doing a little more planning. Creating backup plans may seem like more work at first, but after discovering that your Plan B frequently saves the day, you'll see the extra effort pay off.

21–27 points = practical, but pessimistic. You like the tunes and don't want to change stations. Your great strength is your ability to accurately size up a situation, take action, and, for the most part, control a situation so that it provides an acceptable, if not always positive, outcome. You make plans and backup plans and are rarely at a loss for options if things go awry—which you swear they nearly always do. When it comes to parenting, as with life, you would rather be safe than sorry. You may have experienced some trauma in your life that gives you a fear of suffering through events that you cannot control. Still, you are open to new ideas and often end up enjoying yourself, even if you entered into a project, party, or commitment with less than overflowing enthusiasm. You may be able to enhance your parenting experience by allowing more spontaneity into it, even if you must "schedule" it, such as letting the kids choose the Sunday family activity. Try not to look at other people's plans as being more work for you—for example, "They want a picnic. Great! Now *I* have to go to the store and make the sandwiches. If I had planned this, I would be ready."

28–32 points = overly pessimistic. Turn down the volume. You may have had rough patches in your childhood or suffered through other traumatic events that shaped your wary opinion of the world. Your strength is your survivor instinct, a sense that no matter what life throws at you, you will find a way to cope. However, you may spend too much time simply hovering in the "coping zone" instead of crossing into full-on enjoyment of your life. You may be aware that your decisions are sometimes (maybe frequently) based on fear rather than a more balanced viewpoint. Or, you may genuinely believe that you either lack ability or luck. While you may frequently be gregarious and fun loving, you may also feel cautious and tense in new situations. You may feel like people are always judging you. As a parent, you may suffer big bouts of Mommy Guilt if you feel you've failed your children, even on minor matters. You may lean toward overprotection of them, as well. Be careful. A pessimistic outlook can fuel Mommy Guilt and hamper your ability to enjoy parenting—or any other portion of your life. This may lead to feeling depressed. However, it is possible to learn to change your tune and readjust your attitude toward a more positive beat. You can learn to enjoy your parenting experience more by taking time to marvel at your children—how emotionally strong they are, and how resilient.

CHAPTER 3

THE SEVEN PRINCIPLES OF THE MOMMY GUILT-FREE PHILOSOPHY

1. You must be willing to let some things go.

2. Parenting is not a competitive sport.

3. Look toward the future and at the big picture. Don't become overly hung up on the here and now.

4. Learn when and how to live in the moment.

5. Get used to saying yes more often and being able to defend your no.

6. Laugh a lot, especially with your children.

7. Make sure you set aside specific time to have fun as a family.

Mommy Guilt-Free Principle No. 1: You must be willing to let some things go

By the time we bring home the bacon and fry it, clean the kitchen, put away the laundry, help with homework, and tuck the kids in, all most moms want to do is crawl into bed alone—to sleep. Let's not forget the bills, the miscellaneous phone calls, and, of course, our spouses. Reading about it is exhausting, let alone accomplishing all these things. Human beings were not designed to toil endlessly. We eventually become sloppy, inefficient, and grouchy. This is why so many of us continually make that oh-so-short leap from asking our children to do something to screaming at them—and from screaming to a nice bout of Mommy Guilt. Yelling at the children was named by two-thirds of *Mommy Guilt* survey respondents as a prime cause of regular guilt. While no mother is so perfect that the occasional tantrum never bubbles up from her soul, it is possible to eliminate yelling entirely as a parenting style. (We'll show you how in Part 2 of this book.)

The point is this, if you found out you had only six months to live, would you spend that time defending the carpet against spots? Or would you spend it enjoying your family? We'd guess that filling your ears with the laughter of your children would take priority over rubbing out the chocolate stain on the living room carpet. Still, a serious illness notwithstanding, it is never easy to prioritize things in your life. After all, if everything on your list weren't already some kind of a priority, it wouldn't be on your list at all. Yet mastering the "letting go of things" is one of your premier tools for fending off Mommy Guilt. This alone can lead to such contentment with your parenting work that you float through most of your days feeling like you're doing a darn good job of it all. Furthermore, this feeling can be used as a flotation device to help everyone in the family feel happier and more content.

The safety guidepost: You, as a parent, are responsible for providing a safe environment in which your child can grow and learn. The first trick to helping you prioritize is to ask yourself this question, "In what way would my child be harmed if I didn't do this task right now?" If the answer is, "not much to not at all," you've just found an item that can easily be dropped down the priority totem pole.

Housework is an ideal example. In our survey for this book, 59 percent of participants reported feelings of guilt over not keeping up with the housework. So please, hear this: It is perfectly fine for your house to look as though children live in it—even when guests drop by! You can have toys on the floor, snacks out on the table, and shoes piled up near the door. While we've got loads of advice in Chapter 8 on managing specific housework tasks, for the sake of example, let's use a housework situation to show Mommy Guilt-Free Principle No. 1 by applying the safety guidepost.

Mommy Guilt Scenario for Mommy Guilt-Free Principle No. 1

You had completed a top-to-bottom cleaning of your family room last night at 11 P.M. It is now 7 A.M. and in the twenty minutes your children have been awake, they have had ample time to destroy the room. You see empty food containers on the couch. They dragged a box of toys up from the basement and dumped its contents on the floor, thereby mixing up several box games. Something brown and sticky is now on the wall (chocolate?). To complicate matters, friends are dropping by later this morning, something that both you and your children have been looking forward to for days. You had planned on using your time in the morning to prepare a picnic meal.

You flash back to the night before, where you braved exhaustion and gave up your precious before-bed reading time to clean this room. The kids hardly notice you standing there, ears red from anger, as they watch cartoons and walk past the mess to grab more food from the pantry. You begin to yell. You tell the oldest to start picking up the toys, making sure to put all the pieces back in the proper boxes. He starts to comply but then pouts and stops. Meanwhile, you begin frantically scrubbing the wall and picking up food containers, grumbling as you clean. The kids have moved from passive resistance to arguing with each other and with you. They soon dissolve into tears. By the time your friends arrive, you are frazzled—and although you feel justified—you also feel guilty for yelling.

Mommy Guilt-Free Scenario for Mommy Guilt-Free Principle No. 1

After dinner the night before, you reminded your kids that in order to have a play date, they promised to help you clean the family room. You had given each kid an age-appropriate task, along with clear instructions on what they were to do. While the group of you cleaned the room, you excitedly talked about how much fun the play date would be. Your kids, of course, got constantly distracted from their tasks and needed your help to complete their cleaning portions, but eventually they succeeded and you could do your task, which was vacuuming. In the end, they felt proud of their work on the room and you heaped praise upon them.

All of that pride was forgotten by the morning. It is now 7 A.M. and in the twenty minutes your children have been awake, they had ample time to destroy the room. You see empty food containers on the couch. They dumped the toy box on the floor, and you spot a brown sticky mess on the wall. You are tempted to start yelling, but instead you take three deep breaths to calm yourself. You make a mental note that next time they have a play date, you will set up activities for them to do that will help ease them through their excited waiting period without digressing into destruction. You would like to make the kids clean the room again, so that your friends don't think you live like pigs, but you realize that yesterday's cleaning took a couple hours and if you don't get cracking on making the food, you won't have a picnic to take with you.

So, you ask yourself, is any of this mess harmful? The brown goo seems iffy so you prioritize cleaning that yourself. The toys are not in the walking path, so you opt to let them stay out—they'll be dumped out as soon as your guests arrive anyway. Your kids can certainly carry their own food containers to the dishwasher. Game plan in place, you step in front of the TV, turn it off and say, "Remember how nice this room looked last night? We need to fix some things before our guests arrive."

Mommy Guilt-Free Principle No. 2: Parenting is not a competitive sport

Ever been to the park with your child where all the parents are sitting around telling each other when their kids started walking, or talking, or when they got their first tooth? Who cares! It is human nature to want to compare and contrast but please don't do it over the developmental milestones of your kids. If your child is happy and your healthcare professional has no concerns, great! Take the pressure off yourself and, more important, off your children to hit their developmental milestones as if they were speed trials. Faster truly isn't better. Take it from us. Among our seven offspring, we've covered the full developmental spectrum: eleven-month-old first talker and eighteen-month-old first talker, nine-month-old walker and nineteen-month-old walker, first teeth at four months and first teeth at thirteen months. You know what? All seven kids are perfectly healthy, happy, productive members of society.

It doesn't serve your family's best interest to use peer pressure on your children in an attempt to speed their development only to try and ban peer pressure from their lives when they are teenagers. If you have any concerns about your child's development, ask your pediatrician, your child's teacher, or consider using one of the resources for developmental screenings referred to in the Emergency Guilt-Relief Guide (Appendix C). Should your child be a late bloomer, we ask you to consider these astute words of wisdom, "So what?" No matter the circumstance, from genius to struggling, your children will find their own developmental pace and you will go along with them.

Now, we don't want to minimize the emotional difficulties of parenting a child who needs extra assistance—in fact, we've dedicated Chapter 15 to the topic. But all children—in fact, all people—face difficulties. All of us have areas where we excel and where we don't. Unless you're parenting an alien child from the planet Orak, there will always be a kid in this world who has achieved something faster, higher, bigger, whatever—and one who hasn't. As one wise Mommy Guilt survey respondent put it: *Don't get caught up in the competition with other parents. That's really the source of so much guilt. Enjoy your children and let them be individuals. Childhood shouldn't be a race. The parent who succeeds is the one who has the happy child.*

The germination of this area of parental angst begins during the baby months when parents are eagerly looking for any sign that they've given birth to the next Einstein. Walking is the classic example. Let us clue you in on a little secret—walking is not the sign of intelligence you're searching for. A child who walks at nine months isn't necessarily a genius or a future Olympian. Let's take a look at Mommy Guilt-Free Principle No. 2, from both the Mommy Guilt and Mommy Guilt-Free perspectives, using walking as our example.

Mommy Guilt Scenario for Mommy Guilt-Free Principle No. 2

When Ariel joins her weekly mom-and-baby play group, she sees her friend's daughter, Gabby, taking her first toddling steps. Gabby is only ten months old and her mother is jubilantly showing off Gabby's newfound ability. The child is enjoying the extra attention, but soon grows tired of the effort of walking and begins to cling to her mother. Ariel sets her own thirteen-month-old daughter, Annie, on her feet. She holds onto Annie's hands and walks with her. Annie is the only baby in the group not taking steps on her own. The other mothers offer advice—one insists that the exerciser she bought is why her baby started so young, another says that she spent extra time in the evenings helping her baby learn to walk. Ariel feels guilty—she's been using a playpen, not an exerciser, and she hasn't particularly made an effort to help "train" Annie to walk. At home the next few nights, Ariel works with her daughter, spending extra time holding her up and walking her around, and starts to feel disappointed that Annie plops right down on her diapered bottom whenever Ariel isn't walking with her. She begins poring over her catalog of parenting books looking for more advice. The next week, she skips play group, not able to face all those other mothers.

Mommy Guilt-Free Scenario for Mommy Guilt-Free Principle No. 2

When Ariel joins her weekly mom-and-baby play group, she sees her friend's daughter, Gabby, taking her first toddling steps. She joins the crowd oohing and aahing over Gabby's accomplishment. She places Annie next to her favorite set of blocks and finds a cozy spot to chat with the mothers. The mothers are all gushing over the magical moments of watching their children take their first steps. Annie hasn't been particularly interested in walking, being an expert crawler, and after Ariel contributes that one tidbit to the conversation, she has nothing left to say, so she goes and sits by Annie and helps her build a giant block tower. That night, she calls her sister—who has four kids and is a stockpile of common sense. Ariel wants to make sure she shouldn't be worried that Annie isn't walking yet. Her sister tells her what all the parenting books say—some kids walk young, some don't. "If you've mentioned it to your pediatrician and she isn't worried, you shouldn't be either," the sister says. Relieved, Ariel spends the evening on the floor with Annie, playing favorite games like peek-a-boo and thinking that soon, after Annie starts walking, these quiet play sessions on the carpet will be only memories.

Mommy Guilt-Free Principle No. 3: Look toward the future and at the big picture

All of us want the best for our children—to raise smart, kind-hearted, responsible, loving, hardworking, independent people. These are all desirable attributes, so how do we go about instilling them in our children? We do it by keeping these goals in front of us through years of parenting decisions and by the choices we make in modeling these behaviors ourselves. Simply put, when we look at the future and the big picture, we see this type of person. In every critical situation, ask yourself one question, "How will this help guide my child to become that wonderful person I foresee?"

By the same token, looking toward the future also includes you. Parenting is just one of your roles. As your kids grow older, parenting will vary in its consumption of your time. By having a passion in your life beyond your family, you can increase the joy in your life, generally, and your enjoyment of your family, specifically. We are programmed these days to think the reverse—that time spent away from the family is stolen time and that we should feel guilty about it. But you are your children's primary role model. It is important for kids to learn that to live happy lives, people must regularly engage in activities that make them happy. Children must see that different people enjoy doing different things. If they see you doing something you love, they too are likely to find a beloved hobby, sport, or other activity for themselves. You've now demonstrated for your family an ethic that life is to be enjoyed. Let's illustrate Mommy Guilt-Free Principle No. 3 with a story that is easy for busy parents to relate to.

Mommy Guilt-Free Scenario for Mommy Guilt-Free Principle No. 3

Renee was driving in her car on a sunny Saturday in April, heading out of town to pick up some hard-to-find art supplies. Knowing her plans would not be fun for her family, she arranged for her five-year-old to go hiking with his pals, her nine-year-old to go fossil exploring with his pals, and gave her husband the nod to go mountain biking with his buddies. She was happily driving along, when WHAM! Guilt struck. "I should be spending this great day with my kids," she thought. Busy schedules had prevented them from having a family day in weeks. Although tempted to turn back, she didn't, and at the end of the day, learned Mommy Guilt-Free Principle No. 3 in a big way.

The five-year-old came home bursting with tales from the trail, the nine-year-old had a pocket full of fossils, the dad was happily showing off a few new mountain-biking scrapes, and she had made a great start on a new painting. Sure, the family missed a nice Saturday together, but when she applied Mommy Guilt-Free Principle No. 3 and looked toward the future and at the big picture, she realized that her long-term goal wasn't just a high-volume parenting experience. Renee wanted a family that values its companionship. To do that, each needed to spend time apart from the family. Plus, she wanted her children to explore and discover themselves as individuals. So, she also had to apply Mommy Guilt-Free Principle No. 1, and be willing to let go of some togetherness time, even during a period where there's been precious little of it.

Mommy Guilt-Free Principle No. 4: Learn when and how to live in the moment, rather than in the future

Contrary to being the opposite of Mommy Guilt-Free Principle No. 3, this is its complement. This is the concept of being able to put aside all those to-do lists, stop rushing about, and just be with your children in the here and now. This is especially important because kids themselves live in the here and now. Only adults sit and plan their next meal while eating the current one. Our children give us the best reason in the world to forget about all the grown-up complications in our lives and enjoy the moment. Get on that swing at the park! Go ride the mini-train with your toddler! Play a board game with your preteen. Once you have "let go" of the unfolded laundry waiting in the dryer, you can fully engage with your child while playing. The clothes will wait quietly and patiently until you can get to them.

The here-and-now principle is one that takes a lot of practice. How often do you find yourself thinking about your to-do list while taking care of the kids' needs (getting them dressed, spooning out their macaroni-and-cheese)? Or maybe you find yourself trying to finish a task while your child is chasing you around the house, screaming for you, or attached to your leg? Chances are good that if you just give your child your total, complete, undivided attention—that is, stop what you're doing for ten minutes—he will move onto his separate pursuits with a smile on his face. Our kids really don't need us for very long in a day or, sadly, for very many years in a lifetime. Put down the telephone, laundry, or car keys and play for a little while. Listen to their favorite story for the hundredth time. Play with their dolls. Sing them a song. We guarantee that you will both feel better in a few minutes, your child will stop whining, you will get everything done, and, quite probably, you will have engaged in the best moment of your entire day.

Mommy Guilt Scenario for Mommy Guilt-Free Principle No. 4

As you tuck your son in at night, you feel like you haven't seen him in days. You get a bout of guilt and wish you could bail out of your obligations to have more time to spend with your kids. But that's not possible. You already rearranged your schedule to drive your son to a series of rehearsals for a play he is in. You barely had time to cook and eat dinner before he went to bed. And during dinner, you had to quiz him on spelling words, just to fit it in. Next week, you'll have a hoard of life's duties to make up for, and he's got more rehearsals—no way to schedule some time together then. You sigh—fun time will just have to wait. You wish these moments when you feel like he's slipping away didn't occur so frequently. You feel so guilty over them—are you just clinging? After all, as he grows you'll have to get used to not being the center of his life. You shake your head, and then sadly head back to the kitchen to finish cleaning up.

Mommy Guilt-Free Scenario for Mommy Guilt-Free Principle No. 4

You pick your son up from rehearsal for a play he's in, but before you turn the car on, you turn around and look at him in the backseat. You know if you ask him how it went, he'll answer "fine," but you want to share this experience with him a little more than that. You carefully select a phrase that you know will get him talking, "So, tell me about the scene you blocked today." He gives you the lowdown on that and the rest of the rehearsal as you begin to drive home. While you are driving, you leave the radio off and continue to talk. Later that evening, you call him into the kitchen to set the table. He hums a song from the play and he shows you the dance steps while putting the place mats out. He teaches you the song's words while you make the salad. You sing it together over dinner, sometimes getting up from the table to dance the steps, and then you use the tune to help him cram for his spelling test. The dinner table is the only time he's had to study. As you tuck him into bed that night, you sing one of his spelling words and make him laugh. You've got a new inside joke, you think, as you head off to the kitchen, not even minding that you still have to clean it.

Mommy Guilt-Free Principle No. 5: Get used to saying yes more often and being able to defend your no

As parents, we will have lots of opportunity for confrontation with our kids. We must learn to choose our battles carefully or we will spend the majority of our time fighting. Go back to the second part of Mommy Guilt-Free Principle No. 1: safety should always be your primary concern. This is an easy-to-follow family "rule-making" guidepost since you will automatically be consistent with it, because you will never suddenly bend on a safety rule and allow your child to ride without a seat belt, for instance. Think seriously before responding no to anything else, or creating some new overarching rule for behavior. Is there some reason why they can't leave the table before eating all their vegetables? Can they be allowed to wear mismatched socks to school? If they would rather have the pogo stick than the scooter you came to the store to buy, does it really matter? Your time together as a family will be much more relaxed if everyone makes an effort to give a yes answer first.

I began testing myself, my husband, and my older children. If "no" was given as an answer, the person who said it (self included) had to come up with why. Oftentimes, we found that "no" was being used as a quick, yet unjustified, answer. When everyone saw how ridiculous this was, we all began to say yes more often. We also began to enjoy each other's company more.

Some say that if you give your kids everything they want you will create spoiled kids. The Mommy Guilt-Free Philosophy maintains it's really not that easy to spoil your kids. We believe that if a child grows up in a world full of "yes," confidence will be the outcome. Spoiling—or teaching your children to be selfish—has as much to do with the methods you choose for discipline as it does with allowing your children to occasionally eat popsicles for an after-school snack. If you find that after a day full of hearing "yes," your children throw a tantrum at the one item to which you have said "no," then you may need to institute some sort of system where they earn more instances of hearing yes. But, even when that happens (as it will), you need not automatically revert back to a knee-jerk "no" person. We discuss discipline options in greater detail in Chapter 6.

Mommy Guilt Scenario for Mommy Guilt-Free Principle No. 5

The neighborhood kids are over at your house, so you have six children running around. They decide that they want to do a craft project and ask you if they can paint for a while. You look at the children, envision the mess, and tell them no—you want them to go outside and play in the yard. They balk, beg to know why, start arguing. You remind them that no means no, that you don't have to give them a reason, and after a few more minutes of arguing with you, the friends get sent home, the children get sent to their rooms, and you are alone, still angry. You are also feeling guilty because, now that you've stopped to think about it, you really wouldn't have minded if they used up some of the old art supplies you have stacked in baskets in the playroom.

Mommy Guilt-Free Scenario for Mommy Guilt-Free Principle No. 5

---

*The neighborhood kids are over at your house, so you've got six chil-
dren running around. They decide that they want to do a craft project
and ask you if they can paint for a while. You look at the children,
envision the mess, and make them promise to clean up. They pinky
swear to you that they will, but you are still worried about the mess.
So, you tell them they must work on the driveway. You help them
drag the baskets of art supplies from the playroom to the garage, help
them get set up with rocks on their papers to thwart the wind, and
you sit in the sun overlooking the driveway, reading your book while
they work. No arguing, controlled mess, and, best of all, a few uninterrupted moments of reading time for you.*

Mommy Guilt-Free Principle No. 6: Laugh a lot, especially with your children

A sense of humor is not necessarily something we are born with, and for
some parents, you may have to work at being funny and seeing the world
as fun. Tell jokes with your kids. Laugh with them as they begin their
awkward attempts at telling jokes. Even if you are feeling stressed out, you
can break your own tension and theirs simply by smiling at them, even
when you don't feel like smiling.

Be careful to learn the difference between laughing with them and
laughing at them. Laughing when a child misspeaks a word and makes a
funny sound, for instance, can be wonderful as long as the child is laughing, too. However, if your child doesn't think it's funny, then it's not funny.
Children can't tolerate being teased very well and sometimes parents have
a hard time stopping once they begin teasing because they miss the cues
that tell them the fun is over. While we must teach our children how to
find the funny side of life, we have to show them good-natured humor that
doesn't make another person the butt of the joke. If you don't find yourself
laughing daily with your kids (though most *Mommy Guilt* survey participants report that they do), you need to work on Mommy Guilt-Free Principle No. 6 a bit. Many arguments can be squelched with laughter.

---

*My girls were in a lot of trouble for fighting with each other for about
the hundredth time that day. I had them both sitting on the couch*

listening to my lecture about sisters getting along when my toddler son decided to join us. As I finished talking with one of the girls, he chimed in by repeating what I had just said. It sounded so funny out of his little two-year-old mouth that we all began to laugh. The horror of the moment was over and we all learned something from him. Laughter can be a great cure for a wide variety of ailments.

Let's see how you can put Mommy Guilt-Free Principle No. 6 to work for you with this common morning-time story:

Mommy Guilt Scenario for Mommy Guilt-Free Principle No. 6

Your kids wake up late on a school day. The older one is yelling at the younger one for taking too long in the bathroom. You are rushing about the house making lunches and shouting out how many more minutes until they miss the bus. The kids are wasting even more time arguing with each other over everything—they are tense over being late and are taking it out on each other. You sigh, intervene for the hundredth time, and are ready to collapse from stress by the time they leave. It's only 8 A.M.

Mommy Guilt-Free Scenario for Mommy Guilt-Free Principle No. 6

Your kids wake up late for school. They are tense over being late and are taking it out on each other by arguing. When the older one starts yelling at the younger one for having music on, you start belting out a Broadway show tune that glorifies the joys of music. You ham it up. It becomes a game. They try stumping you with words and you keep coming up with songs, while you help find shoes, brush hair, pour cereal, and pack the lunch box. Then they're gone on the bus. It's 8 A.M. and your day is already humming along.

Mommy Guilt-Free Principle No. 7: Set aside time to have fun as a family

Having fun as a family is more than just laughing together. It's playing together, eating together, doing planned activities together—enjoying each other's company in a variety of ways. Sometimes, it's the one thing we look forward to all week long.

Life is busy these days, no matter who you are and what you do. We work longer hours than ever before. We have hundreds of choices of things to do with our so-called free time. If we don't plan family time together, chances are pretty good that we won't get that time. It doesn't need to be elaborate. Have dinner together at least twice a week. Plan a monthly family outing—anything from a picnic in your own backyard to a family weekend away. Follow your children's lead on this one. They often have great ideas on fun and easy things to do together. Have a family card house–building night. Play board games. Turn your TV room into a mini theater; rent a favorite movie, make popcorn, and curl up together. The only guideline is to find an activity that all of you will enjoy doing and that won't be hard to do if you are following Mommy Guilt-Free Principles No. 6 and 7. Thanks to the interest of her daughter, the family of one of the authors of this book rock climbs together.

It's a sport that all of us can do at our own level and still do it together. We take turns cheering each other on and challenging each other. We do it because it's fun, but it has also built a new trust among us.

You now have seven practical principles to get you through the tough times. Using these principles as a baseline, you are ready to start tackling some of the specific situations that cause Mommy Guilt so that you and your family can enjoy the time you share together.

CHAPTER 4

GIVING BIRTH TO GUILT

Now that we've outlined the principles of the Mommy Guilt-Free Philosophy, we'll take a look at how guilt gets its start. It often begins when you become the parent of a newborn, even earlier, from the birth experience itself.

The good news for parents of newborns is that they can work to sidestep Mommy Guilt. In the same way that they will help their children build healthy lifelong habits, new parents can start from scratch to build the habit of a healthy Mommy Guilt-Free Philosophy.

Guilt and the Birth Plan

For some women, the seeds of Mommy Guilt begin shortly after conception. We're talking about the birth plan. This is that little paper you write up that lets everyone involved in the birth experience know your plans. It includes your intentions for the use of medication, atmosphere of your birthing room, and possibly even the roles that different people will play in this experience with you. In this age of birthing options, the myth of the idyllic birth process is as rampant as the myths about nursing. Mothers sometimes feel guilt over straying from the birth plan. They may have planned to give birth without the use of painkillers, then used them; they may have wanted a home birth, but delivered in the hospital; they may have heard other mothers describe their zero intervention or home deliveries as proud achievements, and feel a sense of remorse or shame that they didn't hang tough enough to get to that same goal they envisioned for themselves.

The truth is that labor and delivery have their own agenda. If the birth of your baby didn't execute according to plan, then you've just gotten your first glimpse of what it means to be a parent—you are not 100 percent in control, nor should you be. Rather than focusing on the experience you missed, new mothers should focus on the unique and equally amazing experience they had. Sometimes, a few minutes meditation in which the mother focuses on that imaginary birth and consciously lets it go can help. A surefire way to let it go is to share your labor and delivery story with other mothers. You probably won't have a difficult time finding another new or experienced mom who will want to talk "baby" with you.

Just say no to the nursing competition

The first little myth for new moms to conquer is this: "The baby is born and I've got my body back." Whether you're a first-time mom or a repeat performer, this fallacy seems to trip up everyone. Except for the fact that your new little one will essentially be another appendage for several months, you're right. For some moms, the method by which your little appendage attaches to your body—suction to the breast—creates enormous Mommy Guilt.

Nursing

Believe us, we know what it feels like to be in the middle of nursing hell—wishing you had read more/read less, used different nursing bras/nursing shirts, talked to the lactation consultant/avoided the lactation consultant and so on. With all the options, advice, and incessant drumming of the importance of nursing, if you happen to be having a difficult time, you can easily feel as if you are to blame. We do agree with the recommendation by The American Academy of Pediatrics regarding nursing for a full year, and many mothers happily follow it. When it does not work for you, though, chalk it up to what life is like and go on knowing that you are doing your level best.

Here's something to remember too: bottles, formula, lactation devices, lactation consultants, the La Leche League International, and so on, existed well before you became a mom. Clearly, millions of women have needed assistance learning to nurse over the years or have needed alternatives to nursing. It also holds true that millions of happy, well-adjusted adults have been reared by mothers who couldn't/shouldn't/didn't nurse them as infants.

The mythology our culture has built up around nursing often doesn't help. At one end of the spectrum is every single cracked and bleeding nipple story that other moms will share with you the moment you see a pink line on your pregnancy test. At the other end is the story about the mom of quintuplets who nursed every single one of her children and still had milk left over to donate to a milk bank (and the wherewithal to pump it!). You'll be regaled with stories of moms who overcame months of pain and misery, mastitis (breast inflammation), and clogged milk ducts. These moms will swear that nursing was worth it all and produced a joy that cannot be experienced any other way. This may be so for these moms, but it doesn't follow that it will be so for every mom. So much has been said on the topic that a new mom can easily believe that nursing nirvana must be every woman's experience. It isn't. Stories like these create vast amounts of guilt if a mom decides to feed her baby via a method other than nursing.

HELPFUL HINT

Nursing and Adoption

If you are a new mother through the adoption process, you may feel inundated with literature about nursing the baby. Your options include attempting to stimulate milk flow in your own breasts, using devices that simulate the act of nursing, and so on. We want to caution you that this can be an area of extreme guilt. Whatever your approach to feeding your baby, please proceed with a Mommy Guilt-Free attitude! If you want to try nursing, your attempts to produce milk are success-ful, and you enjoy the experience, that is great! If these activities aren't "successful," by whatever definition you use, shrug it off and know that many women face the same circumstance, whether their children were adopted or not.

If your choice or the circumstances dictate bottles, know that cud-dling up with your baby, skin to skin, while feeding a bottle will be a wonderful experience for both of you—as treasured as nursing was for other moms. As for missed bonding because of not nursing, we give you the dads. Very few dads nurse their babies (though apparently, a phenomenon called male lactation has been known to occur.[1]) But even without nursing, a whole lot of dads have bonded with their children.

I had a great deal of trouble breastfeeding and switched my child to formula at six weeks. Given the overwhelming barrage of pronursing/ antibottle messages a new mother receives, I was wildly stressed out about my decision, which I now see as being a sensible, generally OK thing to do.

Simply put, while nursing is recommended and is a wonderful way to feed your baby, it can be very difficult for some moms. Some mothers may choose not to nurse for fear of the pain while others might feel completely inadequate because after twenty minutes hooked up to a breast pump, they still have only an ounce of milk in the collection bottle. Others will jump through any hoop to make sure that nary a drop of liquid touches their baby's lips but breast milk. We say that ultimately what matters most is that your baby is healthy and that you feel comfortable about your situation.

Alternatives to nursing

With all this in mind, no wonder nursing can be a new mom's very first exposure to Mommy Guilt. We want to point out that it can also be her first chance to develop her Mommy Guilt-Free Philosophy. As the nursing story in Chapter 1 illustrates, a difficult experience can be the perfect reason to apply Mommy Guilt-Free Principle No. 1 (Let some things go). Even if you don't let them go, they will escape on their own!

For those moms who choose to stop nursing, we hope they also choose not to waste effort defending themselves. They can opt to simply sit quietly while the other moms bombard them with their nursing stories. If you are a mom contemplating how to get out of nursing hell, let yourself feel okay about your decisions. If you decide to combine nursing with formula feedings, allow yourself to feel good about it—remind yourself that what you are doing works best for both you and your baby. The goal is to have a happy, growing baby with a full tummy. Either breast or bottle can get your little one there.

Mommy Guilt can come on fast when we begin worrying about what other people are doing and thinking, rather than focusing on what our own needs are. When this happens, apply Mommy Guilt-Free Principle No. 2 (Parenting is not a competitive sport). One mom in our survey explained her guilt over having to pump breast milk during the workday:

Yes, I am still breastfeeding my child and I feel a tremendous amount of guilt that I need to take time out of my day to pump at work. I pump three times during a normal work shift. Even though I make up the time by staying late, coming in early, or cutting my lunch time short, I still feel guilty that I'm not 100 percent focused on the work at hand. But there's no way I would give up the pumping since I know it's what is best for my son!

If you choose to nurse until your child drinks from a cup, or beyond, pumping at work is necessary. Allow yourself to be relaxed about it. This is a nanosecond of the time you will spend at the office during your lifetime and your employer will hardly be crippled because you are taking a few extra minutes daily in the ladies room (or perhaps in your office with the door closed). No need to feel apologetic—you are entitled to spend the time needed to attend to natural and important bodily functions. This is a classic time to tell yourself: "I am proud to be a mom!"

Bonding

In the late 1980s, it became common knowledge that bonding was something that occurred between a mother and child immediately after a baby was born; similar to imprinting a mother duck on a duckling. We are happy to report that this so-called common knowledge is considered questionable by many researchers. We now know that attachment occurs in different ways at different ages between children and all of their caregivers.[2] A special bond may form at the moment of birth; however, if the mother or child has medical complications associated with the delivery or if the mother is just too tired to cope, this bond may occur later on. Is it a crime not to feel an immediate bond with your newborn? Absolutely not. Take comfort in the fact that many parents commonly feel little more than confusion and fear in the delivery room. Only babies born on TV and movie screens come out pretty, pink, clean, and immediately able to bond with parents. You will have plenty of time to develop a wonderful relationship with your child—you are about to spend countless hours together.

> *After twenty-six hours of labor, I had to have an emergency C-section. I remained awake, but the anesthetics had paralyzed me from the chest down and what parts of me I could feel were shaking violently. When my daughter was born, my husband tried to hand her to me, but I told him, no. After hearing that she was healthy, I couldn't control my arms enough to hold her and frankly I didn't care. He laid her on my chest for a few seconds anyway. She had a fever and spent the first few days in intensive care, as did I. The first day, the nurses kept bringing her to me to nurse and I kept telling them to take her away. I couldn't fully wake up and I was afraid I would drop her. They didn't want to listen and were concerned that I wasn't "bonding." By day two, having achieved a few consecutive hours of sleep, I sat up, took my baby, snuggled her, and tried to learn to nurse her. From day two of her life until now, twelve years later, the two of us are as close as mother and daughter can be.*

Forget the to-do list and go to sleep

So, you now realize that you don't really have your body back. Plus, the body you do have certainly isn't the one you've been fantasizing about. You return from the hospital, your stomach is, with any luck, smaller than when you went in. Your body, though, is a rather yucky mess of blood, colostrum, and sweat, all of which is riding on a hormonal roller coaster. You will be dirty. You will also be forgetful, opinionated, emotional, overjoyed, upset, encouraged, and discouraged. Most of all, you will be tired. Some days, you may not even recognize the person in the mirror (assuming, of course, you have time to look in one). You have a beautiful child in your arms but all you want to do is put her down so you can sleep. Or maybe, you have a funny-looking thing in your arms, with a pointy head, and you are finding it hard to find the little guy beautiful—and feeling guilty about that reaction.

You've been told not to sleep with your baby, because you could roll over and smother him. You've been instructed to nurse your baby every three to four hours, but the thought of being awake that much exhausts you, even if the nursing itself has posed few problems. Feelings of being

overwhelmed and incompetent begin to creep in, and with those, the stir-
rings of Mommy Guilt. How will you ever get through these first few
months?

First, you must realize that there are some things we simply can't control, such as hormone fluctuations. Rather than feel guilty about being
overly emotional, recognize that, except in extreme cases, this is normal
for most women. You have the right to feel the way you do. Cry at that
coffee commercial on television when the boy comes home from college
(one of the authors, Aviva Pflock, did). Allow yourself a case of the complete giggles when you discover you've put the diaper on backward (another of the authors, Julie Bort, did). Scream at your husband when he
innocently suggests pizza for dinner, forgetting your newfound aversion to
melted cheese (a third author, Devra Renner, did).

The goal is to stop yourself from being dragged into parenting exhaustion. To prevent exhaustion in these very early stages, we say, "Sleep when
the baby is sleeping." Stop rolling your eyes, please.

You've already heard it. Your friend, your obstetrician or midwife, the
nurses in the hospital, they've all handed you this wisdom as if it were
magic. Yes, you know they've said it out of love and sympathy. They have
looked deep into your sagging eyes and reminded you. You gather every
bit of strength inside you to respond with a pleasant smile as your mind
spins with thoughts of all the unfinished tasks in your home and world that
you can conquer only while the baby is sleeping.

But, we've got to tell you—don't cast aside this advice. We've promised
to help you prioritize and so we heartily advise, particularly for the firstborn child: sleep while the baby is sleeping.

You need your rest to make sound decisions and to be a calm, caring,
consistent parent. We know the reality of your situation and can tell you
that whatever else needs to be done will wait until after your nap. Those
around you who have been through it might remember how completely
overwhelming parental initiation is. For those who haven't been through
it, you're under no obligation to impress them. This advice is especially
critical if you are planning a minimal maternity leave from your job. Just
keep reminding yourself that these first few weeks are simply that, a few
weeks. The world won't be sent spiraling out of its orbit if you grab a few
minutes of sleep in the mid-morning and the mid-afternoon (after all, you
probably only manage to grab a few during the entire night).

Even if you are blessed with a baby who sleeps a good long stretch at
night, every night—go ahead and sleep while the baby is sleeping. Rest is
key to a positive attitude, and a positive attitude is the underlying structure
that allows you to experience Mommy Guilt-Free Principle No. 4—which
is the golden rule for mothering an infant—"Learn when and how to live

in the moment, rather than in the future." It is those tiny moments, when your newborn rests her head against your shoulder or makes funny faces while she practices working her tongue, where your joy in parenting a newborn will occur. If you are walking around in a total zombie-like state, you will not be able to fully share these moments with your young child.

Just before my second child was born, I thought I would have it all under control. I was experienced, after all. My husband was at a new job and didn't have any leave available, but I still didn't arrange for anyone to come and stay and help me, figuring my eight weeks of maternity leave would be all I needed. By the third day, I was an exhausted wreck. I called my sister-in-law and begged her to come help me, which she did, thank goodness. I handed her the baby and took a nap. When I woke up and took my baby back in my arms, I discovered she had dimples! Took me three days and a nap to see them!

New moms, try to embrace your exhaustion. You've earned it! If you want to sit down at 2 P.M. on a Tuesday and watch TV while the baby naps, do so—even if phone calls need to be returned, thank-you notes written for baby gifts, and your shower taken. No guilt is necessary. Take a cue from endurance athletes, such as marathoners. They include rest in their training. It is the portion of the training process in which the body builds, repairs itself, and strengthens. Without rest, all you get is exhaustion, which is a form of weakness, not strength. After a racing season, some marathoners rest so completely, they barely exercise at all for weeks. Now, would you call a person who had completed a handful of marathons lazy and out of shape for not working out? Then don't assume that a new mom should be fending off exhaustion and using her recovery time or maternity leave to tackle a to-do list.

So, when those precious few opportunities arise when you can put your footsies up, do so with absolute confidence that you have earned this down time! You aren't shirking your duties, you are performing a critical part of the postpartum process—the resting part! A well-rested mom is one of the best things you can hand over to your family.

If that pep talk didn't make you want to plop into the nearest recliner, think of this: once you identify your feeling (in this case, exhaustion), the feeling becomes easier to accept and ultimately control. By allowing yourself to experience the exhaustion, you will be better prepared to recognize "not exhaustion" when it arrives—which it will if it's given the chance.

But, by ignoring exhaustion and pushing yourself to continue moving, working, and accomplishing, exhaustion will increase and can even give rise to feelings of depression. Then the cycle begins—you get tired, you feel lousy because you are tired, you are too tired to do anything, and then you feel lousy because you feel like nothing is getting done.

Guilt and the postpartum blues

While a few hours to a few days of the baby blues is probably a normal shift of post-delivery hormones, you would be wise to discuss these feelings with your healthcare professional. However, if you find yourself exhausted or feeling down for days or weeks on end, or your family and friends have expressed concern about you, then you need to seek professional help. You and your family will benefit equally from this.

Postpartum depression is not a failure. It is not your fault. It is simply an ailment that can and must be treated. Our emotions serve specific purposes and we need to listen to what they are trying to tell us. Sometimes all we need to shake off a down mood is a good laugh, or a good cry. In some cases, we need outside help. If you think there's even a possibility that you need help, move forward to seek it and do so with the confidence that you are not alone.

For crying out loud

The newborn stage is brief but offers an ideal opportunity to help you start on your Mommy Guilt-Free Philosophy. Newborns have minimal needs (food, sleep, affection, and a dry diaper). They don't want a pony ride or an expensive pair of shoes. They don't even care if you've brushed your teeth. So rather than buying into the societal view that newborns are all take and no give, why not view them as all give and very little take? Their existence gives their parents great joy.

This is an appropriate stage to master Mommy Guilt-Free Principle No. 2 (Parenting is not a competitive sport). Are you going to take pride or shame in your newborn's pooping abilities? Nah! Instead, you are going to delight in her tiny wiggling toes, in her little yawn, in her fury when she gets hungry, and in the variety of noises that small body makes. You are going to experience the feeling of comforting your very own crying child. All it takes to experience boundless delight in being a new parent is a slight mental shift: her sole purpose is to be enjoyed by you.

Crying, crying, or crying

While we're talking about comforting a newborn, let's demolish another myth. This one says that mothers become so clued-in to their babies that they can recognize the difference between a hungry cry, a tired cry, and a dirty diaper cry. Maybe that will happen to you (though we doubt it—we think most mothers just get used to figuring out what their baby is likely to be crying about, given the circumstances). But what if it doesn't happen and you really can't ever tell? Should you feel guilty, as if you are not as tuned-in to your child as you should be? Not one bit. In reality, every mother has times when she runs through a list of possibilities in order to figure out what the child needs. (See the "Crying Flow Chart" on the next page.)

In the words of one of the authors, Aviva Pflock: *I am raising three children of my own, providing home visits for other families in my work, and I have facilitated countless play groups for hundreds of families. You know what? I still don't know how to translate baby cries. I do, however, know what to check and what to try. None of the babies seem to have caught on to this so please make sure they don't read this section.*

The dirty secret of new parenthood

Let's look at something else no one seems to dream about in their new-mom fantasies—most new parents are dirty, and they stay that way for weeks to months on end. If you are a new mom and find that you can't get yourself together enough to hit the shower every morning like you used to, you are not alone! Even if you've managed to shower, chances are your darling baby, equipped with a sixth sense of timing, gifted you with some sort of stinky bodily fluid the second after you dried off and picked him up.

Babies rarely give you more than a few minutes between the times they need your attention (and, if you've got other small children, they will be feeling needy for you, too). So, chances are your house's cleanliness is on par with your body's. And then, your friends stop by. Do we need to go on? These all sound like fabulous opportunities to feel completely guilty about your ability (or inability) to handle parenthood. *Stop!*

Daily morning showers are overrated, really they are. Wait until the

Crying Flow Chart

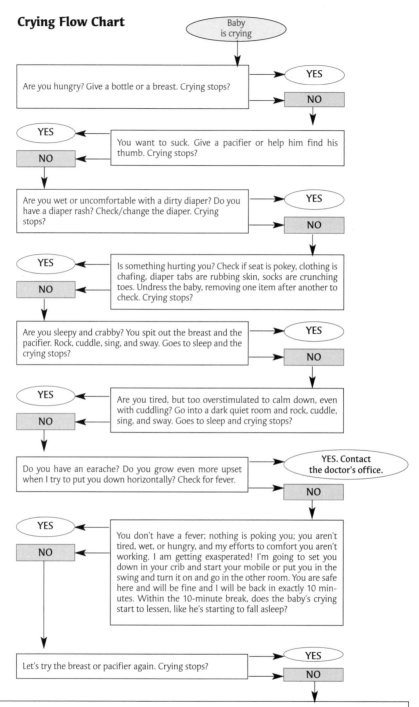

Baby is crying

Are you hungry? Give a bottle or a breast. Crying stops? → **YES** / **NO**

You want to suck. Give a pacifier or help him find his thumb. Crying stops? → **YES** / **NO**

Are you wet or uncomfortable with a dirty diaper? Do you have a diaper rash? Check/change the diaper. Crying stops? → **YES** / **NO**

Is something hurting you? Check if seat is pokey, clothing is chafing, diaper tabs are rubbing skin, socks are crunching toes. Undress the baby, removing one item after another to check. Crying stops? → **YES** / **NO**

Are you sleepy and crabby? You spit out the breast and the pacifier. Rock, cuddle, sing, and sway. Goes to sleep and the crying stops? → **YES** / **NO**

Are you tired, but too overstimulated to calm down, even with cuddling? Go into a dark quiet room and rock, cuddle, sing, and sway. Goes to sleep and crying stops? → **YES** / **NO**

Do you have an earache? Do you grow even more upset when I try to put you down horizontally? Check for fever. → **YES. Contact the doctor's office.** / **NO**

You don't have a fever; nothing is poking you; you aren't tired, wet, or hungry, and my efforts to comfort you aren't working. I am getting exasperated! I'm going to set you down in your crib and start your mobile or put you in the swing and turn it on and go in the other room. You are safe here and will be fine and I will be back in exactly 10 minutes. Within the 10-minute break, does the baby's crying start to lessen, like he's starting to fall asleep? → **YES** / **NO**

Let's try the breast or pacifier again. Crying stops? → **YES** / **NO**

I'm calling for help and advice: an experienced friend, the doctor's office or nurse's hotline, my mother. Maybe you are having a bout of "colic" or just feel like crying for now. We'll go in a quiet room, where I will rock you and let you know how much I love you and keep you company until you feel like smiling again.*

---

* If the child cries for hours, check with your pediatrician. This could indicate an ear infection or other medical problem.

baby is settled down for a long nap (if you decide not to nap yourself!) or when you have someone in the house to help out and treat yourself to a long, hot bath. This is another simple way to find joy in the ordinary. Nothing is more delightful than a hot bath or shower when you are the kind of dirty that can only be accomplished by holding a leaky newborn. When you just can't wait for the ideal time, hop in the shower for a quick rinse. You can even put a baby swing or bouncy seat in the bathroom so you can keep an eye and ear open on your little one. The white noise from the running water may even encourage another nap! If your baby starts to fuss, you can always sing to him while you finish up.

As for feeling guilty that the baby isn't always sweet smelling, realize that at least half of that kid gets washed every time you change her and the other half gets it every time she spits up. Besides, too much soap and water can be hard on a baby's delicate skin. Just by doing the hourly tasks of caring for a newborn, you'll reach the baby cleanliness bar—that the child is clean enough not to become a living petri dish. Though we should point out that even the cleanest babies sometimes suffer from petri dish–like effects. Cradle cap, a form of dandruff, is common among newborns, or sometimes your child will have a yellow tinge to the skin, indicating a touch of jaundice. Such instances are not automatically a reflection of neglect or incompetence on the part of the parents. Your newborn appointments are your help system for issues such as these, and your pediatric healthcare professionals will guide you in treating any newborn ailment that arises. Many insurance plans also offer twenty-four-hour phone service seven days a week where you can ask questions of a pediatric nurse.

The baby doesn't care if the house is picked up

As for the messy house, at this point in your life, our advice is—you guessed it—Mommy Guilt-Free Principle No. 1 (Let some things go). As long as your home isn't a breeding ground for deadly bacteria, call it safe and let it be. If you've been reading this book straight through since Chapter 1, by this point, you may think that we, the authors, are advocating national house slovenliness—and you would be right! To a certain extent. We realize, though, that we all need a baseline of cleanliness to remain sane and healthy.

The definition of a clean house, newborn style

The day before you gave birth, your house could have been pictured in the dictionary under the word *meticulous*. It's now been a couple weeks, and it has degenerated into a mess, but has it really?

Your newborn can't see all that well. He won't complain about the pile of mail accumulating on the living room table. Your newborn isn't mobile. She doesn't need the piles of laundry on the floor in the master bedroom picked up. Your newborn has a limited diet. He doesn't care if every dish, glass, fork, and pot sits in the sink all day until your reinforcements arrive (husband, family member, friend). Your newborn has no white gloves. The dust on the furniture won't offend her. Your newborn isn't concentrating on his sense of smell. He doesn't care if the garbage needs to be taken out. If your messy house is not under a siege of mice . . . if the materials that bacteria love are all contained in the kitchen sink and are dealt with daily (more-or-less) . . . if bacteria is sprouting in plastic containers in the fridge harmlessly contained and out of sight . . . if the garbage is awaiting to be trotted out to the curb . . . guess what? You've got a clean house, newborn style!

Ask for help

If you've already lowered your standards and really are concerned about the green bubbly stuff oozing in your sink, then you probably need to round up some help to get you out of the danger zone. Finding help isn't the insurmountable wall that many people think it is. How many times have you told a friend, "Call me if you need anything." If that friend called for something that was well within your ability to do, would you do it? How would you feel afterward? Chances are you would feel good about yourself. Helping others gives people a sense that they are good people, good friends (or sisters), or good congregation members. It also feeds their sense of karmic justice. If they help someone in need one day, they know that someone will help them on another day.

True, overreliance on other people's help can overstep the boundaries. But let's suppose that this isn't your intention. Let's suppose that you will remain sensible enough not to abuse your friends' good intentions. If so, another issue that may be stopping you from seeking out or accepting help is a strange sense of, "I need to take care of everything myself," when a new child is added to your family.

While we might arrange for a family member to come and stay with us a few days after the arrival of a first child, many of us won't think that same kind of support will be necessary for the second child. We think we should be completely independent ourselves while caring for someone completely dependent on us. Give it up. Graciously accept those offers of dinners from friends, relatives, coworkers, and absolutely anyone willing to do it!

If you need to, call a friend and ask her if she could *puhleese* come over and do the dishes while you and the baby nap—chances are you'll hear her tires squealing, she'll be over there so fast. True, she might not relish scrubbing your pots, but she won't mind. She will be happy to help, as she's probably told you herself dozens of times. People can do your grocery shopping, bring meals to your door, shovel snow from the walkways and driveway, and *certainly* you can find someone to hold and cuddle the baby while you bathe or nap.

I'll never forget the day that two of my friends came to see my newborn third child and spent half an hour folding laundry while we all gossiped about life. Guilt over someone else doing the chore? Not one bit (once they were done). It seemed a little awkward at first, but then I thought to myself, hey, what are friends for?

If you are new to a community and don't yet have nearby friends or family, one great way to find help is to join a local moms' support group. These can be found through national organizations such as Mothers & More, The National Association of Mother's Centers, and other community or religious programs. Your county extension office or human services department may also be able to provide you with a list of support groups in your area.

Also, remember that your new role as parent (or parent of multiple children) is a decision to provide care and guidance for another. It is not the role of maid or cook. It is not your job to keep the house ready for company at a moment's notice. Do you think it is a coincidence that human babies are not mobile? Of course not! We are obviously not expected to have a spotless home in the beginning. We can put our child in a safe place and know that he will not climb onto the countertop overflowing with dirty dishes. We do not need to lavish our visitors with fabulous meals when they come to call.

Will your pride be diminished if you are not able to dazzle your guests—or even keep up with the basics? Tell yourself that nothing could possibly bring a greater feeling of pride than having a happy baby in your home. As for the people who visit and complain about the condition of you or your house, no need to invite them back.

Notes

1. *Wikipedia: The Free Encyclopedia*, Wikmedia Foundation, distributed under the GNU Free Documentation License, edited July 4, 2004, retrieved July 10, 2004, http://en.wikipedia.org/wiki/Male_lactation.

2. Patricia Pendy, *Ethological Attachment Theory: A Great Idea in Personality?* (Evanston, Ill.: Northwestern University, 1998); Robbie Davis-Floyd, Ph.D., *Bonding Period*, "The Birth Scene," http://www.birthpsychology.com/birthscene/ppic4.html (accessed July 10, 2004).

CHAPTER 5

THE START OF FIRST-RATE PARENTING CHOICES (AND THE END OF SECOND-RATE CHILDHOOD HABITS)

Without a doubt, two big sources of Mommy Guilt are our children's eating habits and sleeping habits. More than one-third of *Mommy Guilt* survey respondents named eating habits as a source of guilt. Nearly one-quarter said the same about their children's sleeping habits.

The Mommy Guilt-Free Philosophy looks at these two areas by first recognizing that children will do many things throughout their lives that are outside the control of their parents—even as infants. Eating and sleeping are two prime examples. For all practical purposes, we cannot force food into them and we cannot make them fall asleep. Sometimes, we can't keep them from developing other habits that seem downright nasty to us, although we can help guide them away from these behaviors. Why then does society imply that we can or should? That is where the guilt comes in, because we believe we fail when our children make choices we wish they wouldn't, choices we tried to teach them not to make. But you can't control your children's preferences—no more than your own parents could have controlled your preferences when you were a kid. What you can do is create opportunities for your children to make good choices.

A plateful of eating-habits guilt

Infants, toddlers, and young children will not voluntarily starve themselves to death. A parent's responsibility is to provide a variety of healthy, age-appropriate foods. The child will be the one to decide whether to eat those foods or not. An abundance of literature exists to guide parents toward what are healthy, age-appropriate foods. (If these documents have escaped your notice, ask your pediatrician for some.) That isn't what we are talking about here. We want you to focus on how you react when your child's eating habits are falling short of what you or society expects they should be.

My son was a picky eater. I know I made it much worse because I was so worried about him. I was afraid that if I didn't give him the foods he would eat, he would starve to death. So, I began carting the peanut butter around in my purse. If we went somewhere that didn't have peanut butter, then mommy would have it for him. My son is now almost ten and just this year he began eating meat. I feel terrible that I let his eating take over his life. I wish I had put my foot down in the beginning and made him try other foods. But when you are in the middle of it, you just don't see it.

The guilt trap frequently snaps shut when we second-guess ourselves. We worry that our child isn't eating enough or is eating too much or doesn't look exactly right compared with the neighbor's kid, or isn't riding the center of the chart wave, or, or, or. . . . So, what do you do when you've got a heaping plate of guilt? Put your fork down and read what some of the survey participants had to say:

When teaching your babies how to feed themselves, be patient and have as much fun as they are having. Give them a spoon and don't stress over the mess. Giggle with them as they learn this important skill (otherwise, you'll turn them off).

* * * * *

It's a parent's responsibility to offer three meals and two snacks of nutritious and varied child-friendly, developmentally appropriate foods per day. It is up to the child to eat them. Do not make this into a bigger issue or stress out over it if the kid does not want to eat. The kid will not starve himself. Of course, if the kid really isn't thriving, see a doctor, but that's not a parenting issue, it's a medical issue. Just offer appropriate food and all will be well.

* * * * *

Avoid cooking separate meals for your child. Expect them to eat with the family.

Excellent, sensible advice, and all of it boils down to this: by creating good eating habits early on, a great deal of future guilt can be prevented. Both the parent and child benefit here: mom has less guilt and her child has a healthier diet.

Full means full

Let's tackle another eating-related issue. Some parents believe that requiring children to eat everything on their plates makes sense. However, kids are much better than adults about eating when they are hungry and not eating when they are not.

Children should be encouraged to develop an inner sense of fullness— that is, to stop eating when they feel full. Insisting, or even just encouraging, your child to finish all food served means ignoring that sense and can push a child to overeat. Overeating leads to upset tummies (and possibly to becoming overweight). Instead of focusing on finishing the food on the plate, how about teaching your children to fill their plates realistically? A child's stomach is significantly smaller than that of an adult. A good rule of thumb to gauge serving sizes is to make no portion bigger than the size of the eater's fist. You may learn that your child always eats more or less, but start with fist-sized servings. For a small child, like a toddler, use a smaller plate. The toddler will be able to handle a smaller plate more easily and the smaller size also helps ensure no one will overload the plate with too much food.

The no-thank-you bite

A rule that children cannot tank up on one item until they've at least tried all the foods on their plate also works well for many families. One survey respondent called this the "no-thank-you bite." Once children try the food, they can say "no thank you" to eating more of it. You may also want to introduce new foods one at a time, accompanied by known favorites. This way, you don't have to worry about your children not having enough available to fill them up.

Make it clear that once the meal is off the table, the kitchen will be shut down for the next two to three hours (smaller tummies mean that kids need snacks between meals). If children know that the kitchen will be closed, they may be more willing to eat what is currently in front of them.

My six-year-old took one look at lunch and said, "Yuck, I don't want this." I pointed out that in addition to what he called the gross stuff,

he had some fries on his plate. My son asked to leave the table. I told
him he could leave when everyone was done and reminded him that
the kitchen would be closed after that. He tried to argue with me
about it, and I just repeated, "You may leave the table when everyone
else is done." He sat there for a bit and then lo and behold he began
to eat the "yucky" meal.

Dessert

Now then, what about the all-powerful dessert? The food police are
not going to storm your house if you serve a dessert or if you don't. However, desserts and sweets are a hot button for many parents.

We have adopted the rule that if you are too full to finish your meal
then you are too full for dessert. This does not imply in any way that
you must finish your food. It is not presented in a threatening manner.
It is a simple statement of fact. We also tend to have desserts around,
but they are not offered on a daily basis.

Moderation

We advocate the idea of legalizing and regulating when it comes to
food choices. This means allowing the food but setting limits on when,
how much, why, and where it may be consumed. A child's balanced eating
habits can be helped along tremendously when parents demonstrate that
no foods are "bad" and that all foods should be eaten in moderation. We
even hold the politically incorrect opinion that you should keep some junk
food in your house.

I warned my daughter that presweetened cereal would rot her teeth,
that doughnuts would make her fat. I never bought that stuff for her
when she was little—not even cookies, which I trained her to recog-
nize as the enemy, loaded with artery-clogging fats. I wanted her to
grow up to be healthy and fit, but now that she's a teenager, I can see
this isn't what happened. If someone brings a bag of cookies into the
house, by the next morning, none will be left. If a half gallon of ice
cream winds up in our freezer, I'll see no bowl in the sink—just a big
hole in the middle of the carton, the telltale sign that she's been gob-

bling it down behind my back. Straight from the carton with a spoon, I'll bet. She seems to have no control over herself when it comes to sweets. I think that if I had taught her how to eat sweets in moderation, instead of just forbidding them, it might have worked better.

Putting sleeping-habit guilt to bed

Now that their little bellies are full, they are ready to settle down for the night. At least, we hope they are. We know that we are! When parents don't get enough sleep, we don't function as well as we could. An overtired adult becomes forgetful, inefficient, grouchy, depressed, and easily fatigued. Our kids do too.

Sleep habits are critical for the whole family. We have observed that many children's behavior problems arise because they aren't getting enough good-quality sleep. Children today often operate on adultlike schedules. They go to school or preschool early in the morning, stay after school for sports or extended day care, and then for those with homework, stay up late doing it—or just watching TV. The most recent annual poll conducted by the National Sleep Foundation (NSF) found that children in all age groups are sleeping less than the recommended amount.[1] Children need between ten and fourteen hours of sleep per day, depending on their ages, with infants requiring more, according to the NSF. (For recommendations specific to your children's ages, ask your pediatrician.)

Kids are resilient and may adjust to curtailed sleep, but they shouldn't have to adjust to limited sleep. Children cope better with life—from teething through math tests—when their habits encourage and prioritize enough time for sleep. Likewise, you'll enjoy your rested, happy children more than tired, crabby children.

As with eating, encouraging your child to get enough sleep starts young. Plenty of books dedicated to sleeping habits exist, from addressing specific sleeping issues (bedwetting) to entire bedtime-training methods. In this chapter, we touch on the basics as they apply to our Mommy Guilt-Free Philosophy.

Where should they sleep, your bed or theirs?

Where kids sleep is a hot topic. But we've got oven mitts and aren't afraid to use them! Here are some thoughts on sleep habits offered by our survey respondents:

Some people like the family bed, but we find having our own adult room— and time alone—to be vital and important to our marriage. Only if the kids are sick or scared are they allowed to join us.

* * * * *

We had immense guilt around getting our firstborn to sleep in his crib. We tried everything, including wrapping our pillows around our heads so as not to hear him. Then a very wise friend from India questioned why Americans choose to separate from their children when they need them most. From that day forward, our baby slept with us and everyone slept. We did the same with our second son. Both decided when they were ready for their own beds.

* * * * *

Never get in the habit of falling asleep in your child's room or letting them sleep with you—unless you want to do that for a long time.

* * * * *

I firmly believe in having your child sleep in his/her own bed and started that habit from day one. My child slept in his crib with me in the guest room next door. When he cried, I immediately came to him, but he got used to sleeping in his own crib and has been sleeping peacefully through the night since he was eight months old. He is most happy in his crib and is a well-adjusted child.

* * * * *

Sleeping habits were my godsend. I started them at birth and put them in their own bed always at the same time. If they had a bad dream, I would go in and lay with them instead of letting them come into our room. If they wanted to sleep in our room, they slept on the floor next to us. That lasted about a month and they thought their bed was much better so they stopped coming in our room.

We think it makes sense to do whatever will allow your family to get plenty of high-quality sleep. If you feel guilty over listening to your child cry on the nights she has trouble falling to sleep, then you may choose to bring her into your room or join her in her room. Note, however, that whether she sleeps in her own room or with you, this may become the sleeping arrangement your child expects for days, weeks, months, or even years to come. When trying to decide what to do, ask yourself: "Will this habit be something that I will want to live with or will we end up making ourselves nuts trying to undo this later?"

Tell me, how can a three-foot-tall person take over a king-size bed? Our son has been having nightmares since we moved into our new home and he now wants to be in bed with us. It is a disaster. My husband and I find ourselves hanging off the bed while our son is spread-eagle on our bed and snoring away. We are both exhausted, our son is raring to go, and we are ready for him to go—right back to his room!

Is it selfish to want to have your bed all to yourself? No. Your children know you love them, even if you don't share your bedroom with them. Is it "cheating" to go the easier route, and just let the youngster in your room? No. If everyone is happily getting a good night's sleep, you've made the right decision for your family. But when you are immersed in Mommy Guilt, you can easily lose perspective. So remind yourself that the goal of bedtime is for everyone to get plenty of sleep. Then make your decision accordingly.

Bedtime rituals

Children need bedtime rituals to help set the scene for sleep. Respondents to our survey offered the following advice:

For good sleep habits, you need to be consistent. Parents need to do the same bedtime routine each night and at the same time.

* * * * *

Good sleep habits: always do the same routine from early on. Start bed early (around 7 P.M.) and find a calming routine so the child knows what to expect when it is time to sleep. Always put your child into bed awake (and at the same time nightly) so she isn't dependent on having you with her to fall asleep.

See a pattern? Consistency and sameness. To a child, a consistent routine offers security and comfort—children like to know what is going to happen. Even if your work schedule or a special occasion means a slight digression from the norm, an established routine is the key.

While we have no magical bedtime routine to offer you, we can give you some guidelines on creating practical ones for your own family. Believe it or not, even tiny infants enjoy a good read. A parent's voice is soothing to a child, so reading to your children remains on the tried-and-true list. If books don't grab your fancy at bedtime, try singing favorite bedtime songs, saying prayers, hugs and kisses, or any combination. For those nights when you aren't going to be home to carry out the routine, try writing down directions for whomever is putting your child to bed. If your child is old enough, you can come up with a bedtime ritual together for the nights you are away so the child knows that even though you aren't there, you were still a part of making it happen.

Avoid long, drawn-out bedtimes in which a child pleads for one more book, hug, or kiss—and gets it. This encourages the child to resist sleep once tucked into bed and can lead to Mommy Guilt in countless ways. If you give into the "one mores" you reinforce the begging and before you know it, you've got an hour-long, complicated bedtime routine that includes entering and leaving the room two, three, or more times. This drawn-out routine can make you feel like you are doing everything you can think of to comfort your child so that she'll sleep but failing. It can also be exhausting for the parent yearning for a few minutes peace at day's end. When bedtime seems to take forever, a parent may grow impatient and then begin to yell, which certainly doesn't help a child get to sleep.

I was home alone with our three year old. I had just finished the bedtime routine when he asked for another book. So I read another book. I might as well have agreed to bob in and out of his room like a yo-yo for the next three hours because that's what I did. One more kiss, one more glass of water, one more hug, one more question. When my husband came home later that night, he passed our son's room and I noticed the silence. "YES!" I thought, "He's finally sleeping!" But when I tiptoed past my son's room on the way to my own, I heard him call out in a very chipper voice, "Mommy?"

Oral habits

Among the most guilt-inspiring habits to sprout in the first year of life are oral fixations—otherwise known as bottles, pacifiers, and thumbs. All of them serve a purpose in the beginning. All of them can be hard or impossible to snatch away when the time comes. If your child uses any of these methods and doesn't drift out of use on her own, here is some general advice for when to take action and how. Of course, if you are concerned about the role these play in your child's physical development, we recommend consulting a doctor or dentist.

The bottle

As soon as the skill of cup drinking is accomplished, we believe stopping the bottle cold turkey works best. You can begin to introduce a cup around six months and have your baby bottle-free by fourteen months. At this young age, you are likely to feel worse than your child about getting rid of it. As with most habits, the longer you wait and the longer you drag out the quitting, the harder it will be. If your child is particularly attached to the bottle, there may be a few days of crying and tantrums to let you know he isn't happy. Once you get through this phase, though, it's done. No more bottle.

Need a little support to help you transition? Try telling your child, "The bottle is gone. How about a song and a cuddle in the rocking chair?" Offer a soothing alternative to help alleviate a child's anxiety. When you have decided it is time to launch Operation Bottle Drop, try to pick a time when life isn't particularly more stressful than usual; a time when you will have few disruptions distracting you from the mission. Repeat this mantra to yourself, "He can whine and he can cry but the bottle will be going bye." Giving your child more hugs and some extra undivided attention during this time may help you both feel better.

The pacifier

Pacifiers have their time and place but when your child begins to talk, it's a good time to pull the plug. Pacifiers are a bit easier to get rid of than thumbs, since they aren't attached to the end of your child's hand, but this is not to say that the Mommy Guilt is lessened. It isn't. Babies do need to suck but most really don't need a pacifier past age one. As with the bottle, we think cold turkey around age one is a good rule of thumb, oops, pacifier. If you need some help, though, try one of these tips. Let your child know it is difficult to understand her with the pacifier in her mouth. You may want to clip the tip of the pacifier, making it less satisfying to suck. You might also want to try and interest your child in a trade. Each time he reaches for the pacifier, ask him if he'll trade it for a toy you are holding.

Thumb sucking

Thumb sucking is similar to using a pacifier because it soothes an infant who needs to suck. After infancy, toddlers may use a thumb for security or for when they are tired or upset. The difference with the thumb over the pacifier is that you can't remove it from a child's hand. The role you will most likely play in breaking this habit is to be the distracter. Any time you see the thumb go to the mouth you can try to hand your child something to hold. It is also perfectly appropriate to let your child know, in a very matter-of-fact way, "Hey, I can't understand you, please take your thumb out and tell me what you want me to know." This is different from nagging and teasing, which will definitely only lead you to a power struggle and may result in the opposite reaction from your child.

How to get off the habits trail

While eating and sleeping habits are two primary areas that cause Mommy Guilt, they certainly aren't the only ones. As you've seen, oral habits, particularly thumb sucking, are also the subject of a great deal of parental angst.

Then there are hair twirling, nose picking, nail biting, pencil chewing, and countless other behaviors we'd prefer our children didn't engage in. While doing these things may not get in the way of achieving greatness, they may interfere with peer relationships and socialization. If your child wants to and is ready to stop, he may do so relatively easily and without any input from you. But if your child's habit is such a part of him that he can't imagine life without it—or he wants to stop but can't find the strength to do it alone—read on.

While the Mommy Guilt-Free Philosophy is generally one of pleasant acceptance, we do feel that there could be situations when you will want to say, "I'm disgusted, and I won't take it anymore!" At this point, we suggest taking an active role in helping your child move on to a different stage, one we like to call, "Cut that out!"

In Chapter 6, we're going to generally pooh-pooh reward systems (otherwise known as bribes). But rewards do have a role in stomping out bad habits. Rewards are prizes that are not related directly to the behavior itself. When you are ready to implement a reward approach, it must be clearly defined and nonnegotiable. When using rewards for habit breaking, you must jump right in and notice whenever the child has a period without engaging the habit. In most cases, simple praise and affection is reward enough. So always start there. But if you feel extra incentive is needed, know that for many children, waiting days or weeks to gain a big reward won't be enough incentive to stop the habit when the urge strikes. Be prepared to give out small rewards that grow bigger as more success is achieved. Gaining stickers to get a toy is the classic example of small-to-big incentives.

One more word of advice on breaking bad habits: If your child is slumped over pathetically, dying to engage in the habit, and you take pity by saying just this one more time—you'll have just undone all your prior work. Whatever suffering you witnessed before will be longer and worse the next time around. Your child will now hold out the hope, no matter how many days go by, or how many times she hears you say no, that you will change your mind and say yes. So, be firm. That's the best way to make the heart-wrenching-ness of it all short lived. This is when you recall Mommy Guilt-Free Principle No. 5 and understand that defending your "no" benefits you and your family and alleviates the Mommy Guilt.

Note

1. *2004 Sleep in America Poll,* March 2004, the National Sleep Foundation (www.sleepfoundation.org), conducted by WB&A Market Research.

➤ PART 2 ◀

The Stuff of Guilt

CHAPTER 6

YIPPEE! GUILT-FREE YELLING

The *Mommy Guilt* survey found that yelling at the kids is the No.1 guilt-inducer. That is not especially surprising, but it is disconcerting. We own the voice box; we should be able to control its volume. When we opt to crank up the volume and holler at our offspring, we feel Mommy Guilt.

About one-third of our survey respondents say that they fight with their kids daily, with another 38 percent admitting to being in yelling matches a couple times a week. Yet a whopping 60 percent of survey respondents feel guilty about yelling at their kids with 47 percent reporting that it makes them hit their highest level on the Mommy guilt-o-meter.

Clearly, most of us yell, but most of us don't want to yell. So why do we succumb and lose control? For some, it stems from being reared in a household where parents routinely yelled. The guilt is incurred when these moms remember how awful it felt to be the object of their own parent's yelling. If this sounds like you, then the Mommy Guilt-Free Philosophy can help you cease perpetuating the cycle that could create another generation of yellers. Some moms yell when they lose patience with their kids, giving into the lure of emotional immaturity by responding to their children's tantrums with one of their own. The Mommy Guilt-Free Philosophy asks you to examine how you yell, why you yell, and what you want to do about it. You can learn to choose a different, non-yelling approach and save your vocal chords for when you really need them (like when you cheer your kids on).

Yelling over the line

Please note that there is a difference between losing your cool and being verbally abusive. Simple yelling focuses on the child's behavior, not the child. It expresses the parent's frustration regarding an action: "You poured a glass of milk on your brother's head! That is not something we do!" In contrast, a verbally abusive reaction might go something like this:

"You idiot. You know better than to pour milk over your brother's head! If you ever do that again, you can find somewhere else to live. You are one sorry kid and I don't know why you can't do anything right."

If you find that your yelling includes threats, insults, and/or cursing, know that you have crossed the line into verbally abusive behavior and it's got to stop. Verbal abuse is highly damaging to your relationship with your children. Many programs exist to help parents who are on the edge of being abusive—or over it—stop this destructive behavior. Your local human services or county extension office may have a list of anger management classes available in your area. Taking a parenting class or spending a few sessions with a therapist could also help.

Since the majority of parents are not being verbally abusive, let's assume that your yelling isn't that kind. Although it may be frequent, let's say that yelling doesn't constitute the major way you interact with your kids. Let's assume that you only lose your cool on a quasi-regular basis— maybe at certain times of the day (the dinner rush hour) or only under certain conditions (children who refuse to get ready for school and are constantly missing the bus). Let's further assume that you yell when you lose your patience with your kids, and that you lose patience when you feel like your kids are behaving poorly. For you, we have good news. You can eliminate this yelling and, therefore, nix that guilt entirely. All you need to do is fill your parenting toolbox with a few more options besides yelling. In the words of a survey respondent:

Listen patiently and without distraction to your child, especially for school-age children. It will be helpful in figuring out how to help them. If discipline is needed, think first. What do you want them to learn? Are you just thinking about how you are feeling and what you need? In other words, yelling at the child may make you feel better, but will it help the child change his or her behavior?

The above advice nicely sums up the Mommy Guilt-Free approach to yelling. Engage Mommy Guilt-Free Principle No. 3 (Look toward the future and at the big picture) by focusing your energies on behavior modification instead of parental frustration release. Behavior modification is nothing new, and no doubt you've heard of it or have been using it, even if you didn't happen to know the technical term for it.

Your four basic discipline tools

Nearly all behavior modification techniques revolve around four methods: praise (also known as positive reinforcement), natural consequences (learning by experiencing the logical outcome of decisions/actions), rewards (using prizes of some sort to motivate someone to engage in the behavior), and punishment (negative reinforcement) of which yelling is one form.

Positive reinforcement

Positive reinforcement means paying close attention to your children's behavior and praising them when they are doing what you want them to do. Positive reinforcement is truly a magical tool in your Mommy Guilt-Free arsenal and a surefire way to put Mommy Guilt-Free Principle No. 3 (Look toward the future and at the big picture) into action. Once you begin to use positive reinforcement on a regular basis, you'll feel as powerful as an Olympic weight lifter. But before we get into the specifics, let's focus on the word *reinforcement*. This technique does not suggest gushing compliments over your child's every waking act. It is about helping your children recognize the specific behaviors that you expect from them.

To grasp the strength of positive reinforcement think of it this way, you may know what you *don't* want your child to do, but that is only half the behavior modification battle. Alone it gets you nowhere. It's the absence of an action. You can't teach an absence and your child can't learn how to do it. So what exactly is it that you *want* the child to be doing? Figure it out (make sure it's realistic), then, the moment you see that action, smile and give big praise.

Marcy hates to sit still, but we go to synagogue every week and we feel that at eleven years of age, she should be able to sit still for an hour and a half. I decided to try positive reinforcement. As soon as Marcy sat down, I complimented her on how quietly she did that. Then every few minutes I leaned over and told her what an awesome job she was doing. After the service ended, I made sure to let Marcy know how proud I was of her and I made sure to compliment her behavior in front of our rabbi. At night, I told her again how proud I was of her behavior at services. After a while, Marcy began to think of herself as a child who does a great job sitting through a service and is proud of herself, too.

When you turn your parenting attention toward the positive, you will see that positive attracts positive. You will find yourself naturally gravitating toward Mommy Guilt-Free Principle No. 6 (Laugh a lot with your children). You will also find that your praise will be heard far louder and longer than any yell you could possibly resonate.

Natural consequences

Allowing children to experience natural consequences is difficult for many parents. We fear that our child will be damaged from the experience or blame us for what happened to them as a result. Yet choosing to engage the natural consequences tool doesn't mean tossing your children out into the cruel world and making them fend for themselves. It does mean allowing them to experience the logical, natural results of their own decisions and actions. Along with positive reinforcement, natural consequences are another powerful Mommy Guilt-Free alternative to yelling.

For instance, if your child refuses to put on shoes in the dead of winter, fine. Let her see what it feels like to have cold feet as she walks to the car. Take the shoes along with you, and once she has had enough cold she will ask for them.

I warned my son that we would be shopping at the mall for a present for Granddad's birthday party and that we couldn't come home until we bought it. I asked him several times if he had to go potty, and once, seeing him dance around, I even walked him into the restroom. Being three, he refused to go, or even try. Maybe ten minutes later he had an accident. He got to walk around in wet clothes for another twenty minutes while we bought the gift and got ourselves out to the car. Then I told him to put his wet clothes into a plastic bag and wipe his bottom and legs off by himself with the cleansing wipe before he could put on the spare clothes. No yelling, no punishing, just some simple directions to get him to resolve the situation.

As long as you are not putting your child in any danger, go ahead and let him learn. Unlike yelling, punishment, or reward systems, natural consequences internalize the feelings associated with behaviors and usually do fit as the ideal discipline for the action.

Reward systems

Reward systems, also known as incentives (or sometimes known as bribes), are another behavior modification technique but are tricky to implement appropriately and therefore parents should limit their use. Reward systems are about trying to encourage a behavior by offering incentives (toys, treats, an extra bedtime story, and so forth) when certain milestones in that behavior are reached. They are clearly distinguished from natural consequences because they are an external motivator that has nothing to do with the action itself.

In Chapter 5, we discussed how rewards can be used effectively, but now we want to emphasize the tricky part of using them as an all-purpose behavior modification technique.

Reward systems nearly always work great at first, which is why they remain popular with parents. But they frequently lose their punch quickly and can then backfire. Human nature being what it is, if people regularly engage in the behavior that earns the reward, the prize begins to feel like an entitlement and then resentment can bloom between the reward giver and the recipient.

Janine's school-age kids simply wouldn't clean their rooms. Every Saturday, she would send them into their rooms to clean and two hours later even the basic tasks were unfinished. She would start yelling, they would be put in time-outs—none of which made the rooms any neater. Janine decided to implement a sticker system. When her children completed a cleaning task in their rooms, they got a sticker. At the five-sticker mark, they got a toy. It worked! The first day she tried it, they earned all their stickers and they happily went out to the toy store to buy their rewards.

The next week, however, the kids wanted to negotiate. Surely, picking up their shoes was worth a sticker on its own, wasn't it, Mom? Soon, they were only partially picking up their rooms, but wanting stickers every time they did the tiniest thing. Although their rooms were not fully cleaned, over a couple of weeks they had managed to earn five stickers anyway and they wanted their toy. Feeling trapped, Janine bought the toys. She refused at the next five-sticker-but-room-still-messy mark. She told her children that they had to get the whole room clean once a week to earn stickers. Her kids got mad, accusing her of changing the rules and being unfair. Not only that, Janine noticed that they had started talking a lot about toys, planning for their eventual rewards. Every time they went to the store, they asked if Janine would buy them a toy—promising to clean their room after she bought it and getting angry when she said no. Where she had once had sweet children who didn't think much of toys except around their birthdays and holidays, she now had whining toy-coveting monsters—with dirty rooms.

Rewards are most effective when used for short periods of time when trying to reinforce a new behavior or help a child learn, or unlearn, a habit. As soon as you find the focus is always the reward and not the behavior, you would be wise to try another technique.

Punishment

Punishment—or negative reinforcement—of which yelling is only one form, can be powerful, but also damaging. One typical outcome of a parent using punishment is that afterward everyone feels terrible, child and parent alike. The purpose of negative reinforcement is to create a bad feeling/consequence associated with a particular behavior so that a person will shy away from doing the behavior again.

We say negative reinforcement has a place in parenting, but a limited place. The classic example is grabbing a child's hand when you see that hand reaching for the stove burner. You might also shout, "no!" loudly when you see your child about to stuff a fork into an electrical outlet. When safety is the issue and a quick response is needed, negative reinforcement is an appropriate tool to take out of your toolbox. If yelling is reserved for only the most egregious transgressions, when you pipe up, your child will get a clear indication of how big a deal this is and how upset you are.

Yelling is a short-term solution. Behavior modification systems will help yield long-term results. Now, we know there will be times when you still yell. Hey, we do too! The important thing to remember at these moments is the power of an apology. That's right, apologize to your children when you make a mistake. Parents often worry that apologizing will make them appear weak. Not so. Apologizing teaches children that no one is perfect, and when mistakes are made, people must accept responsibility for them. Like we said in Mommy Guilt-Free Principle No. 2, parenting is not a competitive sport, so apologizing for a mistake is not admitting defeat.

The 3Cs: calm, consistent, caring

Positive reinforcement, natural consequences, reward systems, and punishment are methods of discipline. Discipline does not mean punishment. It actually means "to teach." No need to feel guilty about disciplining our children as long as we are teaching them what we expect from them and what they need to expect from themselves. That is where the 3Cs come in: calm, consistent, caring. The words alone bring feelings of comfort and serenity. They are another key to guilt-free discipline because they emphasize that your behavior stays in control throughout any situation.

Remain calm: It is the first step listed on many emergency cards and posters. It is the first thing people tell you to do in an otherwise frantic situation.

Be consistent: It is not fair to change the rules in the middle of a game, nor is it an effective way for your children to learn the rules.

Show them you care: Your children know you love them, but they will also respect you when your love for them means treating them with respect, too. Does the following situation seem familiar?

You are trying to get out the door to take your kids to a movie with friends. Your son refuses to find his shoes and your daughter needs her purse. You finally scream, "I told you we're in a hurry. Get in the car!" However, immediately following that outburst, your son goes into full tantrum mode and your daughter stomps out the door, slamming it behind her. Well, that went well and now you're going to be even later because he still doesn't have his shoes on and he's now also refusing to stand up. You grab him and his shoes, force him into his seat and get yourself in the car under the ugly glares of your daughter. You meet up with your friends and feel terrible about the way you handled the entire event and the resulting attitude of your family. In retrospect, you are sure you could have handled the situation better if you hadn't been on such a time crunch.

Since time always seems to be of the essence for parents, we must assume that we will never have enough of it and figure out how to not let its scarcity undermine our efforts. In this case, what would happen if we just remember the 3Cs?

You are trying to meet your friends for a movie and are rushed. Your son has no shoes and your daughter is frantically looking for her purse. Instead of insisting that everyone hurry up, you quietly ask your daughter a few questions to jog her memory about her lost purse (When did you last use it? Did you leave it in the car?) and tell her she has a minute to track it down while you deal with shoe boy. You have let her know that you understand the importance of her purse by assisting her in trying to locate it. She will then have to decide if she can live without it. You then kneel down to inform your son that he is not allowed in the movie theater without his shoes on.

If he still won't put them on then you must make a decision. This is the hard part. You *calmly* state one final time that shoes are required in the theater. If he wants to go, he must put them on. Whatever you say next, you must be *consistent* and follow through on. You present the options in a respectful, *caring* tone of voice, not as threats:

Option 1. No shoes, no movie. He puts them on and you go.

Option 2. No shoes, no movie. He still refuses. You inform everyone that you will stay home. Your daughter manages to politely convince her brother to put his shoes on and you go.

Option 3. No shoes, no movie. He still refuses. You inform everyone that you will stay home. Your daughter tries to help, remains calm, is also unsuccessful. You praise her for being a great helper and make arrangements to somehow get her to the movie. (You're a parent, you'll figure something out even if it means she goes on a different day or to a later movie.)

Option 4. No shoes, no movie. He still refuses. You inform everyone that you will stay home. Your daughter immediately goes into tantrum mode and you inform her that she could have responded in a more helpful manner and the movie will wait until a better time for everyone.

Option 5. You decide it makes no sense to spend valuable time arguing about shoes and put your shoeless son in the car with your daughter, take the shoes with you, and figure everyone will be calmer once you get to the theater. Once at the theater, if you can put the shoes on without a battle, the story is over. If not, you find yourself facing similar options as above, in a new location.

All of the options have a critical similarity! No yelling, no loss of control, no power struggle, and *no guilt*. You remain in control of the situation by remaining in control of your own behavior.

One last thing to keep in mind is that you choose whether or not to participate in a fight with your child. By employing the 3Cs, not only will you spend less time fighting, you will demonstrate to your children how to approach life's difficulties with their own calm, consistent, and caring attitudes. That will yield big dividends with your family for years to come.

CHAPTER 7

THROTTLE DOWN THAT TONE OF VOICE, PART TWO

In Chapter 6, we discussed some strategies to approach discipline without yelling. Now let's address several circumstances that would try the patience of even the calmest moms: tantrums and other misbehavior in public places, backtalk, and being ignored by the children. A mom can spare herself a load of guilt in these situations by employing some empathy and putting into practice some of her best Mommy Guilt-Free tools. In all these situations, the best course of action is to demonstrate to your children what behavior you want from them, give them ways to practice that behavior, and pile on the praise when they meet your expectations.

Making public places guilt-free spaces

Like a private company that goes public, children's behavior in public is difficult to predict, and the younger they are, the harder it is to get a read on future performance. As parents, it is our responsibility to try to read the market report and then evaluate whether we want to invest in taking our children into the public sector. There will be times when it will be in everyone's interest not to put them out on the floor, unless you can trade them!

Tired, hungry, or ill children almost always behave poorly in public no matter how old they are. If you cannot postpone your venturing out until the child is feeling up to par, then your best option is to cut your child some slack. A public outburst, argument, or tantrum might be in your immediate future. A lot of the guilt surrounding this behavior focuses on what others think and often has little to do with our children at all. Sometimes, a mother feels guilty over how she handles a stressful public outburst as well. Take comfort in the fact that every parent faces this situation at some time.

Avoid the inevitable

A great deal of Mommy Guilt over your children's public behavior can be avoided simply by doing that—avoidance. Avoid situations that are going to expect too much from your child. For instance, avoid taking your toddler to any restaurant that doesn't own a highchair. Until your kids are old enough, save the leather-chair, cloth napkin experience for an adults-only evening. On the other hand, you won't want to limit yourself to the fast-food experience, nor should you. Plenty of family-oriented restaurants exist where wonderful people not only cook your food but also bring it to you, take it away, and wash the dishes for you. Be prepared though, if you haven't already experienced the delight of hateful glances from other restaurant goers, you probably will along your parenting path—even in family-friendly dining establishments. So when you do, repeat to yourself, "No one in this place was born an adult." Taking breaks in a restaurant by walking around a lobby or out in the parking lot does wonders for a child and is another great way to get him comfortable with his surroundings. When children feel comfortable, they are less likely to misbehave. As long as your child is not throwing food or screaming, ignore the nasty looks and enjoy your meal. The Mommy Guilt-Free Philosophy views the family-oriented restaurant as a fun destination in itself as well as a training ground for the eventual foray into the cloth-napkin place.

Another great way to avoid public battles is to prepare your kids for what is about to happen. As you make your way to the destination, begin to narrate the trip for your child. One of the authors of this book, Devra Renner, narrates these excursions in the voice of an airline attendant, which gets a laugh from her kids. More important, her children also remember what she said because it was funny. Through this narration, you can let them know the purpose of the trip, how long you expect it to take, where your child will be, and with whom. If shopping is involved, you can also tell them what will be purchased and for whom. The more detailed the better. You can start this preparation game when your children are infants to get you both used to it.

When you combine avoidance and preparation with what we call a "stepping-stone" approach to age-appropriate experiences, you are once again living Mommy Guilt-Free Principle No. 3 (Looking toward the future and big picture). There is also a healthy dose of Mommy Guilt-Free Principle No. 1 (Letting some things go)—in this case, trips to age-inappropriate venues. There is also the opportunity for plenty of Mommy Guilt-Free Principle No. 6 (Laughing a lot with your children). The stepping-stone approach allows you to teach your kids the public behavior you expect of them in small, age-appropriate steps. As they grow and demonstrate increasing mastery of public behavior skills—such as self-control, "indoor" speaking voices, and adhering to the behavioral rules of the venue—you can safely and enjoyably expose them to a broader variety of places and circumstances, fine-tuning your behavioral expectations as they learn. This allows everyone to enjoy their experience while practicing the expected behaviors.

A stepping-stone approach to movies might look like this: drive-ins for toddlers, matinee films for preschoolers, early evening movies for school-age kids. For live theater, you might want to begin with child-oriented productions like cartoon-character ice shows, move on to regional theater, and then progress to the young people's concerts offered by the symphony. Remember, the idea of the stepping-stone approach is to be able to place age-appropriate expectations on them—not adultlike ones.

My friend and I took our toddler girls to see one of those kiddie ice shows. The music started and the toddlers began to sing and dance in the aisles. The four of us were laughing and having a good time. Then I saw HER. The grandma behind us was giving us the evil eye over allowing our toddlers out of their seats. She was making her grandchild sit quietly. The smile dropped from my face. I felt so guilty! Was my child's behavior ruining the experience for other audience members? I whispered to my friend about it, and she just shrugged. Her message in that shrug was that this is a kid show. If the grandma wanted quiet, she could have gone to the symphony. After that, I didn't worry about grandma. I taught my child how to politely say, "Excuse me," when walking past others in the row. I let her enjoy the performance in her own toddler way, dancing in the aisle.

We also like a proactive approach to learning proper public behavior—practicing at home. Children like to play let's pretend, so why not role-play going out to eat or seeing a show with your children. Point out appropriate behavior that you want your kids to model, even if it's the pretend patrons of the pretend restaurant you have set up in the living room. "See that girl, she is sitting so nicely at that table." Or "See that little boy, he is talking so quietly." Or "See that mommy, she is eating with a fork." If you teach your children what is expected and practice it with them, they may not act like unruly urchins in public. They will simply act like children.

Taming the beast

If at all possible, we recommend taking your children out when they are at their best, and to us, best means sniffle-free, rested, and fed. We recognize that this is an ideal, and there will be times when you must brave the elements and schlep that runny-nosed, tired, or hungry kid around. However, before you put the car in drive, think avoidance, do you really have to go to the grocery store at 8 P.M. with your children in tow—even if you are out of milk, bread, cereal, and all things resembling breakfast food? It may take some creativity on your part, but maybe you can scrounge up some breakfast and leave the food shopping until morning. Leftover pizza can be a breakfast food! (For a list of Mommy Guilt-Free pantry recommendations to help you through these moments, see Appendix B.) On the other hand, what if your entire home is devoid of toilet paper? Arm yourself to enter the shopping zone.

A trip to the grocery store can be akin to walking through a den of snakes unless you've got a plan in place to deal with the invariable cries of hunger and "I want that" from your children. If your child is old enough, "preshopping narration" can include telling him items on the list. Then he can help you find them on the shelves. This engages him in the shopping experience, rather than allowing him to get bored, zeroing in on all the low-shelf goodies you have no intention of buying, and brewing up a public tantrum when you inform him that 100 packs of gum are "not on our list." We also recommend you give your child a little snack en route or bring along something she can eat while you shop. Don't worry about whether your child will eat dinner or not. What's more important, one dinner on just that day or buying the toilet paper that you are completely out of with a minimum of fuss?

Let's say your child couldn't eat before shopping and you have no food on hand when the stock begins to crash at the store with many loud screams of "I'm hungry!" Go ahead and buy some food from the store's deli—even if your child insists on junk food. Let your child eat while you quickly finish shopping. You might ask whether this is giving into a tantrum. Won't I feel guilty about giving in—almost as guilty as I'd feel over dragging my screaming child through the store? Remember Mommy Guilt-Free Principle No. 5 (Get used to saying yes and being able to defend your no). If you entered a warehouse of food with a hungry child, you've got a great reason to say yes and ample opportunity to take action. When you take control of the situation, you can avoid a power struggle and an escalation of the problem.

If you worry about what other people will think about your screaming child or your junk-food solution, here is a sampling: Some of them will be thinking, thank goodness the screaming stopped. Some of them will be thinking, poor child, she's hungry. Some of them will be thinking, poor mother, I remember the days! Still others will be thinking—doesn't bother me, she's not my kid. All of them will be thinking about getting through their grocery lists and getting out of there, just as if you and your hungry child weren't in the store. Who cares? What they think doesn't matter. And that's the crux of dealing well with public tantrums, no matter where they occur.

If they happen in the store . . .

If they happen at the doctor's door . . .

If they happen in the no-parking lane . . .

If they happen on the air-o-plane . . .

You need to take action so you won't go insane!

The people you encounter in public will probably never be in your lives again and are in no danger from the loud noises emanating from your family. Don't worry about them. Once you stop focusing on them and start focusing instead on your child during the situation, guilt will evaporate.

When my youngest daughter was a toddler, the frustration of life would build up in her and there was no avoiding the storm. I learned to watch for tantrum signs, like scanning the clouds to predict rain. But I didn't always read the tantrum weather right. One day, we were shopping when the tantrum came pouring out. She flung herself on the sidewalk in front of the store door— people had to step over her. I debated carrying her kicking and screaming to the car, but then I thought about how hard it was to be a two-year-old, with no control over your life. So I sat down on the sidewalk next to her and let her scream. After about five minutes, I asked her if she wouldn't mind moving out of people's way. She refused. We sat. A few minutes later she got up and plopped herself out of the doorway. We stayed for another twenty minutes, her screaming, me sitting. Strangers mostly gave me that "I've been there!" smile, but a few were annoyed. I didn't care. When she was done, I held her and wiped her face. I gave her a very short version of the "Was it worth it? Do you really feel better?" speech. Then we continued our shopping and had a great day.

Before you begin to doubt our sanity, we will also tell you that there are times when you must decide to cut bait and leave. For instance, if your child is throwing food in the restaurant, or this is a repeat tantrum in the marshmallow aisle, realize you are being had and that it's time to leave. Leave as quickly and as quietly (on your part) as possible. Focus on your escape. Looking around apologetically is wasted effort. Every parent on the planet has had to do this at one time or another; you are simply taking your turn—you weren't the first to pass this way, and you won't be the last.

While you may be tempted to yell or lecture your child while still at the venue, refrain. If you do yell at your child in public, you probably won't be looked upon sympathetically by others. Of course, it doesn't matter all that much what these strangers think of you, but please realize that they probably aren't going to empathize with both a tantruming child *and* her tantruming parent. One of you needs to remain in control and it really should be the grown-up.

The outcome of your discipline efforts should not be public humiliation of the child. Many children will already feel embarrassed about losing control in the grocery store, even if they don't tell you so. What you want to concentrate on is getting the behavior under control, yours as well as your child's. Adding public humiliation into the mix may create a resentful child who will not want to go to the store again. Some children are like elephants, with long memories. Best not to make this moment any more memorable than it needs to be. When everyone is calm, in the car or at home, address what happened. In delaying your reaction until the moment is over, you will also give yourself some time to cool down. Once calm, you can take inventory as to the reasons for the meltdown and address them.

In the words of one of the authors, Julie Bort: *During my daughter's first plane ride, the change of routine, the stress from traveling, and little ears that wouldn't clear set her off. She started screaming. People around me grew agitated and annoyed. I forced myself not to let their glares get to me, telling myself, "Who cares? I'll never see them again and if they can't have tolerance for a crying child, they don't deserve my sympathy." I gently rocked her and comforted her while she howled. I told her I knew how hard it was for her. In a few minutes, she fell asleep. At the end of the trip, an elderly couple from across the aisle who I had imagined were among the most annoyed stopped me in the aisle. They complimented me on how I handled the situation and declared me "a very good mother." That really boosted my parenting confidence.*

When you are confronted by a tantrum and you keep your emotions in check, you will be the "mom who really kept her cool when her child was so out of control." This will boost your self-image. Do you remember Lamaze? Now is a great time to use it! Take deep breaths and concentrate on your breathing. It will give you time to calm yourself and think of an action plan for ending the tantrum.

Busting backtalk

Somehow a rude comment from a child can make a mom flip her lid and fast! We know a mom who didn't believe in spanking but slapped her child across the face in an instantaneous reaction to a rude comment. Want to bet that this mom spent the evening with an acute case of guilt?

You don't have to put up with rude kids—in fact, you absolutely need to stomp out any behavior in which your child treats you or anyone else disrespectfully. The way to eradicate this behavior is to model for your kids how you expect them to speak to you. That is, talk to them with the respectful tones you expect them to use with you. When they venture into rudeness, stop it. Explain to them that rudeness is unacceptable. Then model the correct way they should phrase their comment, and have them restate it, using respectful words, in a polite tone of voice.

When my kids were nine and seven, we went through a period where everything they said to me was an argument or rude, in content or tone of voice. I would get angry, my husband would jump to my defense, and the kids were constantly being lectured and sent to their rooms. While I wanted them to understand that rudeness to me was not okay, I also wanted to live in a happy household, where my kids were not constantly in trouble. So I initiated the "Yes, Mommy" rule. The only thing my kids were allowed to say to me was "Yes, Mommy." Literally. That was it. When I told them the new rule, they greeted the idea with looks of rebellion. So we practiced it for a good fifteen minutes. I said, "If I say, 'Go clean your room,' you say, 'Yes, Mommy.'" I made them repeat it: "Yes, Mommy." I tried other phrases, "Time for bed." They said, "Yes, Mommy."

"Are you working on your homework?"

"Yes, Mommy."

"Can I throw spinach in your hair?"

Giggling, "Yes, Mommy."

For the next two weeks, they couldn't talk to me unless they first responded with, "Yes, Mommy." I rewarded them by making a game out of it, thinking up silly things for which they had to respond "Yes, Mommy." But it also worked. The tone of voice and respect I wanted was modeled and practiced until it became habit. To this day, when they slip into the rudeness, a couple hours of "Yes, Mommy" clears it right up!

Everyone in a family deserves respect and consideration. If you see that your kids are having a problem with this idea, first look and see if you are contributing to the problem. If you haven't been modeling respectful behavior lately, it's time to start. Also, remember to heap on the praise when your children get it right.

Handling the selective-hearing dilemma

Your five-year-old child is playing on the floor in the other room and you ask her to go wash for dinner. A few minutes later, you're still waiting for her to wash and report to the kitchen. You call out to her again. More minutes pass. Finally, you storm out to the other room, yelling, "This is the third time I've told you to wash for dinner! You need to learn to do what you're told!" The child looks up at you astonished, and then gets defensive. "I didn't know you wanted me to wash up. I didn't hear you."

You shout back, "I was standing three feet away from you. You weren't listening, you were ignoring me. For that, you can go to bed tonight without watching any TV."

She storms off, and as you cool down, you feel guilty at your outburst and wonder why your child always pushes you to the point where you lose your cool.

Welcome to the wonderful developmental milestone of selective hearing. Selective hearing is common among kids age five to seven, but can begin as early as four and last until the child is twelve. It is one result of your children's growing attention span and their interest in the world. Understand that your children are not deliberately ignoring you. They are only so fully concentrating on the task at hand—playing, for instance—that they tune out everything else, including your voice issuing instructions. In other words, your child really didn't hear you.

HELPFUL HINT

Too Much Selective Hearing

While selective hearing is a normal developmental stage, if it seems extreme, it may indicate that your child is having a physical or emotional problem. Tell your pediatrician if you feel that your baby often tunes you out. Messages from your child's teacher indicating that your child is having trouble paying attention in class should be treated seriously (remember, she deals with kids your child's age all day long). If you cannot easily break your child's concentration—a touch on the shoulder doesn't illicit an immediate response—that could also be grounds for a doctor's visit.

Selective hearing isn't an automatic sign of disrespect. The child's brain zeros in on the object or subject and tunes out the world—much the way you do when you are reading a novel or watching TV. Yelling really won't help. As a child grows older and learns the skill of multitasking, she may begin to give you quicker attention when you request it. However, better methods exist for dealing with selective hearing than demanding your kids keep an ear open for your instructions at all times.

When you begin to notice selective hearing, you need to stop the habit of yelling instructions from one room to another in the house. (The telltale sign that you've encountered selective hearing is when the child claims not to have heard you.) Go to your child and touch him gently on the shoulder. When he gives you his attention, then give him your instructions. Ask him to repeat those instructions to you, just to be sure he processed your words. Also require your children to come to you when they need your attention and to wait for you to give them your complete attention, too, before they start speaking. One of the authors allows her kids to enter her home office while she is working at any time. They stand by her chair as a signal that they need to tell her something. As quickly as she is able—typically within a minute—she stops what she is doing and acknowledges them. Let your kids know how to politely get your attention, and use the same polite methods when you are trying to reach them. For sharing instructions such as doctor appointments, phone messages, or chore lists nothing beats writing it down. Not that you want to become a personal secretary, but a central message board can help you communicate instructions.

Of course, understanding selective hearing and leaving messages on the board won't help you out when you've got to get your kids in the car, *now,* and they are tuning you out. So get creative in coming up with methods to get your children's attention without yelling.

My three children were in the throes of selective hearing and I was absolutely going crazy, feeling like I was yelling all the time. So, I bought a whistle. Three whistles became the call to the car. The first was a warning to get their shoes on and be ready to leave. The second meant "you better be on your way to the car." The third was, "I'm walking into the garage now, you better be sitting in the car, or running to it." I also bought a megaphone that I use to get my children's attention. When I'm not using it to get their attention, I make up silly cheerleading routines to entertain them. They think the megaphone is hilarious.

Day camps deal with selective hearing by training their kids to perform responsive calls, chants, or clapping games. If the counselors need everyone's attention, they begin by calling out, "Hey you," and the kids must all reply in unison, "Hey what!" Or they clap the rhythm of "Shave and a hair cut" and the kids reply by clapping the rhythm "Two bits."

Once you realize why your kids don't ever seem to hear you, you can come up with clever, fun solutions to encourage them to recognize when you need their attention. No need to yell. Also remember with selective hearing, it's just a phase—this, too, shall pass.

During the preteen years, your children are capable of hearing you again even when they are busy, but selective hearing becomes an issue of finding the best time to talk to them. At times, they are very distracted by what is going on their world. They are becoming more adultlike. Just like you are unavailable at times during meetings, phone calls, or handling a plumbing crisis, you need to have the same kind of respect for your preteen. When your preteen is on the phone, it's not a good time to talk to him about plans for the weekend.

You've now learned some Mommy Guilt-Free strategies for eradicating daily yelling matches with your kids (and weekly ones, too!). With these strategies, plus the tools outlined in Chapter 6, you've given yourself a volume control knob on your voice box. When the yelling voice is throttled down, you'll be able to cultivate laughter in its place.

CHAPTER 8

A PARENT'S GUIDE TO (ALMOST) STRESS-FREE HOUSEKEEPING

A home that looks like a tornado's aftermath is incompatible with a relaxed, comfortable home life. But—make no mistake—an immaculate, uncluttered, white-glove-inspected home is equally incompatible. The Mommy Guilt-Free Philosophy strives for a realistic balance in all things, housekeeping included. Make that housekeeping *especially*.

Housework is the responsibility of everyone who lives in a house, not just the moms. Yet, moms are driving themselves bonkers in their pursuit of dust bunnies. This is their number two area of guilt (after yelling), with 59 percent of our survey participants naming living in a messy house as a source of guilt. It ranks high for parents of toddlers as well as for parents of preteens—and for every age group in between. Almost half of the moms surveyed went so far as to name it as the area that causes them their most severe feelings of guilt. This compares with only 19 percent of dads who feel severely guilty about a messy house—although 38 percent of dads who participated in the survey name housework as an area that causes some guilt.

The chief household officer

Not only are moms suffering severe Mommy Guilt because they think the house is too dirty, they are also feeling the pain over spending so much time trying to get the housework done! Our survey respondents say they spend as much time running the household (as the "chief household officer") as they do interacting directly with their kids. Forty-six percent of the moms surveyed report that half or more of their day is spent being the chief household officer (CHO). In contrast, dads say that they spend more time with their children than on CHO tasks. One-third of the dads report that the mom does the CHO job pretty much solo (while less than 1 percent of the moms credit the dad as the sole CHO).

Moms feel frustrated because the never-ending job of housework is just that, never ending. They feel guilty because the hours spent with dust bunnies are viewed as time taken away from being with their children. A couple of respondents share this advice:

I just acknowledge the guilt and try to deal with it at the time it occurs. For example, when I feel guilty about not spending time with my kids while I'm cleaning or preparing dinner, I'll drop what I'm doing and play with them for a few minutes—it calms them down as well—especially the four-year-old.

* * * * *

The best advice is to try and balance your time with what you have going on. Ignore the housework and play with your kids whenever you are home. They are only small once and you have the rest of your life to clean your house.

Sounds simple. It can be! The Mommy Guilt-Free Philosophy believes that these two uses of time—housework and interacting with the kids—are not mutually exclusive. Simply engage your children in the housekeeping *with* you. Obviously, babies from birth to sixteen months shouldn't be expected to help keep the house clean, and while eating the crumbs from the floor does help clean the floor, we're not sure this counts.

But as soon as the child becomes a toddler, walking and capable of following simple instructions, the kid can help out. Trust us on this. The Mommy Guilt-Free method to (nearly) painless housekeeping is not only simple but also practical and *possible.* Intrigued? Peel off those yellow latex gloves and read on (or jump ahead to the box "Kids Love to Help" on page 82). In this chapter, we've got a scrub bucket full of ideas to help you attack the clutter and wash away the guilt.

Sanity Keepers for Household Dirtiness Run Amok

While kids can help with many housekeeping tasks, some tasks need more adult involvement than others. When you find yourself responsible for the tasks listed below, here are some tips to help you cope guilt-free:

➤ Try not to go to bed with dirty dishes in the sink. Stepping into a clean kitchen can make the day much smoother.

➤ Consider how much time you have in relationship to the task you are about to tackle. If you don't have time to complete the entire task, see if it can be broken down into manageable segments that can be done over time.

➤ Keep a set of bathroom cleaning supplies in each bathroom, including sponges, rags, paper towels, a toilet bowl brush, and so forth. Cleaning a toilet bowl and wiping down the counters to achieve "surface clean" takes only a few minutes if all the gear is at hand.

➤ Accept that clutter happens but doesn't have to happen everywhere. Inform family and friends that a specified kitchen countertop must remain clear of clutter at all times (not all horizontal surfaces need to be used for storage). Try giving each family member a bin or other designated area where each can toss their own personal clutter.

➤ Teach your child from the start that a new game cannot begin until the other game is put away.

➤ Try the "ten-minutes-first" rule with yourself. Spend the first ten minutes of any available time during the day sorting through clutter. Do it first. Stop after ten minutes. This is enough to whittle away at the piles that magically appear, and even stop some from forming.

Stop expecting royalty

The first step in conquering housekeeping guilt is to create a realistic schedule for basic maintenance. Realistic is defined, in part, by your household project-management style. (See the quiz at end of this chapter called "Are You a Keeper-Upper or a Catcher-Upper?") The word *realistic* is also defined by your expectations. If you expect to maintain cleanliness in a state we call "ready for royalty," we suggest you activate Mommy Guilt-Free Principle No. 1 (Let some things go) and lower your standards. Ready-for-royalty cleanliness is the kind of clean achieved right before guests arrive. It is a special bubble of time in which your house could be photographed for a decorator magazine. Ready-for-royalty cleanliness doesn't last even a few hours unless you have banished your family from the home. It is one thing to keep a single *room* in your house in a ready-for-royalty state—such as that otherwise-unlived-in space known as the living room—it is quite another to expect the entire house to remain in that condition. We feel that maintaining a minimum is the way to go.

We highly encourage you to consider for your minimum something we call the surface clean. You would be amazed at how much nicer your house will look if you run a quick vacuum over the portions of the floor you can easily access and wipe down the shiny surfaces (sorry, this does include the toilets). Trust us, we've all done it and called the house clean! In Chapter 3, we offered you the safety guidepost as a guide to general household rule making. Surface clean complies with the safety guidepost. You want your kid to play in a safe environment. Vacuum up the lint balls before the baby eats them and clear the counters before your preteen eats the leftovers off them. Once you've removed dangers like food poisoning, choking, and lint ingestion, safety is achieved. The rest of the mess is simply proof that you would rather be looked up to as a great mom, than a great maid. Besides, which do you think leads to a more enjoyable parenting experience, if the house is a mess and your kids get to play with you, or if you've spent more time cleaning the house than playing with your children?

Kids doing their fair share

Then again why not combine the time you spend cleaning up with the time you spend with your children? This approach is not only easier than it sounds but also a great way to implement Mommy Guilt-Free Principle No. 6 (Laughing a lot with your children).

The way we attend to housekeeping duties influences our children's participation in keeping their home clean. If we constantly follow them around, picking up after every little thing they do, they will naturally begin to view us as the maid whose job is to keep their environment spotless.

When a child is able to follow a one-step command and walk with an object in hand, she is ready to help. A two-year-old can manage to toss a toy into a bin. Help her out by having a low, wide, large toy box that everything can be tossed into without much effort on her part. While the toy area does need to have some order to comply with the safety guidepost, there is no need to make huge drudgery out of keeping the area tidy. An easy way to keep this area under control is to limit the amount of toys you need to put away. In addition to encouraging an attitude that cleanliness does not matter, too many toys in the area put kids at risk for injury and can be a breeding ground for bacteria following an illness. (For more tips on age-appropriate tasks, see the box "Kids Love to Help: A Household Responsibility Guide.")

Take a serious look at the toys your kids actually use and see if they have outgrown any of them. While your kids are picking the toys up off the floor, have them toss the lesser used ones into a bag which you can then donate to a local children's charity (get rid of cleaning guilt and teach your kids a lesson in helping others). Try rotating toys into and out of their toy area, cleaning them after they are removed and before they are stored away. Dunking toys into soapy water is also a task you can do with your child. Simply remove and clean one or two toys every few days and throw them into a box in a closet. Toys that reappear after being banished to the closet box will regain appeal and seem "new" again.

Books are certainly another item that even very small children can learn to pick up. Remember that your children are not librarians, though, so revel in the fact that they got the book on the shelf. Abandon your expectation that the book should be perfectly aligned with the other books, alphabetized, or ordered by subject (even if you've gone to all the trouble of labeling each spine with the appropriate Dewey decimal system number). Willy-nilly stacking of the books on the shelf is fine for toddlers through grade-school kids and beyond that, you'll be in such practice with Mommy Guilt-Free Principle No. 1 (Let some things go) that you won't remember how to use the Dewey decimal system yourself. In fact, you may need to chant Mommy Guilt-Free Principle No. 1 as a mantra while you clean house with your very young children, at least until you learn to rejoice in their less-than-perfect idea of clean.

Now that my children help with the household tasks, I find that I am a much happier mom. Instead of feeling like the maid, I now find it fun to talk about how much my kids help around our home. Granted there are tradeoffs, like not being too picky about how a job is done. I have learned that if I let my preschooler help with cleaning, I need to redefine what the word "clean" means. Preschool clean means he will spray tons of glass cleaner at one time, use one paper towel to wipe at it, and he will repeat this until boredom sets in. Having your child help means that instead of saying "Oh my gosh, what happened here?" You readjust to "Wow sweetie, it smells so clean! Good job!"

Kids Love to Help: A Household Responsibility Guide

The Mommy Guilt-Free Philosophy emphasizes enjoying your children by matching your expectations of their behavior with age-appropriateness. The following chart represents suggested age-appropriateness of common household tasks. By mapping tasks to a child's developmental and emotional abilities, you avoid frustration for both you and your child. Obviously, you know your child best and may feel your child is or isn't ready by the ages listed here. (But what the heck, you may want to try the list as it is before fine-tuning it—your kids might surprise you!)

AGE	ACTIVITY
17–24 months	Can now pick up and put away one toy at a time under direction and help from a grown-up; can help a grown-up toss clothes into a washer or dryer.
2–3 years old	Can now choose clothes and dress with little-to-no assistance from a grown-up, can stack books on a shelf, help set the table, fill a pet's food dish, put clothes in a hamper, water plants.
4–5 years old	Can now use a handheld vacuum, dust, make a bed, empty wastebaskets, bring in the mail, clear unbreakable dishes from the table, can help to load and unload non-breakable items from the dishwasher.
6–7 years old	Can now sort laundry by color and put in piles, match socks, sweep floors and outside decks/walks, set and clear the table, rake leaves, wipe kitchen and bathroom countertops, run a vacuum with supervision, put clothes in drawers, strip and make a bed, with supervision.
8–10 years old	Can now load dishwasher, put away groceries, vacuum, mop, clean hard surfaces (dusting, windows, bathroom counters), engage in simple unsupervised cooking tasks (make a sandwich, wash fruit, etc.), engage in more skilled cooking tasks with supervision, fold and put away clothes, walk pets, take out the garbage, read to younger siblings, wash themselves in the bath/shower.

10–12 years old	Can now complete loads of laundry from sorting through folding with little to no supervision (teach them to separate the reds & whites first though!), clean all fixtures in the bathroom unsupervised, mop and surface clean, wash windows, wash car, cook a hot meal with supervision, prepare a cold meal without supervision, unload the dishwasher, complete longer/multistep projects with little-to-no supervision (organize a bedroom).

Remember, too, that a child's brain does not kick in with "Warning! Warning! You have made an uncontrollable mess that will drive your parents crazy and take a week to clean up." Periodically remind your child to put some things away. Include this in your realistic schedule, and be specific. Until at least the fourth grade, a child hasn't developed the maturation to perform project management, so telling him to clean the family room and hoping he'll notice what you are doing and follow your lead rarely works. For toddlers through preschoolers, tell the child to pick up a specific item (a book) and put it in a specific place (the book bin). School-age children can be expected to pick up categories of items—books, toys, clothes, and so forth. You may also break the task down by asking them to pick up items according to color, shape, size, or some other more fun, imaginative criteria. ("Pick up the items that rhyme with the word 'hook!'")

Speaking of fun, the more you approach joint cleaning time with a sense of fun and humor, the more all of you will enjoy this time spent together. Housework won't be categorized as dirty, awful, exhausting, or unrewarding work unless you cast it in that light. Young children think mopping and doing windows is a blast!

My Brownie troop and I spent a weekend camping in the backyard. I had prepared enough directed activities for them to earn four badges. As part of their training to go on a real trip to a camp with no electricity or plumbing, they had to prove they could do the work part. They helped set up their tent, cooked their own meals, and cleaned up. At the end of the weekend, I asked them to perform a skit about their favorite part. They ignored all the fun badge activities I had prepared for them and chose to re-enact the cooking, sweeping, and dish washing! I was dumbfounded. It occurred to me that directed activities are standard for six-year-olds, but they are rarely given full responsibility for their own caretaking. They relished it. I learned not to be so quick to do "the work" for my kids. Young school-age kids want to help—I should let them!

Take advantage of this magnificent opportunity by allowing school-age children to help; however, you need to adjust your expectations to be satisfied with a young child's interpretation of clean. Call on the magic of positive reinforcement discussed in Chapter 6 and pile on the praise in equal portions to the effort, not to the result. Taking the shirt out of his hand to show him the "right" way to fold it, or following up with instructive criticism while refolding, will only reinforce the message that cleaning is not something he does well, so why bother? Mommy the maid will show up to clean up. Instead, try throwing on some tunes and boogying down with your children as you bust that grime together and straighten up that mess. Think fun—and fun you shall have.

If you are worried that you will turn your children into servants by making them responsible for cleaning, douse yourself all over with Mommy Guilt-Free Principle No. 5 (Saying yes more often and defending your no). You have every reason to say yes to kids doing their fair share, and no reason to refuse them. Plus, kids really do love to help as much as they love to be messy. When you encourage them to help, you teach them how to be responsible for their environment and allow them to try even if it falls short of what you would do. You will be looking toward the future and the big picture (Mommy Guilt-Free Principle No. 3), and you will avoid becoming a servant in your own home. In addition, you are teaching them daily living skills that they will need once they leave your nest and make one of their own.

Quiz: Are You a Keeper-Upper or a Catcher-Upper?

Your housework will be smoother for you and your children if you draft your plan to match your management style. Without taking that step, you could be setting yourself up for guilt. Plans that don't match your natural operating style are difficult to follow long term—akin to the guilt we feel on January 5 when our New Year's resolutions are mere memories. This quiz is designed to get you to think about how you like to operate.

Read the following pairs of statements. Then select one statement per pair—either a or b—that best describes you:

1a. I rarely read more than one book at a time, preferring to complete one before starting another.

1b. I frequently read several books at a time, picking up one or the other depending on my mood.

2a. When it's my turn to do dishes, I prefer to do a whole day's worth all at once rather than constantly dealing with them after every meal.
2b. When it's my turn to do dishes, I prefer that my sink and countertops remain clear of clutter. Dirty items are placed immediately into the dishwasher after they are used.

3a. If my household gets behind on the laundry, I may catch up by washing it all, but then it will frequently wind up in baskets waiting to be folded or put away.
3b. If my household gets behind on the laundry, I will make sure there is adequate time to wash, dry, and put away each load before I start it.

4a. When paying bills, I collect them all, write all the checks and mail them out—typically once or twice a month.
4b. I write bills several times a week, paying them based on when they are due.

5a. I prefer to plan out the week's meals in advance, so I know exactly what ingredients to defrost or have on hand well before I have to start cooking.
5b. I rarely plan dinners, preferring to cook whatever I'm in the mood to eat each day.

Score: Give yourself one point for every "a" statement and three points for every "b."
5–8 points: You prefer "catching up." You are happiest when you can do a task from beginning to end before moving onto the next task. You would rather wait until a task is large enough to consume your entire attention, and you may find it exhausting to flit from one task to another. If you are interrupted from a task, you may not get back to it, and then may feel overwhelmed and guilty when looking around at a list full of half-accomplished items. When prioritizing your commitments, allow yourself plenty of time to complete a task in one continuous period if at all possible. Do laundry one or two days a week, for example, rather than attempting a load a day. Pick a specific time during your day when you can do the dishes—for instance, in the evening after dinner. Take one day a week or perhaps one day a month

and call it an errand day, in which you can accomplish, start to finish, all the little items that pile up during the month—returning library books, going to the pharmacy and dry cleaner, and so on. Always spend time enjoying the feeling of accomplishment when a task is done and don't start another task until you've savored that moment.

9–11 points: Your style depends on the task. While you may prefer catching up overall, you may also realize that some tasks can spin out of control so quickly that you would rather deal with them in smaller doses. Note which tasks you complete on a regular basis and which tasks pile up and never seem to get completed. Apply the advice from "catching up" to the tasks that never seem to get done. If you feel stressed out and guilty when unfinished tasks begin to accumulate, you may actually be best suited to operate completely as a "catching up" person. If you routinely finish tasks from which you are interrupted, but feel overwhelmed when a task grows so large it cannot be completed in a matter of hours, you may be best suited to operate almost completely as a "keeping up" person.

12–15 points: You prefer "keeping up." You would rather engage several tasks at once than feel like you are wasting time doing a solo task. You find it easier to tackle maintenance than initial organization, and may feel overwhelmed when a task gets too far behind. If something cannot be completed, or at least seriously progressed, in a matter of hours, you may get frustrated. Break large tasks up into small components that can be done in minutes to hours. For instance, do one—and only one—load of laundry per day, finding a time of day when you can fold it and put it away. Note the sense of completeness when the task is done. Prioritize emptying the dishwasher, so that it remains available for dirty dishes as soon as they are made. View other cleaning tasks in their smallest possible components such as cleaning one toilet (not all bathrooms), and make sure you accomplish one to three of those tiny tasks daily. Always stop and notice the sense of completeness when each task is done. Keeping-up people can easily feel guilty over never finishing enough work—the key here is to redefine "enough." Give yourself a couple of times per week to be able to accomplish errands such as returning library books or going to the dry cleaner. If you find yourself loaded down with so many unfinished tasks that guilt is creeping in, stop initiating any new task (even that one load of laundry per day), until you can complete the ones you've already started.

CHAPTER 9

THE GUILTY GOURMET

What's for dinner, Mom? The question alone is enough to make you lose your appetite. Does it seem as if the moment you cross your kitchen's threshold, suddenly everyone needs your attention? For some moms, the stress gets so hot, it boils over into regular predinner fights with the kids.

Maybe it is simple exhaustion that makes you steam. You are at the end of your busy day. You are tired. You are hungry. Cooking is more work (even if you enjoy it), and it creates the obligation of cleaning work after it. Your kids are tired and hungry, too. If after-school activities kept you running, the clock is ticking. Hurry up and cook! Hurry up and eat! Hurry up and get your homework done! Hurry up to bed! After that, a nice little postmeal mess awaits you in the kitchen. No wonder dinner has become a dreaded hour for so many moms—it leads to fights, tears, anger, and Mommy Guilt.

Maybe the nightly meal planning stresses you out. Even on the days when you have the foresight to take something out of the freezer by 8 A.M., you never know if the dinner you cooked will be greeted with raves or rejection. After all your hard work, will your children turn up their noses and demand peanut-butter-and-jelly sandwiches?

We hear you. More than one-third of Mommy Guilt survey respondents named their children's eating habits as a source of guilt. (For 14 percent, it causes their highest level of guilt.) Moms feel guilty over allowing junk food for dinner, a lack of veggies in the diet, or worrying that kids are eating too much or not enough. Now, toss that guilt with a stress vinaigrette of finding time to make and eat dinner every day, and you've got a fresh serving of Mommy Guilt waiting for you.

Chapter 5 covered Mommy Guilt-Free methods for helping your children build sensible eating habits. This chapter will touch on peaceful alternatives to predinner stress, handling the picky eater, and surefire methods for meal planning, even for superbusy weeknights. We've got a pantry full of suggestions for managing the craziest time of day—dinner time—with a dollop of enjoyment, and zero added guilt.

Prevent predinner pandemonium

Do you find it difficult to get your kids out of your hair (or out of your arms, or off your leg) long enough to cook for even fifteen minutes? Whether you have been with each other all day or everyone has walked through the door at the end of the day, tummies are growling but the kids are also clamoring for your attention. Now, the Mommy Guilt-Free Philosophy says bring on the attention! Ignore the uncooked food for a little while longer and spend the first fifteen minutes of the dinner hour playing, hearing about your children's day, looking at what they brought home, or pulling out the pots and pans for your toddler to bang on. That's Mommy Guilt-Free Principle No. 4 (Learning to live in the moment). If ever a perfect time existed to engage Mommy Guilt-Free Principle No. 4, this is it! After fifteen minutes, we predict that you will be rewarded by the cooking gods who will bestow upon your children the feeling that they have spent hours by your side. You will not only get more time to cook, but you'll be interrupted less often and can remain more relaxed while sautéing.

If fifteen minutes isn't enough to fend off interruptions (and the guilt created by shooing your children away from you), understand that your kids are not intentionally trying to sabotage your meal-making efforts. They want to be with you. So let them be with you. Hand them a meal preparation task and make dinner together—you're back at Mommy Guilt-Free Principle No. 4 again, living in the moment. When kids participate, you get the best of both worlds. Kids who help cook the meal are more likely to eat and enjoy the meal. Happy diners make for enjoyable dinners. Kids will also learn to appreciate what goes into preparing dinner and will be able to assume more meal-making duties as they grow. (See the box "An Age-Appropriate Guide to Teaching Your Children to Cook.") And look-y here! You've just squeezed some precious daily family time out of the most hectic hour of the day. Turn on that radio, dance around the kitchen, clang those pans, and sing songs. It can be a lot of fun to prepare food, as well as a great end-of-the-day stress reliever.

Sometimes meal-preparing stress, and the guilt that accompanies it, is not about your child wanting you, but wanting food. Hungry children are rarely patient, cheerful children. So, don't tell your mother, but we say abandon the idea that eating before dinner is a cardinal sin. Why not have kiddie cocktail hour? Offer the kids fruit, veggies, cheese, or other healthy snacks along with some milk, juice, or water. They can even snack while they cook—don't you? Don't worry about ruining their appetites. Look at it this way, do you feel guilty when you go out to eat and order an appetizer before your meal? Babies and toddlers, in particular, need to eat small frequent meals. If you are concerned that snacking will prevent them from eating dinner when it is served, institute the "company way." Ask that they keep you company at the table while the rest of you eat. The dinner hour is often the only time of day that a family shares together while not engaged in other activities. It provides an excellent opportunity to catch up on family news and just stay in touch with each other.

An Age-Appropriate Guide to Teaching Your Children to Cook

The following chart is a guideline as to what types of cooking your kids might be able to handle as they grow. But this is only a guide, dependent on your child's development. Be prepared to monitor your child closely as he or she tries out new skills in the kitchen and always put safety first.

AGE	SKILL THEY CAN LEARN
2–4 years old	Putting food on plates, stirring cold foods like cake batter.
5–6 years old	Peanut butter sandwiches, measuring flour with supervision, breaking eggs. Safe food handling such as washing hands after breaking eggs.
7–8 years old	Toaster oven foods, microwaving safely. Following a recipe. Cleanup.
9–10 years old	How to use a properly sharpened knife for food preparation and at the table. Sautéing and using the oven with supervision. Safe food handling such as washing veggies.
11–12 years old	Practice using a knife. Using appliances like food processor, blender, electric egg beaters safely. Safe food handling of raw meats.
13 years old and older	Cooking safely with less supervision. More advanced knife skills (julienne carrots, for instance). Clean up, including stove and washing knives.

Put an end to the personal chef syndrome

Do you find you are a personal chef, making separate dinners for the adults and the kids or even for each individual? (Peas for your son, green beans for your daughter, fish for you, a burger for your spouse. . . .) Most parents do not like to eat jarred baby food, so the idea of separate meals begins innocently enough. However, by the time children reach age two, they can eat most of the things you eat.

Maybe your personal chef days began when you discovered your child had food allergies. Or maybe it began the day you cried uncle and simply started serving peanut butter sandwiches for dinner because it was the only food your child would eat. If you are the family's personal chef and you don't mind doing it for the next three to eighteen years then, by all means, do what you enjoy. If, however, you find yourself stressed out over the extra work, resenting it, or feeling guilty when you "fail" to go to the extra trouble, it's time for a change.

Even a very young child can eat the family dinner. So bring your baby to the table.

I bought this portable baby food grinder. I would bring it with us to restaurants and just grind up whatever we were eating and feed it to our son. I had parents zooming over to me asking me what I was doing and when I told them, they said, "Oh wow, that's a great way to get your kid to eat what you eat." I thought so too. I also believe, although I don't have any statistical proof, that both of our kids are open to eating a larger variety of foods because we fed them this way.

The same tactic works for home meals. Make one meal and cook some of the vegetables a little longer so you can mash them up. Your baby can enjoy eating what you are eating and you'll be instilling a lifelong dinner-time habit—a meal cooked family style, not restaurant style. This has the added benefit of getting them to try new foods (without insisting) just by being at the table with the rest of the family and following your example.

So, the next question is, how do you get your children to stop being picky eaters? The answer is that you don't. Only your children can decide which foods they like. Your part is to offer them a variety, and politely—without a battle—encourage them to try and keep trying. Not only do taste preferences change over time—even for adults—but volumes of research on picky-eater behavior shows that children often need to be exposed to a food between 10 and 30 times before they decide that they like it. In contrast, recent research has shown that many mothers only expose their child to a new food 2.5 times before concluding that the child doesn't like the food.[1] The Mommy Guilt-Free Philosophy encourages you to avoid food power struggles, no matter how good the intentions or how high the nutrient count of the food in question. On the other hand, children can be expected to try a tiny bite of all foods they are served, even the ones they've tried and hated before.

If they don't want to eat a food—and even if they resist trying—don't worry about it. If they are hungry enough, your chances are greatly improved that they will both try and like the food, but you can't control their hunger, either. At the same time, you are not their personal caterer, something both you and your child must understand. If your child insists that he will only eat cheese crackers, do not cart around a package of cheese crackers to every event you attend for fear that he will not eat if you don't. In other words, don't be your child's picky-eating-habit enabler.

Dealing with food allergies doesn't automatically mean a parent must assume the role of personal chef either. You can create a core list of recipes that are safe for your allergic child and that the whole family can enjoy. If you feel guilty over making the entire family eat expensive, specialized food when only one person must, sit down with a cookbook and do a little planning. Many regular recipes can be structured so you can set aside a portion of the food to be allergy-free, before adding the cheese, croutons, milk, or other allergens. Maybe cost isn't your concern, but you feel guilty making all family members adjust their palate when only one is required to. Treat these foods as you would any other new food, incorporating them into your pantry and recipes until they become family favorites.

My youngest daughter cannot eat wheat. Over the years, her older sister has learned to enjoy many wheat-free foods. It took her many tries before her taste buds adjusted to, for instance, rice pasta, which looks like wheat pasta but has a different taste and texture. Today, they'll both be happy with a bowl of chewy angel hair rice noodles and alfredo sauce. The whole family does not restrict itself to a wheat-free diet, but we do plan around it—adding croutons to the salad after it is served on the plate, making one spaghetti sauce and cooking two kinds of noodles, wheat and rice, and so on.

Once you've opted out of the personal chef syndrome, engaging your children in the new routine will help. Your children can help you pick out your list of standby recipes that the whole family will enjoy. They can help you shop for the food, and they can take on at least some small tasks to help you prepare it, if not outright cook it with you. Mealtimes also offer one great method for implementing Mommy Guilt-Free Principle No. 7 (Set aside specific time to be together) because everyone needs to eat!

Teaching Your Children to Cook

Children love to cook. The dinner a child cooks will be the dinner the child eats. Even toddlers can help cook dinner. But in our overly busy lives, we often don't make time to teach our children to cook because we all get to eat faster when the adult does the work. Many ten-year-old children are still afraid to use knives because no one taught them and let them practice. With supervision, by that we mean demonstrating and monitoring for safety, children can cook entire meals. Your child will grin with pride as your family eats the dinner she cooked, filled with unevenly cut onions. To you, those onions will taste just fine!

I sprained my ankle one afternoon and couldn't stand. I sat in a chair shouting out the cooking instructions for dinner while my kids did the work. They were delighted to be helping me in my hour of need and even happier about being in almost total control. They knew I couldn't just step in and take over the work. When we were done eating and they had cleaned up, they told me: "Wow, what a lot of work! No wonder you get tired, Mom!"

Meals for families on the go

For families with school-age children, another area of stress is simply finding time to eat dinner, let alone cook it. With soccer practice, gymnastics, drama class, scouts, plus homework—who has time to eat? We've heard of mothers who bought Crock-Pots that plug into the car cigarette lighter.

We'd caution that if this type of Crock-Pot sounds like a good idea, you may be overscheduling your children. In our opinion, school-age children should not be doing more than two extracurricular activities that occupy more than two days a week (a topic we will discuss in more depth in Chapter 17). Yet even if you limit activities to two per child, if you have more than one child, you will have plenty of nights where the hours between 3 P.M. and 7 P.M. are extremely hectic. If you don't have help—available spouse, carpools, childcare workers, etc.—you don't have someone to do the cooking while you do the schlepping.

HELPFUL HINT

The New Kind of Dinner Clubs

Some parents have developed dinner-sharing programs. The group settles on a menu. Everyone takes turns cooking enough dinner to feed all the families. Arrangements are made to deliver or pick up the dinners. These can work quite well for families who are also carpooling together. This idea might be worth mentioning to your friends!

You need a backup plan that gives you options for feeding your family when you have next-to-no time to cook, without stressing you out until you morph into the yelling, maniac mom, hitting the high mark on the guilt-o-meter. And so we give to you a five-part strategy for lower-stress, higher-enjoyment meals during ultrabusy nights. With these tricks, you will be transformed into smiling Mom the Magnificent, pulling dinner out of a hat. Drum roll please . . .

1. Love thy freezer

Cook extra portions on the nights you can cook and freeze them for instant, nutritious microwaveable meals. Freeze some in single-serving portions, too. A vacuum-sealing food-saving system is ideal for this. Vacuum sealing removes air from the package and protects food from freezer burns. If you don't have one of these, you can vacuum seal your own food. Place the food in a zip-lock freezer bag, and force out all the air before sealing by carefully lowering the bag into a sink of water. Then freeze.

Tips for Happy Frozen Foods

Most cooked foods freeze well including:

➤ Pasta dishes.

➤ Soups, spaghetti meat sauce, stews (omit potatoes—see below).

➤ Chili, lentil soup, beans and rice, other bean-based dinners.

➤ Cooked chicken breast and homemade chicken nuggets.

➤ Pot roast.

➤ Turkey—remove and freeze stuffing separately to reduce risk of food spoilage.

➤ Deli meats.

➤ Dough-wrapped sandwiches. (Use bread dough from the bread machine, store-bought frozen dough, or tins of refrigerated biscuit dough. Roll out to a 4- by 6-inch ball, stuff with fillings such as meats, cheeses, pizza fixings, or sautéed veggies. Bake per package or recipe directions until bread is lightly browned before freezing. Wrap in a paper towel and microwave on low setting to reheat.)

The following items do not freeze well:

➤ Cream, cream cheese.

➤ Hard-boiled eggs.

➤ Deep-fried foods (unless you don't mind that they can become soggy when reheated).

➤ Cubed cooked potatoes, which can get rubbery or dissolve. Mashed, whipped, or candied sweet potatoes will freeze well. If making stew to freeze, add cooked potatoes to the reheating phase.

2. Rapid-fire recipes

Write a list of five to ten recipes that your family likes, can be prepared in minutes, and are made from staples that are kept on hand. Make sure you keep items for this list stocked at all times and you will always be able to put a dinner on the table in minutes, even during rushed times. We've drafted a list of suggested food staples to keep in the house at all times in Appendix B.

Busy nights are not ones when you want to wing dinner. By creating a short list of about ten quick-cooking dinners made from household staples, all you will need is fifteen minutes to put dinner on the table. Each of your recipes should offer several easy variations.

This is the time to use convenience foods, but remember that while foods such as seasoning mixes, white rice, canned soups, or sauces are great for fast-cooking dinners, they are typically less nutritious than home-made alternatives. So limit the nutritional hit by sprucing them up with fresh veggies and meat and serving salad, fruit, and other nutrient-dense foods.

3. A snack fit for a meal

For school-age children, make the after-school snack hearty enough to be considered a meal. Have it ready on the table when your kids come home, or ready in the fridge to be grabbed and eaten on the go. Sandwiches, fruit, and low-fat chips make the perfect travel meal, and can be prepared the night before. In fact, many healthy foods are available in mobile forms. You needn't give up the convenience just to get the vitamins. Baby carrots, string cheese, trail mix, whole-grain bagels, cups of yogurt, milk cartons, beef or turkey jerky (for protein and iron, although some brands are high in salt), are all examples. To further promote the Mommy Guilt-Free technique of having everyone help with the household tasks, have your older kids prepare their own snack. Sometimes they will surprise you and offer to make a snack for you and their younger siblings, too!

4. A dinner of fast-ing

For speedy weeknight dinners, consider using fast food sparingly but effectively. To fend off a guilt attack over routine use of fast food for dinner, try to limit your children's unhealthy food choices to one item per visit. For instance, ask them to choose from among fries, soda, and a milkshake. If they want fries, they can choose milk, juice, or water to drink. If they want soda, they can choose a salad with their cheeseburger. Most fast-food restaurants offer brochures that list nutritional information. You and your children can look at these together. The nutritional information also gives you backup to defend your "no" (Mommy Guilt-Free Principle No. 5) if your child wants to argue that a milkshake is a healthy choice. You can add variety by including take-out items, too. Many eat-in restaurants are becoming increasingly takeout friendly as well, so that may also be an option. Tell your children ahead of time that fast food or take-out food is the evening's plan. Get your children's food order before dropping them off for their after-school activity, and pick it up just before you get them.

5. Junk food or junk-free

Another way to relieve eating-habit guilt while still throwing a speedy dinner on the table is by effective use of prepackaged foods—shelf or frozen. However, use these foods sparingly. For the most part, the entire category contains tons of sodium, fat, sugar, and unpronounceable chemicals. In addition, even foods marketed as organic or natural can lack nutritional value. Still, like fast food, prepackaged foods can be an effective part of the Mommy Guilt-Free dinner plan. The trick is how often you turn to them—and what you buy. If you rarely tell your kids to break open a bag of snack chips, when you do, you will do so guilt-free. What kind of frequency rate constitutes "rare?" Well, if such items need to be replenished through your routine trips to the store, you would have to say you eat them routinely, instead of rarely.

Note

1. B. R. Carruth, Ph.D., and others, "The Phenomenon of 'Picky Eater': A Behavioral Marker in Eating Patterns of Toddlers," *Journal of the American College of Nutrition* 17, no.2, pp. 180–186 (1998), www.jacn.org (accessed Nov. 17, 2004).

CHAPTER 10

FAMILY TIME AND THE FAIR-FIGHT ZONE

Mommy Guilt-Free Principle No. 7 advises you to set aside specific times to be together as a family. But what if your family time is marred by constant bickering among your children? How do you balance family time *and* one-on-one time with each of your children (in an already loaded schedule)? What's fair in dividing your time not only among your kids but also among the household responsibilities and financial resources, too? Maybe you are about to add to your family and are having a bout of Mommy Guilt over that. As long as we're talking about family issues, what about feeling guilty over issues with the extended family, living far from grandparents, or other situations?

Yes, we're talking about the messy, sticky, complicated world of family dynamics, and the awful guilt it oozes. While no family is ever entirely mess-free, we can help you minimize the destructive, guilt-inducing power to increase the harmony in your home. Let's start with getting your children to stop fighting with each other.

How to Sideline Second-Child Guilt

You are about to add another child to your family when suddenly it hits you like a rock between the eyes. How could you be doing this to your oldest child? You are forever altering this child's world by adding someone who will be competing with him for your attention, time, money, and love.

I was the second daughter, and from the moment I was born, my sister had intense feelings of rivalry toward me. Of course, I didn't understand what rivalry was when I was a small child. All I knew was that my older sister was always mean to me. My mom promised me that my sister would grow out of her feelings and that one day, we would be friends. That never happened. As adults, we stopped speaking to each other altogether. So while I was pregnant, I worried a lot about how my oldest, Margaret, would react to the new baby. I prepared her in all the usual ways, with books, videos, discussions. I wanted to make sure that Margaret knew that her baby sister would never replace her, but would be another family member to love. I always called the baby "our family's baby." I looked for ways to include two-year-old Margaret in the excitement. Margaret picked out the baby's layette set, helped decorate the baby's room, performed caretaking for the newborn—helping to bathe her, to close the tabs on the diapers. As much as possible, I concentrated on Margaret over the baby. I let Margaret climb on my lap while I was nursing her sister. I handed the baby to others and held Margaret (figuring the baby didn't care who burped her). I am happy to report that my daughters are, and always have been, the best of friends.

What an effective way to help her toddler adjust to the new baby from the start! Ignoring the necessity of preparing the first for the arrival of the second can haunt you and create enormous feelings of guilt. Adding a second baby sometimes makes moms feel they have to hurry their first child's development. They want to move their toddler out of the crib or get their toddler potty trained. Lighten up! If your child's not ready for a bed or to ditch the diapers, don't push. Your newborn will be just as happy in a bassinet or in a borrowed crib. Toilet learning can be stressful (or at least messy) enough without buying into an unnecessary sense of urgency. So, you have two in diapers? Not only is that perfectly okay, it really isn't more work (no matter what people say). Your kids will get out of cribs and into cotton underwear when they are ready.

Fighting fair

So, what exactly did we envision with Mommy Guilt-Free Principle No. 7? Do we see every family chuckling together over nightly dinners, or delightful evenings gathered around a 1,000-piece jigsaw puzzle? Nah, we see a reality where children will be fighting over the level of milk in their cups and jigsaw puzzle pieces will be flung across the room by the toddler while the rest of the family moans in exasperation. Such family scenes can lead moms to feel terrible about the quality of their family time—that their attempts to organize enjoyable family time ends in disruption or arguments.

But arguing is normal and not automatically a bad thing. Disagreements can bring about positive changes in a family. It's a way for individuals to express emotions and indicate to others that their needs are not being met. It can foster change and growth. If we all got along and agreed on everything, nothing would ever be different! Still, there are ways to argue that are constructive, not degrading or purposefully hurtful.

Rules of fair fighting ought to be established in your family and modeled by you and all other adults who live in the household. It is important for children to see that people can have disagreements, discuss their differences of opinion, and come to a resolution. When adults model fair-fighting rules, children grow up learning them. We are not advocating knockdown, dragged-out fights in front of your children, nor arguing about adult issues in front of your children. However, showing your children that Mommy never calls Daddy names during a disagreement teaches your children that name-calling is never necessary.

Of course, before you can model the fair-fighting rules, you first need to establish them, discuss them, and post them in a central place. You can even read them aloud to younger children if a fight begins to turn nasty. While your family may want to develop its own set of rules, here are the basics:

Fair-fighting rules

1. Keep to the issue at hand and do not bring up past mistakes that have already been resolved.
2. Name-calling will not be allowed.
3. All parties must keep their hands and feet to themselves.
4. Use "I" statements instead of blame statements (Example: "I feel mad when my toys are used without asking me" versus "You made me mad when you took toys out of my room without asking!")
5. Respect the code word. Agree on a family code word for when the argument begins to violate any of the previous rules, or someone feels too hurt or out-of-control emotionally to follow the rules. When the code word is spoken, the argument is suspended. Sometimes, if you agree on a particularly funny, nonsense code word— for example, "ticklemeyer" or "beanburst"—it can be a wonderful tension breaker.

*My eleven-year-old and I seem to butt heads on a regular basis. We
both wanted to stop, so one of the things we did was to come up with
a code word, elephant. Whenever one of us feels like we are getting
too angry we shout out, "Elephant!" This shocks us both into silence
and often causes us to stop fighting and start laughing instead.*

Fair fighting encourages productive disagreements, which helps alleviate Mommy Guilt. It requires that everyone focuses on the way they treat
each other during a squabble. By staying focused on the issue, people can
move more quickly to a resolution.

Siblings' squabbles

"Mom! She hit me!"

"Well, he bit me!"

"Well, she took my toy!"

"He sat on my book!"

"She left it in my room!"

Sound familiar? Sometimes your children will act like beasts, particularly to each other. The more you understand how children operate, the
better equipped you will be to guide your children in their relationships
with their siblings. Notice we said *guide*. Your children didn't get to choose
their siblings and you cannot *control* their relationship. They can love each
other, tether a family bond, and still not like each other much. Understand
that it is up to your children to determine what kind of sibling relationship
they will develop. Some siblings grow up to be very close; others do not.

If you have a sibling, you may have experienced rivalry yourself and be
eager to avoid it among your own children. Your Mommy Guilt can be
relieved when you remind yourself that history does not have to repeat
itself. The relationship you had with your siblings will not automatically be
the one your own children have with each other. Your children are not
you.

The Mommy Guilt-Free attitude that children are individuals and
should be treated as such, goes a long way in curbing sibling rivalry. Furthermore, if you always teach your children to treat each other with respect, they will still fight but they will rarely be tempted to hurt each other
deliberately. Whether rivalry is at the core of fighting or not, siblings can

learn to treat each other with kindness. If you achieve polite behavior between them, you've done a lot toward helping them grow that relationship into friendship.

As with many areas in the Mommy Guilt philosophy, relieving the guilt associated with sibling fights begins with data collection. Have you ever quietly observed a fight in progress, by staying out of it and seeing how your kids come up with their own resolutions? Or do you tend to jump in immediately, assess the cause, and mete out judgment? If you've never been an observer before, it may be time to try. The next time the shouting erupts, position yourself out of sight and watch.

Many parents assume that children fight because they are angry. This is true, but anger is often not the first emotion a child feels and acts upon. The first emotion is typically pain, such as hurt feelings, jealousy, frustration, or even physical pain. Once this happens, a child will do something about it. Don't interfere unless you think the situation is going to come to blows or if someone is crying or otherwise emotionally out of control. Hitting, biting, or violating safety must be stopped immediately. The kids must be reminded that people are not punching bags or chew toys. When children act violently, they should be held accountable for their actions.

As for verbal disagreements, try not to jump in immediately and dole out a resolution. Be especially wary of issuing a ruling that punishes one kid and not the other. You'll avoid a case of guilt later if you find out your ruling was unjust. Keep in mind, too, that when parents quickly step in, don't get all the facts, and assess blame, kids quickly figure out that this is an effective way to get a sibling in trouble. When the finger-pointing begins, remind yourself and your children that an argument takes two people. One of them could have opted not to get involved, or could have ended it. Children as young as three years old are capable of understanding this. Often, simply listening to your children's grievances and offering some sympathy and hugs (and humor, if appropriate) is enough to soothe hurt feelings. Once you've gotten a chance to observe a conflict, you will quickly realize the importance of being a slow-motion mom when responding to a fight in progress. Perhaps the kids will resolve their differences before you get on the scene.

If more intervention is needed, go on to mediation. Mediating fights is another way to implement Mommy Guilt-Free Principle No. 3 (Look at the big picture). A mediator's job is to help all parties create their own resolution to a disagreement, unlike a judge, who hands down rulings. By playing mediator instead of judge, you are teaching your children valuable, lifelong conflict resolution skills.

When mediating, keep your own voice and actions slow, calm, and controlled. Explain to your children that everyone will be heard, but interrupting is not allowed. Your goal is to learn whose feelings got hurt and why all parties think the fight happened. This will give you an indication of how much mediation you may be called on to do. You don't want to solve their conflicts for them, but to walk them through the steps of identifying all viewpoints and coming up with their own resolution.

My brother, Uncle Dave, brought the girls some toys. It didn't take long for them to start fighting over them. Uncle Dave was about to go out and buy duplicates (something our mom always did), so each niece would have the same, but I told him not to. Been there. Done that. It never works. I sat both kids down and asked them if they wanted to abolish the family rule that said we couldn't touch things that didn't belong to us without permission. I reminded them that without this rule anyone at any time could walk into another's room and take anything. I also asked them if they wanted to live in a house where no one shared. That would mean no one could ever play with another's things. The two thought about it and decided to voluntarily share the toys Uncle Dave had brought. They saw they were both willing to compromise. Over the years, the two became adept at negotiating many of their resolutions with no intervention from me.

Children are children

Try to look at the world through your child's eyes. Children are not miniature adults. They should not be expected to behave like adults for long periods of time. As parents, we need to give very young children a safe environment in which to explore and grow. As our kids get older, we also need to consider an environment that does not encourage conflict. When they are in situations where they become bored, they will likely entertain themselves by fighting. Admonishing them for fighting in the car, on a plane ride, or at religious services won't solve the problem. Be proactive, take along boredom-busting activities (lots of them), and you'll easily get rid of a whole bunch of fights. You will also treat yourself to a more enjoyable experience.

Whenever we take a plane ride, I make sure that my toddler gets to run around the waiting area for a little while. I make sure that he isn't yelling and screaming, he's just moving. One day a woman complained to me about it saying, "I can't believe you are letting your child run around in an airport boarding area!" I shrugged and asked her, matter-of-factly, "Which would you prefer? That he kicks the back of your seat like mad for the next two hours or that he runs around the boarding area and gets worn out?" The woman smiled at me and replied, "Smart mommy!"

When children aren't feeling well, or when they are under pressure at school, irritability and aggression tend to increase. When excessive household fighting breaks out, take a closer look at what may be happening in your child's world. Evaluate the activities of the last twenty-four to forty-eight hours. Did she have enough sleep? Have candy, soda, or other empty calories been a large part of your child's diet lately? Has she had a substitute teacher this week? Children often do not have the language skills or social know-how to articulate the things that are upsetting their lives. Sometimes they don't even realize themselves that a change of routine—and not the incident that caused the argument—is stressing them out.

If you suspect that the behavior is rooted in something more complex than the disagreement at hand, talk with your child privately during a quiet time. Just before bedtime or during a car ride may be ideal times to ask questions. You may discover that a headache is to blame for the last several hours of difficulty. Discovering such underlying causes doesn't excuse your children from accepting responsibility for behaving badly to each other. It will, however, help you with mediation. Kids might be more willing to compromise and move on when they understand each other. If they know the crabby one is crabby because she has a headache and will be expected to apologize when she feels better, they may be more forgiving. If the irritability seems to be lasting for a long time, or is getting worse, that certainly warrants a call to a pediatrician.

One child at a time

One of the joys of parenthood is spending time alone with each of your children, interacting with them as they grow. However, moms with more than one child often feel a lot of guilt on this count—worrying that they don't give each child enough individual attention.

I feel extremely guilty about not having time to spend alone with each of my kids. My oldest was an only child for a long time and I remem-

ber how much of my attention she got. Now, even when I try to do things alone with her, the toddler jumps in or the boys start fighting. I feel awful about it.

The Mommy Guilt-Free Philosophy focuses on balance. Your children don't need so much one-on-one time with you that they feel like they don't have siblings. They just need to know that your attention will be there for them regularly, and whenever they especially need it. We suggest that you try to include a few minutes of daily alone-time rituals, a weekly activity together (even a ten-minute one) and an annual big block of time for each of your children.

The easiest way to create daily alone time is to slip it into your routine. This could be tucking your child in at night or helping her get dressed in the morning. This is when to execute Mommy Guilt-Free Principle No. 4 (Learning to live in the moment). Slow your pace down, and focus your attention on your child and the childcare task at hand. Forget about your burgeoning to-do list for now. When you do, you will find that these daily few minutes will become extremely powerful for both you and your child. This is when your child will have a chance to share the day's events, exchange private jokes, discuss squabbles with other family members or friends, and so on. Keep your child's emotional style in mind. If your child gets worked up easily, bedtime won't be the right moment to discuss a bad experience at school. If your children share a room, think creatively about how to work in this daily alone time. Some families do individual nighttime hugs and kisses in the living room.

In addition to daily minutes, add in longer periods of alone time about once a week. This is important for all children, toddlers through teens. Do an activity you both enjoy together: baking cookies, throwing a baseball, playing a duet on the piano—put it on the schedule like any other event and find childcare for your other children if you need to. If a week or two passes and you realize you haven't done an activity with each of your kids, you know it's time to prioritize that, even over family time.

Try to plan an annual mother-child weekend away together, if possible. If you can clear the house of other family members so the two of you have full run of the place, you can pitch a tent in your backyard or living room and spend the night there! An overnight in a local hotel also works well. Mother-child weekends can be an especially helpful way to reconnect with a child inching up on puberty who is suddenly telling you that he doesn't want to talk to you about his life. It is also a great way to heal the wounds from a prior disagreement.

Relationships are built by experiences over time. When you give time to them, stronger bonds develop.

Fair but not equal

Fair does not mean equal, and the sooner your children and you realize this, the sooner the "that's not fair" accusations will stop flying around. Parents feel a heavy burden of guilt over trying to make everything equal among their children. One-third of our survey respondents named dividing time, financial resources, and the chores in a fair manner as a source of guilt, with 14 percent saying it caused them to feel their highest levels of guilt.

> *Justin is my third grader and Natalie is in preschool. I was helping Justin with his homework and Natalie came into the room. She began to whine and complain that she "never gets to see Mommy." I felt awful. I had spent an hour with Justin, so I stopped helping him with his homework and played dolls with Natalie for an hour.*

Sometimes a mom has to explain to herself and her children that although she is giving more time (or more food, clothes, etc.) to one child now, she is not being unfair. When her other children need more of her time (or more food, clothes, etc.), she'll be right there, attending to their needs, too.

Getting hung up on spending equal amounts of money on each child is also a source of Mommy Guilt. Do not buy into the pressure that says if you purchase something for one you have to buy the same item for all. Kids are individuals and will feel more appreciated when purchases are made with their own interests and needs in mind. Monetary worth need not be the focus either. When it's birthday time, they simply want what they want; sometimes it is something expensive, sometimes it isn't. We aren't saying that children need not understand that toys cost money, we are saying that cost doesn't need to be the central focus of selecting "fair" gifts.

Now, let's see how the fair-but-not-equal viewpoint can be applied to divvying up the family responsibilities. Unless you are running a family farm, you probably give your children fairly easy-to-accomplish, reasonable workloads for their contributions to home maintenance. You tell one child to take out the garbage and clean the kitchen table. You tell another child to pick up the toys from the family room. The first one balks—accusing you of being unfair for giving her two tasks—which she figures to be twice the work. The Mommy Guilt-Free response is to point out that no one is being treated like Cinderella and any household responsibilities are given out on the basis of age and ability. Remind your children that it takes everyone's help to keep things running smoothly at home.

Over time, you are treating all of your children fairly, even if on any given day one child does more work, and this very well may happen, because older kids are able to do more. Each is being held to the same long-term objective: to be a contributing member of household maintenance and, eventually, a responsible adult.

Preferential guilt

Maybe you feel guilty because you worry that if you don't make everything the same for each child, your kids will accuse you of favoritism. You might also secretly worry that you gravitate more easily to one child than another. Fear of favoritism is another area that can rocket a mom right off the Mommy guilt-o-meter. Realistically, since your children are individual people, you may actually get along more easily with one and have to work harder with the others to have a relationship.

My youngest son, Mark, and I just seem to click. He is organized yet easygoing and flexible at the same time. Just like me. My older son, David, is so different. He just seems to flail around in search of himself and he hates any changes. I never know quite what to say to him as I never was like that. David gets along very well with my husband but I never feel like I understand David. I understand Mark, and this makes me feel very guilty that I am somehow shortchanging David.

The Mommy Guilt-Free Philosophy says to give yourself a break. Preference of some types of personalities over others is pretty much human nature. Feelings of preference in regard to your kids doesn't have to be as big of a deal as you may have been taught to believe. Many times, for many parents, such feelings are fleeting anyway, particularly when they relax about them. Think of it in terms of your adult relationships. You call one friend up and ask her to attend a movie with you; you call another friend for a lunch date. You enjoy both friends, you just feel like spending time with one or the other on a particular day. The same happens with parent-child relationships. One day, you want to hang out with your oldest child, another day, you can't wait to do a project with your youngest. Your kids may even be swinging on a similar pendulum. Haven't you ever felt like you had "most-favored-parent status" on Monday but that your name was mud by Wednesday?

The important thing to remember is to find areas of interest you can share with your children that will foster a bond. As a team of two, you can choose to do activities together that interest you both. Better still, you can both learn a new activity together. This helps curtail any parental desire to be the expert or to set yourself up as the powerful, all-knowing one while interacting with your child. (If you have no idea how to roller blade, you can't be issuing instructions to your kid on how to do it correctly, now can you? You'll both be wobbly together.) As long as the activities you engage in are ones you both enjoy, this time together will help assuage any guilt you might feel over personality clashes.

HELPFUL HINT

An Objective Opinion

If you recognize that you always seem to (or want to) spend a hugely disproportionate amount of time with only one child—or away from one child—consider speaking to an individual or family counseling professional. An objective third-party opinion could be enormously beneficial. Part of the Mommy Guilt-Free Philosophy is admitting when you need more help and getting it. Doing this will give you guilt relief!

Several Mommy Guilt-Free Principles can also help. Mommy Guilt-Free Principle No. 4 (Live in the moment) can help you focus your attention on the delightful parts of your relationship with your child, not the frustrating aspects. Mommy Guilt-Free Principle No. 5 (Say yes and better defend your no) can help you identify times when your own negativity adds tension between the two of you. Mommy Guilt-Free Principle No. 6 (Laugh a lot with your child) is a surefire way to make your times alone together more enjoyable.

Mothers: you, yours, and his

No discussion on Mommy Guilt-Free families is complete without discussing the mother of all relationships—yours and his. The origins of guilt between adults and their parents are as numerous and varied as fingerprints. Here are a few that lend themselves to Mommy Guilt.

Grandparents gone wild

Not knowing how to handle uncomfortable situations with grandparents is often a source of Mommy Guilt. Moms may feel immobilized in addressing issues, worrying about hurt feelings, or someone becoming offended. One example is the mom who feels her own mother was (or is) too critical, and believes that grandma is now being too critical of her grandkids.

Pay attention to the child, not the adults (including yourself). Often the relationships between grandparents and grandchildren are less conflicted than those between parents and children. Your kids may be able to tune out Grandma's criticism in a way you never could. They might love her company. Many grandparents have figured out what didn't work with their own children and will not pull that same garbage with their grandchildren. Instead, they give their grandkids the best of their parenting skills. But if your child is being made to feel uncomfortable, Mommy Guilt can be squashed by taking on the role of the child's advocate. Think through what you need to do to protect your child from being hurt. You are an adult now, and you can tell your mom to back off. If you find that to be too confrontational, you can also assist your child in leaving the room without making a huge fuss about it.

Certainly, talking to the grandparent can be a good choice. Keep in mind that the goal should be to let it be known that her behavior is confusing or damaging to your child. Grandma may not change her opinions, but you can always tell her that it would be more helpful for her to write down a list of her criticisms and give them to you instead of listing them aloud to her granddaughter.

If a grandparent is not willing to stop or make reasonable changes in harmful behavior, you have an obligation to limit contact. This goes for any adult whom you have determined to be causing your child unnecessary distress. Some people or relationships are harmful and limiting contact or staying away may be the only real option. If this person is a grandparent, you may feel your guilt telling you that limiting contact is selfish. Ultimately, you need to consider the health and well-being of your children.

After all, you wouldn't repeatedly expose your kids to a stranger who caused them harm. Why feel obligated to expose them to harmful people just because you share the same gene pool?

Here's another thought to make these decisions more palatable. When you advocate for your children and take steps to prevent them from being hurt, you send an empowering message that ill-treatment should not and will not be tolerated from anyone. When you model how positive relationships are created, your children learn how to build positive relationships.

The guilt of living far apart

In our transient society, extended families are extending ever farther apart. Our parents are more likely to have remembered a time when most of the family lived close by. Family get-togethers occurred routinely and not simply because someone was being born, getting married, or dying. The Mommy Guilt that occurs from moving away from your parents can be an awesome load, particularly if the grandparents exhibit an attitude of blame.

My husband, two sons, and I were living within two hours of my in-laws. When we moved halfway across the country, I felt extremely guilty that I had wrecked my kids' relationship with their grandparents. My in-laws refused to visit us, behaving as if, since we were the ones who moved, it was our job to bring their grandchildren to them. For many years, all of our vacation time and all of our extra cash went toward visits with them. After a while, I grew resentful of this. Many of my friends lived far from their parents and that didn't stop those grandparents from making an effort to be in their kids' lives.

Before allowing Mommy Guilt to consume you because you moved away from your place of origin, keep in mind that planes fly both ways, phones work from either end. Ultimately, what you want is successful communication between all parties and in order for that to occur, messages must be sent, received, and confirmed. While it is not your sole responsibility to create communication between your children and their grandparents, being willing to give in a little here and bend a little there is helpful in achieving the overall goal of maintaining a relationship. Families all over the nation live apart and remain emotionally close. If they can do it, so can you.

Have a brainstorming session in which you come up with ways to stay close other than traveling. Letters? E-mails? Phone calls? Videotapes? A monthly live videoconferencing session over the Internet? Tailor the communication style to the personalities involved. This will result in a plan that people can follow more easily. You may love to write letters but hate talking on the phone. Grandma may be all phone and no writing. So you write; she calls. Don't be pulled into some kind of scorekeeping of who called last, who wrote most, and so on. You may not be able to stop others from playing scorekeeper, but you can deflect unproductive conversations about it by making it clear that everyone is free to communicate in the way he or she most enjoys. Do your part to always welcome their communication, no matter its form or frequency.

CHAPTER 11

HUSBANDS AS FATHERS

We've all heard the saying that if you want to get something done, give it to a busy person. Busy people are that way because they know how to multitask. And doesn't the word *multitask* describe what most moms do? Moms can schedule four dental appointments over the phone, then while on hold, click over to the other line and confirm a hair appointment. This, while simultaneously making two peanut-butter-and-jelly sandwiches. This is simply the way moms operate.

Linear Versus Multitask Thinking

Most people have heard that various areas of our brains are dedicated to specific tasks. Now, whether the male linear/female multitasking belief is accurate is the subject of some argument. Likewise, generalities don't apply to individuals. Many men are champion "multitaskers," while many women operate far better by finishing one task before starting another. However, looking for linear versus multitask thinking will help you decide how to guide your children when they need your help. For instance, say that you've observed your daughter becoming overwhelmed by her homework, and you notice that she has it spread out in front of her, jumping from math to geography to spelling. She is attempting to multitask, unsuccessfully. By helping her learn to work on one item at a time (a linear approach), putting all tools from one task away before starting on the next one, you can show her how to experience less frustration during homework time.

Observe the work habits of your family members and see if they naturally gravitate to multitasking or linear methods. Notice how they operate when they feel successful and how they operate when they get frustrated. When cutting the lawn, does your spouse ever stop the mower to pull a few weeds that are in the way? Or does the grass always get cut completely first, then the trimmer and then the weed pulling? How about you? Simultaneous weed whacking or not? Knowing this linear/multitasking tendency about your spouse, your sons, and your daughters could save you loads of future frustration. Watch yourself, too. If you discover that a family member's work style is different from yours, what makes you the expert on the best way for the person to accomplish the task? Why not just ask for the results and leave it to the person to accomplish them?

Not only do many moms try and do it all—they end up getting far too bogged down in doing it. In reality, many daily tasks performed by moms can be performed by someone else—such as the dad—and many mothers could save themselves a lot of guilt by sharing more of these duties with the children's father. Yet women frequently find it hard to let go of the control zone, even (or maybe especially) to the other person who is equally the parent, the dad. Women are bombarded with messages that seem to tell them that good moms are the ones who are in charge of everything, and the expectation is that anything related to childcare or household tasks is the mom's domain.

New moms particularly find the delegation of childcare responsibilities hard to do. They feel like they've got to present themselves as "mom to the world" as soon as they give birth, and prove that they can do it on their own. More seasoned moms have trouble when they have had their finger on the family pulse for a long time. They worry that if they let go, pandemonium will result. Not true! If you left town tomorrow, your family would figure out how to get to the dentist without you. More important, you are not in this child rearing thing alone and bringing the dad in as a full partner is not about him muscling in on your territory. Full partnership will not only make you feel better but it will also benefit your family. Conversely, staking out your territory as sole parenting services provider will nearly always lead to exhaustion, feeling stressed-out, and, most assuredly, a whopping case of Mommy Guilt.

Lisa and her husband, Ron, had their first baby and all was perfect with the world. Ron worked full-time for a large company and Lisa was on maternity leave from her job. During this time, Ron's company allowed him to work half-days so that he could assist Lisa with the parenting responsibilities. A typical day would have Ron walk in the door, give Lisa a big hug and kiss and then ask how the day was *going and how he could help. Lisa would then hand over the baby to Ron. Ron would coo at his little baby and talk to her. Lisa would hover and say, "Ron, you are talking to her too loud, she needs to go to sleep now." Then Lisa would scoop the baby out of Ron's arms and head to the baby's room. Ron was left standing there wondering why he bothered to come home to help. Lisa would become aggravated at Ron and complain that if he wanted to help, he could at least "do things the right way."*

The "right way" according to Lisa, that is. But Lisa, like so many moms, was trying to create a parenting dictatorship. And we all know what happens in a dictatorship. It spurs revolution and, sometimes, assassination. You can't have a dictatorial relationship with your parenting partner and expect that person to "help" you. What will happen is resentment.

A mother who operates on the my-way-or-the-highway plan may not only damage her relationship with her husband but also thwart her husband's relationship with his children. We know of one five-year-old girl who called her grandmother on the phone one day, crying, "Grandma, come over, Mom left me alone!" The grandmother, knowing her daughter—the child's mother—would never do such a thing asked a few questions. She soon discovered that Dad was actually at home at that very moment, in the garage working on the car. Over the years, the mother had been so controlling of the interactions between father and child that by the time the child was five, the two had practically no relationship at all. The daughter felt as if she was left alone while she was really in the care of her father!

If you want him to help, let him help

We know that ultrabusy moms are not intentionally trying to stomp out the relationship between the children and their fathers. Many think they are even trying to encourage that relationship—never getting the clue that orchestrating father/child time from the sidelines hinders it from developing on its own.

Relationships need room to grow and flourish. This means two things: First, dads will have to learn by trial and error what works and what doesn't—just as you did. In other words, he doesn't need the mom to tell him how to pack the diaper bag, or why he should feed the kid a snack between school and soccer practice. If he gets it wrong and a blowout or meltdown occurs, he'll learn—just as the mom did. Second, it means accepting that things will be done differently when the dad is in charge of parenting. A dad will choose different activities to do with his kids. A dad will choose different meals to cook and different reasons for visiting the fast-food drive-through instead of cooking. Dads may have their own thresholds regarding discipline, expectations of behavior, and how they joke around with their children. This is okay. This is downright good! This is called having a relationship!

While consistency in child rearing is a wonderful thing, consistency doesn't mean "sameness." Your children will quickly learn the dad way and the mom way. They'll learn the grandma way and the grandpa way. They'll learn the first-grade teacher's way and the second-grade teacher's way. Just as you did while you were growing up. In reality, no matter how controlling a mother tries to be, a dad will approach things differently— and will often come up with better solutions to household issues, too. It is impossible for a mom to turn her husband into a replica of herself.

Another great truth is when you step out of the scene and observe your husband being a father, you may find that he will often handle situations just as you would have handled them. If he opts to handle them differently, this does not mean disaster for the family. It simply demonstrates that there are many means to reach the same end.

My husband has several busy seasons a year when he has to work a lot. During those times, he always gets very grumpy. When he comes home, he immediately starts yelling at the children over every little thing. He wants them to pick up their toys from the living room. He wants them to help with yard work. He wants them to be quieter while he is watching TV or reading. I always felt he was being unfair to the kids, so I spent a lot of time intervening. Then he would get mad at me. We'd fight and he'd accuse me of undercutting his authority with the children. One day, I got so exasperated, I shut up. I told myself that the kids wouldn't be damaged for life if I did nothing while my husband yelled at them just this once. When they came to me, crying, instead of stepping in, I told them to work it out with their father and I left the house. When I came back, I found my husband in my son's room, having a heart-to-heart with the kids. He was explaining, in a totally calm voice, what he wanted them to do (all reasonable requests) and why. The kids listened and, low-and-behold, even picked up their toys! I realized that when I constantly stepped in, I was only enabling my husband's bad mood, and setting myself up as the bad guy in his eyes. Without me around, he quickly figured out that he had to change tactics to get the cleanliness, help with chores, and quiet he wanted. Being an adult that is, of course, exactly what he did.

You want to see any of the authors go into a rage, just let us hear someone say a father is baby-sitting his own children. Dads are not baby-sitters; they are parents! No one would ever dream of telling a mom that she is baby-sitting her own children when she stays home with them while dad goes to poker night with the guys. Why, then, do we often hear people say, "Dad is baby-sitting tonight." Maybe it's partially due to the fact that we often treat them like baby-sitters. We review bedtimes and appropriate foods, we suggest activities to keep the kids entertained in our absence, and we let them know how to reach us and when we will be home. How silly is that?

A couple of us went to dinner and a movie with another mom friend. As we left the car to go into the theater, the friend was trying to decide if she should set her cell phone to silent. We reminded her that her daughter was home with Dad and he was as capable as she was of calling 911 in an emergency. If anything else came up, he would handle it. The phone remained in the car and the three of us had a wonderful evening out with each other.

So kick off your shoes, relax, and let Dad do his thing. Now, this should not be confused with leaving him out on a limb. If you see a major landslide headed toward Dad, throw him a rope and pull with all your might to complete the rescue, just like you would want him to do for you. Other than that, a father can certainly figure out how to rustle up a kid-friendly meal or to come up with some games to play before bedtime. Yes, he will do things differently from the way you do them, but who cares? It will all get done!

When Doing Nothing Is Doing Everything

Attaining family harmony means butting out and letting husbands be fathers. But maybe you don't know what you need to stop doing. If you really want to resist any controlling urges and watch your man shine as a dad, read this list. Some suggestions may be helpful for your own situation.

- ➤ Plan days, evenings, or weekends that will get you out of the house and away from parenting responsibilities—trusting that your husband will survive without you.
- ➤ Stop referring to your husband's time as a solo parent as "baby-sitting" either to him or to others.
- ➤ Meal planning can happen without you; let whoever is feeding the family decide what to eat.
- ➤ Skip the instructions for your spouse with the exception of relaying health/safety information such as when medicine needs to be administered.
- ➤ Share the kids' schedule with him but sharing doesn't mean doing the logistic planning. If he needs to bring one kid to soccer at 4 P.M. and one to Scouts at 4:15, just inform him with the confidence that he will manage it. If there is a carpool available, you can share the information, but you need not make the arrangements.
- ➤ Avoid calling him to check in. Gently resist taking calls from him asking for "how-tos" as well. Respond to such calls by telling him you know he will do his best and you are sure it will be great.
- ➤ Get rid of the idea that you need an accounting of events upon your return. If he opted to skip soccer practice or Scouts to ease his day, that's his parental choice. (You have likely made similar choices in the past—and if you haven't, view this as a lesson—it is okay if your sanity overrides your children's schedules.)
- ➤ If Dad's choice to skip an extracurricular activity has upset the children and they complain to you, tell them, pleasantly, to take it up with their father.
- ➤ Let your appreciation be known on any items that you thought he handled especially well—just as you would like someone to notice and appreciate you for a job well done.

Dad's special brand of guilt

At the beginning of the book, we touched on the idea that Daddy Guilt may seem nonexistent. That's not to say that dads don't ever feel guilty.

First and foremost, you must forgive yourself. As long as you carry around your guilt, you will not be able to express your love effectively. I had a lot of guilt from several years ago when my wife and I had gotten into a fight. I ran out into a snowstorm. The image that burns itself in my mind is my daughter running to the door ahead of me (I did not realize she was listening) and barring the door with a chair in the hope that I could not get out. I moved her and the chair aside and ran outside anyway. My family is happy, but I still occasionally see that image of her by the door.

While the particulars of this dad's guilt-inducing incident are not universal to what all dads might regret, the guilt that dads feel tends to center on specific circumstances or actions, not the kind of generalized feeling that we have described as Mommy Guilt. In fact, according to the *Mommy Guilt* survey, twice as many dads as moms reported no feelings of parental guilt at all.

That doesn't mean they are automatically less stressed as parents. Dads are definitely concerned over the impact of their parenting decisions. They worry that their decisions will affect everything from their children's eating habits to their SAT scores. Sexist as this may sound in our politically correct era, men and women often see the world differently, with men more focused on the here-and-now physical moment while women are analyzing the undercurrents of emotions. This translates into moms interpreting their parental stress as "guilt" while dads interpret their parental stress as "frustration."

If a child is crying, the dad might demand in an angry tone of voice (frustration) to be told exactly how, in detail, the series of events led up to the crying. The mom might be focused on how upset the child really is, whether it is an indication of physical injury or hurt feelings. She may be feeling bad that she wasn't available during the "traumatic" moment to prevent the event while the dad is analyzing why it happened at all.

Just because Mom always fixes every little bump with a hug and a kiss doesn't mean that Dad can't make things better with words of "shake it off, little guy." All people show love and compassion in different ways. The Mommy Guilt-Free Philosophy is to embrace Dad as Dad with the assurance that his way is just as meaningful as yours. *Different* does not automatically equal *better*, nor does it automatically equal *worse*.

Communication between the guilty and the frustrated

Dads are great role models and the more active a dad is in the parenting of his children, the more likely those children will grow up to be responsible parents themselves. The more children see their parents working as a team to parent them, the better off they will be. Even in cases where parents are divorced, making sure that parents present a united front regarding parenting issues is beneficial to children. So how do Mommy Guilt and Daddy Frustration come together to create a healthy environment in which to raise children? They meet in respect and trust.

It is imperative that Mom and Dad agree on major parenting decisions such as the family's fair-fighting rules (see Chapter 10) or curfew times. These decisions need to be presented as a united front. The mom who allows herself to trust that the dad is every bit as capable of achieving the ultimate outcome with his methodologies as she is with hers will find herself a far more relaxed, Mommy Guilt-Free parent. A few simple communication techniques often help. Try having your discussions with the dad about major parenting issues without your children around. This will allow you to create a united front. To get the most out of these discussions, try talking about specific issues, rather than in abstract terms, and try not to wander down the road of accusations or blame. If the two of you approach your discussions in a calm "we're in this together" manner, then you should be able to develop your strategies together. If you find that you and your partner are always on two different sides of planet parenthood, seek help in the form of parenting books, a parenting class, or even a third-party mediator or therapist. Parenting is a tough job and, as we've said before, it's okay to seek out objective, third-party help if you need it.

One more word on the united front: while we all love and adore our children, children can be manipulative and may bank on their ability to divide and conquer if one parent doesn't know what the other parent is doing. If an important issue comes up when a private, parental powwow isn't immediately possible, tell your children that you need to discuss this topic with the other parent and the two of you will get back with a response as quickly as you can. The catch phrase, "Wait until your father gets home," is not an ideal term to toss out, though, as it implies that one parent has more power than the other. United and equal is what you need to be aiming for when you are co-parenting.

My son Danny came in from baseball practice and asked if we could order pizza. I thought nothing of it and agreed. My husband then screamed from the other room, "No pizza! I already told Danny no pizza because while we were at the game, he wanted a hotdog. I bought it for him and he didn't eat it." I felt really bad about telling Danny no after I already said yes, so I ordered the pizza anyway. I didn't think it was such a big thing, but my husband was pretty angry with me. He accused me of undermining his parenting. I gave it some thought and realized that I really could have told Danny that he needed to wait until his dad and I discussed what the dinner plan was going to be. I apologized to my husband and we agreed to check with each other, when reasonably possible, to make sure that our son wasn't playing us against one another.

CHAPTER 12

SCHOOL-YARD GUILT

"Back to school"—how can these three words create Mommy Guilt? Well, let's start with the exhaustive shopping for clothes, shoes, and school supplies. Once school is in session, the stress just keeps on coming. Countless forms must be filled out, checks written, bedtime rituals remembered, morning-time rituals remembered, back-to-school nights attended, and numerous other extracurricular activities begun (all of which require more forms, fees, and sometimes doctor appointments).

Back-to-school time isn't just expensive, it's draining. Overnight, the more relaxed summer plan is replaced by early rising and what feels like a nonstop stream of school-related schedules. Plus, we remember our own school experiences and hope our children experience the best and are spared the worst. You aren't alone in feeling this way. One-third of *Mommy Guilt* survey respondents with children old enough to attend school named school-related issues (selecting a school or academic programs, finding time to volunteer) as a source of guilt. Eighteen percent said it was a major source of guilt.

So sharpen up your pencils and grab a notepad. Today's lesson is the Mommy Guilt-Free approach to school.

Choosing guilt

Once upon a time, parents didn't agonize about whether their child's school was the "right" one. The neighborhood you lived in pretty much determined the public school your child attended. Everyone knew which neighborhoods had the premium schools and which had the struggling schools. If your neighborhood school wasn't a good match for your child, your choice was to take on the cost of private school or move to a different neighborhood. Not anymore. "School choice" has arrived in most states, and while options are wonderful, they bring with them a guilt-inducing downside. The responsibility of school selection is heaped into the laps of parents who now worry immensely about their decisions. They feel that if they choose wisely, their child flourishes, but if they misstep here, their child will be shortchanged, academically or socially. This pressure may leave many moms sitting in Mommy Guilt detention.

Charters, Choices, and Laws

Most U.S. residents no longer have to move or receive an inheritance to have a wide range of choices for schools. Most states have enacted open enrollment laws in one form or another that will allow you to choose which public school your children attend. Laws vary on the approval process for student transfers—some are mandatory, some are voluntary, some apply only to in-district transfers, some to intra-district. As of December 2002, forty-four states had "open-enrollment" laws on the state books that allow parents to transfer their children to a public school of the parent's choice.[1]

I live in a beautiful neighborhood, a showcase of restored houses from the 1800s. The people are great, too. My street is loaded with doctors, lawyers, and high-powered city officials. But the schools worry me a lot. Rougher, higher-density neighborhoods border my area. I'm concerned about drug use and violence at the public schools, and they have really high student-to-teacher ratios. When my children were in preschool, all the other parents started buzzing about school selection—and I started to get frantic. My friends said that the best private schools sometimes have a two-year waiting list. If you don't start the process by the time your kid is three years old, forget it. Kids have to undergo tests evaluating their intelligence and skills. Children who are labeled as "gifted" by these tests are the ones accepted into these "better" schools—you can't even get on the waiting list until your child is tested and placed. I can't tell you how many nights I've spent awake wondering what to do. Maybe I should get my kids to somehow hurry up and learn to read, or maybe we should move from this house and area that we love to somewhere with better public schools. For now, I've enrolled my kids in a private school nearby, which is costly and doesn't offer a sports program. I have no idea if I'm making the right choice.

The Mommy Guilt-Free Philosophy encourages an outlook that will not cause guilt over decisions made honestly and with good intent (even if they turn out to be mistakes). When the time comes to tackle school-related guilt, the best course of action is to empower yourself with knowledge. By researching your school choices and making well-informed decisions, you are certain to find a great situation for your child.

Selecting a school

Before you can have back-to-school angst, you've got to have a school to be anxious about. If you live in a community that has more than one elementary, middle, and/or high school, you've got some legwork to do. Expect to get a real workout, too, because you may need to repeat this process every few years: for preschool, grammar school, middle school/junior high, and high school, and prior to moving to a new community.

When researching a school, begin with a list of what you feel is necessary and what you feel would meet the needs of your child. (See the box "School-Selection Checklists" below for a list of questions to help you out.) Next, create a list of the schools in your vicinity or the area in which you will be moving.

We move a lot. So every time we move, we take out a map and put a pin on where we live and where we work. We then draw circles around these pins to equal the longest commute we are willing to make for schools. After we do that, we research all of the schools within the scope of these circles and that is where we begin to list the schools that we will check out for our children.

School-Selection Checklists

Assessing your school needs

1. Can I provide transportation myself, or do I need to rely on the school's transportation?
2. If I choose a private school, how much tuition can I afford to pay?
3. Do I need before-school or after-school child care?

4. Do I desire a preschool program at the same location where my school-age children attend school?

5. Beyond reading, writing, and math, what other kinds of programs are important to me (arts, music, physical education, second language, science, geography, etc.)?

6. What kinds of extracurricular programs would I like to see my child have an opportunity to enjoy (dramatic, visual, or performing arts; science projects; intramural or competitive sports)?

Assessing your child's needs

1. Does my child work well independently or does he need a lot of direction and personal attention?

2. If my child should need extra help academically, what programs are available for that?

3. How much time can I reasonably expect my child to dedicate to homework?

4. What track record does the school have in dealing with my child's special needs?

About the district

1. How does the state rate schools and what is the district's overall rank?

2. How does the district compare with the national averages in areas such as standardized testing, spending per student, teacher/student ratio?

3. What are the school's boundaries and bus schedules? What time must my child leave in the morning to make the bus and when will she return?

4. Does the district have any charter schools? What are their educational philosophies?

5. Does the district have any specialized academic schools and where are they located (international baccalaureate, bilingual, language immersion, etc.)?

6. What is the district's policy about school choice and what are the deadlines for applications?

About the school

1. What do other teachers in the district say about the school?

2. What do other parents say about it?

3. How old is the facility and how well maintained is it?

4. Is the playground equipment new? If not, what are the plans
   to update it?

5. What is the typical student/teacher ratio?

6. Who is the principal and how long has he or she been there?

7. How long have the teachers been there (long tenures usually
   indicate stability and happy teachers)?

8. Is there a volunteer requirement? How much time is required?
   (Charter and other private schools often mandate volunteering.)

9. Does the school have a computer room? How old are the computers? Are computers in the classroom as well?

10. Does the school have dedicated staff for the library, the com-
    puter room, physical education, the arts?

11. What special academic programs does the school offer and
    what are the requirements for a child to be eligible?

12. What special nonacademic programs are included and what
    extracurricular programs and clubs are available?

13. How has the school scored on standardized tests and what does
    the principal say about the school's approach to standardized
    testing?

14. How are standardized test scores used?

15. What methods are used to evaluate student progress?

16. What "vibe" does the school give you? Is it a quiet, pleasant,
    controlled place filled with smiling, relaxed-looking people?

Gather the facts

You are now ready to gather information to help you select a school.
The Internet is the place to start your search. If you don't have access to
the Internet, plan on hitting your local library. Web sites are available that
will give you loads of statistics on school districts and individual schools,
too. They include reports on items such as how the district (or individual
school) compares with the national average, information about standardized test scores, per-child spending, the student/teacher ratio, and so on.
A particular district's own Web site can offer a lot of information on things
such as school boundaries, bus schedules, results of state-wide standardized tests, and so forth. Individual school Web sites can also give you an
idea of what the school year might be like, the educational philosophy, and

homework policies. To find these sites, just type the name of the school district into a search engine, and start clicking from there.

Remember, however, that statistics themselves tell only a partial story. If a school ranks average on its standardized test scores when compared with other schools, this could indicate a mediocre school, but not necessarily. Likewise, those that rank high on such scores don't necessarily indicate superior academics. Statistics are wily things, easily manipulated. A school with lower enrollment—generally a good thing—may struggle to achieve a high overall score because, with fewer students, each student's score carries more weight. A couple of low scores skew the entire average down. Still, those scores are an important part of your overall background research to help you in your next step—talking to people.

Ideally, you should talk to teachers in the district, the principals of prospective schools, other parents, and kids. Finally, you should bring your child along to visit your last few choices, if possible.

I was new to the neighborhood and new to the idea of school. My four-year-old, Alex, was very eager to start kindergarten in the fall. After much research, I narrowed my choices to two: the school in my attendance area and another public school the same distance from my house. When we entered the first school, Alex looked at the cluttered classroom and innocently asked me why these kindergarteners didn't put away any of their things. When we went to the second school, Alex was thrilled to see a beautifully organized space full of fun activities to occupy his school day. My choice was easy.

Listen to your gut

Your gut feeling is a good judge. A school may shine online or on paper, but the principal may not impress you. Your instinct regarding your feelings about the principal can and should carry weight in your decision. Check out the average tenure rate for teachers—one of those statistics available on the Web site. It is telling about a school's principal and politics if the teachers remain for years on end or if there seems to be a revolving door at the teachers' lounge. If the teacher tenure statistics are nowhere to be found, add that question to your list of things to ask others about. The same advice holds for gut feelings about teachers, the atmosphere of the school, and so on. If something about the place gives you pause, try to find out why.

After you make the leap and enroll your child, you are not quite done. You still may need some onsite validation. Accomplish this by doing things such as volunteering in the classroom, talking to other parents at the bus stop, or making an appointment with your child's teacher. Children in a new school environment won't always be accurate informants, so do the legwork yourself to find out the score. If you decide your choice isn't panning out, rather than wallowing in a bout of guilt, you'll be in prime position to take action.

Selecting academic programs

One day while volunteering at school, I overheard a discussion of a new advanced math program. My daughter, a math whiz, was never included in the evaluation testing for it. I took action, talked to the teacher and the principal, and politely but firmly insisted that they test my daughter. I wasn't surprised when her test score showed that she was a good candidate for it. I'm sure that if I didn't intervene, my daughter would never have been placed in the advanced math program.

It isn't enough these days that you must handpick your child's school, you also need to be on the prowl for the many programs schools offer, academic and otherwise. Be an active partner in your child's education. If you feel that your child is a candidate for a program that hasn't been offered to her, ask the teacher about it. You know your child. If she likes to be challenged, help your child and your teacher find appropriate challenges.

Moms sometimes remain hesitant to be proactive in this way, believing that doing so is stepping on the teacher's toes. Most teachers, however, welcome an involved parent. As long as discussions you have with the teacher are conducted in a positive manner, never centering on blame, you can expect your teacher to welcome and respect your input. The two of you have the same goal—a high-quality educational experience for your child.

Similarly, if you see your child struggling academically, talk with the teacher about available tutoring or special assistance. Mommy Guilt often results when children are not achieving academically or socially at the level of their peers. By seeking out services for your children and getting them help, you are not putting a stigma on their permanent record. You are doing the responsible thing by getting them the extra help they need. Enrolling your child in these programs will make you feel proud that you are taking a proactive role in your child's emotional and educational well-being. Your teacher or principal should have lists of specialized academic programs. Ask for them. Treat your school as a smorgasbord of opportunity filling your child's plate.

Being a familiar face

What about volunteering in the classroom? Feel guilty just thinking about it? Too much? Too little? Not at all? Give yourself a break from the Mommy Guilt. Work, other commitments, and having to divide your time among your children are all valid reasons for not being the room mother. Teachers will tell you that they will take whatever time you have available to give, so just give what you can. If you have a child who begs you to come into his class because he sees other moms doing it, take comfort in the fact that just one brief visit to his classroom is enough to let him know you are interested in his school life. Note, too, that school volunteering can be a lot of fun. Kids are entertaining people when you spend time with them.

Sometimes merging a workday and a school day can't be accomplished. Another way to volunteer is to offer to bring home a class activity to cut out or assemble, or contribute your professional services to the school in some way. Computer professionals can design a Web site; small-business owners can invite the class to the business for a tour; doctors can donate tongue depressors for a project—the list of possibilities is endless. The school's parent-teacher association (PTA) will also have an abundance of volunteer opportunities within the boundaries of your abilities and schedule. You don't have to be president of the PTA; it's just fine to dip your toe into volunteering in very light ways, such as overseeing a booth at the annual school fair or baking (or buying!) a cake for a fund-raising event. You may find that some years you have more time to offer, and other years you have less. Keep in mind that being supportive of your children's school experience is what really matters, not the number of PTA committees you run single-handedly every year.

Whatever you do, pick something enjoyable to you. With so many choices of how to be involved, this is a lot easier than you might think it is. By the same token, feel free to say no to projects that turn you off. By volunteering for activities that you find fun, and only activities that you enjoy, you not only assuage your Mommy Guilt, you achieve Mommy Guilt-Free Principle No. 6 (Get a few laughs along the way).

Starting the guilt-free homework adventure

I'm never really sure how much assistance I should provide when it comes to homework. If I help too much am I taking away from my child's learning or giving her an unfair advantage on her grades? If I don't help enough, I feel so guilty watching her struggle when the answers are so obvious to me. Plus, my child is always doing homework right before dinner or when I am trying to put the younger kids to bed—I just don't have time to sit down and help her.

It's time to turn the homework adventure Mommy Guilt-Free. As a general rule, the Mommy Guilt-Free Philosophy views homework as 100 percent your child's responsibility. That is not to say that you have no obligation in the process (in fact, some schools ask parents to check over and sign homework) or that the child won't need help from time to time. But if you view it as 100 percent your child's job, then most of the guilt associated with it decreases. That said, you aren't off the hook entirely, so let's look at how to achieve the homework-help balance.

Have you ever helped your child with homework, only to get an angry or resentful reaction instead of gratitude? Keep a look out for the signs that your child may not need the amount of help or the type of assistance that you are giving.

I used to sit down with my son at the table and do his homework with him. It would take hours and it almost always ended up with one of us in tears. I couldn't understand why something that was so easy would take him so much time. It became a real power struggle. He'd insist he could do it alone, but I could see that he was making mistakes, and I insisted on checking his work. If he came home with really low grades, I would feel so guilty that I didn't make him listen more carefully to me.

Back off, Momma! It's called homework, not momwork. It is meant to be done at home by your child; to teach kids responsibility and study skills as well as have them practice, on their own, the material they learned in class. Homework is not about creating a list of correct answers to ensure they make an *A* grade.

Help with Homework

The purpose of homework is to develop children's independent study skills and to give them a chance to practice the material learned during the day. These tips will help you help your child with homework:

➤ Embrace the concept that homework is 100 percent the child's responsibility, including remembering the assignment, knowing when the assignment is due, and turning in the assignment. It's not your responsibility to drive forgotten homework to school. She'll learn in a hurry not to forget it.

➤ Ask very young children, grades kindergarten to third, if they have placed their homework into their backpack each night, but don't place it into their backpacks for them. Helping them to think like a responsible person is your job—picking up their slack is not.

➤ Creating an environment that promotes study habits is a way to help with homework. For younger students, someplace close to you works well, such as the kitchen table. Older students can be expected to work on their own at places like the dining room table, on the floor in the family room, or a desk in their bedrooms. Encourage your child to keep work areas clutter-free.

➤ When buying school supplies, buy some for home use as well. Put them where your child can reach them and put them away without your help.

➤ Help your child develop a study style. Some kids need to finish one thing at a time where others will need to take a break and work on something else for a while.

➤ For long-term assignments, set up a bulletin board somewhere for important school assignments to be posted and a calendar of their due dates.

➤ Let your children know that you are their support staff. If they need a ride to the library, you are willing to help; however, it is their responsibility to let you know ahead of time and not five minutes before they want to be there.

Your role is to let your children know you are available to help if they want your help. You can let them know you will answer specific questions or interpret the teacher's directions with them, if they get stuck. Talk to the child's teacher to ensure that you understand what the overall purpose of the homework is and how you can best support that purpose. Is the goal of homework responsibility, with an emphasis on turning in the work? Is the teacher trying to reinforce a specific learning skill so that the assignment will be graded for accuracy? By being informed yourself and limiting your involvement, you are less likely to find that you are either reteaching a lesson plan without the notes, or you are undermining your child's ability to problem solve. While you don't want your child to become so frustrated that he gives up, if you do homework "with" him nightly, you are not allowing your child to be 100 percent responsible for his own work. Find a balance. This may mean being in the room, but not at the table.

Dealing with social crises

Inevitably, the day will come when your school-age child stomps into the house and crumbles into tears over a fight, snubbing, or other falling out with another kid. Or maybe one day you find yourself worrying over why other kids don't seem to call your child to play. Maybe you're fuddled over why your child doesn't seem interested in making friends. Extreme flare-ups of Mommy Guilt can be caused by these and other types of social issues:

➤ The kids who do call seem to be odd, misfit types to you.
➤ Your child still hangs out with the same two kids he has played with since kindergarten, not forming new friendships from school or the other activities he is involved in.
➤ You notice that your child seems to be hanging out with kids who are bossy and sometimes outright mean (and maybe even following their lead).
➤ You get a call from another parent upset over something your child did/didn't do during a play date.
➤ Another parent asks if you would invite her child over to hang out with your child—but your child really doesn't like this kid.
➤ You moved over the summer. Your child is the new kid and doesn't seem to be making much headway with new friendships.

We mothers feel guilty that social traumas were somehow caused by us not paying enough attention or not properly socializing our children when they were younger. We feel enormous guilt when our advice backfires and makes the situation worse for our children. We are frustrated when our child ignores our advice and the problem remains. We lose sleep. We hold long powwows with our friends to discuss and brainstorm the problem. Even when every fiber in our bodies tells us to intervene, we aren't sure when, how, or even *if* we should. The Mommy Guilt-Free Philosophy on peer problems is simple: Making friends is your child's job. Your job is to help your child grow the internal mechanisms for developing positive, strong friendships.

There will come a day when you must step out of the role of play date coordinator and allow your children to make their own choices when it comes to friends. You want your children to consistently select friends who bring out the best in them. In order to do this, your children must be free to choose—to say yes and no to friendships. Being able to refuse friendship with a kid she doesn't like sounds obvious, but many parents unwittingly try to force unhealthy friendships upon their children.

I wanted my daughter to be able to play with the neighbor's daughter. They are the same age so I figured it would be a great match. After many times with my daughter coming home in tears, I realized the girls would never be friends. They were just too different.

Handling peer problems and solutions

Before you go charging in to fix any peer problems that occur in your child's life, take stock of your own history. If your child isn't complaining of an issue but you clearly see one, ask yourself how your own childhood experiences are coloring your view. Are you pushing "popularity" onto your child, worried that he is missing out on the best part of childhood? If you struggled with making friends, are you anxiously looking for signs that your child is able to make friends? If you hung out with kids who were "bad influences," are you always on the scout for that situation among your children's friendships? Recognizing your biases will help you act as an objective "friendship consultant" when you feel you must step into action.

Brainstorming possible solutions with your child

If a friendship goes bad or you see something that isn't working out well, try problem solving with your child to get to a workable resolution. This may help your child learn that friendships sometimes need attention, or that there are times when another child isn't acting like a friend. Listen carefully to what your child has to say. Then gently assist her in thinking through the problem. Walk through possible outcomes of proposed solutions until your child finds a resolution she believes will work. Avoid dictating a course of action to your child.

My third-grade daughter, Colleen, was coming home every day upset. All of her friends from last year were in another class, and they weren't saving a seat for her at lunchtime while she waited in line to buy a hot lunch. She had to eat with the second graders. Colleen and I discussed several solutions—calling friends on the phone to ask them to save a seat, approaching them at morning recess about it. Colleen came up with the idea that if she took a cold lunch for a few days—no matter what was on the hot lunch menu—she could get to the table faster. I agreed to pack Colleen's lunch for her. Mission accomplished! Within a few days, the others were remembering to include Colleen at their table.

Conducting a mommy reconnaissance mission

My fifth-grader didn't seem to be doing well socially. He never seemed to make new friends. Occasionally he played with some kids he has known since first grade, but other boys didn't call him. I asked him about it all the time and gave him loads of advice, but none of it ever seemed to make a difference. I felt incredibly guilty that I couldn't help him.

It's time to head to the playground and take a firsthand look. If you see that your child is happily playing with another, give a sigh of relief and know all is probably well. If you see your child wandering around all by himself, a quick call or a short note to your child's teacher expressing your concern should get you the information you need to figure out what is going on with your child and his friendships.

Talk with a variety of adults who interact with your child when you are not around including teachers, religious education teachers, coaches, Scout leaders, and the like. Keep in mind that time, place, or circumstance may change a child's behavior. A child may be popular with kids at school but not at hockey practice. Oftentimes, even bullying behavior varies according to the situation. A child who is bullied at school may turn around and be a bully while at summer camp. Ask these adults, in general, what they have observed regarding your child's social skills and the particular crisis being addressed.

Use the parenthood pipeline to gather feedback from other kids in the class. Carefully choose another parent or two, explain your concerns and ask if the parent would discretely talk to her children. Ask for assistance in finding out how your child is viewed by his peers. Do other kids view him as a "geek"? Does he play with other kids or hang out by himself? Tailor the question for the situation.

Bringing it to the attention of an expert

If you think your child is suffering from an issue that is beyond your scope, many school districts now have "social skills" coaches and nearly all have some sort of a counselor or school social worker available. Make an appointment, initially for you alone to discuss the issue, then for your child if necessary. If your school offers no such service, give your pediatrician's office a call for suggestions or a referral.

Also understand that children need to make their own way. You need to be aware of the boundaries of when to create situations for your child to make friends and when to back off. If they are not showing signs of being anxious about their friendships—they are most likely comfortable with their relationships. Many of the crises that occur in a child's friendships are momentary, they may need a sympathetic ear or have a need to vent. What they don't need is for you to prematurely spring into action and call in the reserves in order to save them.

Social Crisis Solutions

Using the Mommy Guilt-Free Philosophy on social intervention, and the suggestions in the "Handling peer problems and solutions" section in this chapter, let's work through some solutions to the following social crises.

Problem: The kids who call to play seem to be odd, misfit types to you.

Investigation shows: Your child is happy and is making good grades.

What to do? Keep your mouth shut on your opinions of his friends, and get to know the kids better. Volunteer in the classroom or during

Scouts or take them all camping. Maybe they are quirky, funny, intellectual kids who are very nice people.

Problem: Your child still hangs out with the same two kids he has played with since kindergarten, not forming new friendships from school or the other activities he is involved in.

Investigation shows: Your kid would like more friends but says he doesn't know how to make them.

What to do: Brainstorm with your kid. Try to find situations in which your child can interact with others within his social comfort zone. Maybe he'll want you to talk to the teacher and see what opportunities there are for group work, for example. Maybe he'll be okay with letting you set up an opportunity for less direct interaction with others. For example, he might like the idea of inviting a classmate out to a ballgame better than a one-on-one play date at your house.

Problem: Your child comes home with another story about how her best friend told her she wasn't her friend anymore.

Investigation shows: Your child forgets that she was upset.

What to do: Nothing, but keep your ears open. If the two haven't worked out their differences on their own, you can brainstorm with your daughter on ways to work it out. You can also brainstorm with her about things to do to help her develop other friends, should this relationship continue to be volatile.

Problem: You notice that your child seems to be hanging out with kids who are bossy and sometimes outright mean (and following their lead).

Investigation shows: Your child is uncomfortable with their meanness, but insists she likes these friends.

What to do: Discuss possible solutions and role-play them with your child. If your child does not indicate that it is a problem, address the issues that you can control. Let it be known that being mean is not a quality that is acceptable behavior in your household and reinforce what is expected from her: being polite, kind, and considerate.

Protecting your perfect angel

To you your child may be perfection, but no one actually is perfect. Defending our children's behavior at every turn is becoming a disturbing trend. Other people need to be comfortable with our children. If adults in a position to know, such as teachers, indicate that your child has a problem—is excessively introverted or aggressive—take that information seriously. Do the homework outlined in the "Handling peer problems and solutions" section above with an open mind to find out what is going on with your kid. Keep in mind that your actions must illustrate that your intent is to collect facts to get to the root of the problem. Whenever possible, avoid both defending and blaming anyone until you have all your facts and you feel you may have the full story. Mommy Guilt seems to take on a life of its own when we feel our kids are in crisis. When we can act as an objective crisis consultant—as opposed to a rescue worker—we cease blaming ourselves or taking on too much and, in turn, feel less guilty.

Note

1. *StateNote: School Choice State Laws*, compiled by Todd Ziebarth, updated May 2003, Education Commission of the States (ECS). www.ecs.org.

CHAPTER 13

WORKING ON GUILT

Every parent works. Whether it's inside the home, outside of the home, paid employment, or a volunteer position, it all involves work. This chapter will cover strategies for adhering to the Mommy Guilt-Free Philosophy while dealing with the morning, noon, and night of work.

Who do you think suffers more guilt, stay-at-home moms (SAHMs) or work-outside-the-home moms (WOHMs)? The answer is neither. Results from the *Mommy Guilt* survey showed no appreciable difference in the frequency and severity of guilt between the two groups. In fact, many of the same parental issues caused equal (and high) amounts of anxiety for both groups. Whether parents have outside jobs or have made running the household their primary job, they endure a lot of stress.

Happiness and Work

The *Mommy Guilt* survey finds that work situations do not impact most of the issues over which parents feel guilt. (See Appendix A for the full report on the *Mommy Guilt* survey.) However, the type of work environment did correlate with some interesting differences in reported happiness.

For the category of happiness, 60 percent of survey participants said they were "mostly happy," 22 percent are "very happy," and only 1 percent reported being "very unhappy."

> ➤ 18 percent of those with **full-time outside jobs** claimed to be "very happy" and 1 percent "mostly unhappy."
> ➤ 24 percent of **stay-at-home parents**, declared themselves to be "very happy" and 1 percent unhappy.

> The happiest of all groups are the parents who have full-time paid jobs, but perform them **full-time from their home offices**. A full 38 percent of folks in this group say they are "very happy." One percent were unhappy.

Work—the guilt-ridden choice

One of the ironies of parenting is that the work situation is so frequently a no-win Mommy Guilt situation. WOHMs, who may feel good about their situation overall, often suffer pangs of guilt over the hours they spend away from their children. In fact, "spending too much time at work" is the No. 1 cause of guilt for WOHMs who participated in the survey (named by over 50 percent). Work commitments cause residual guilt, too. WOHMs worry that they have less time to volunteer at their children's schools or that their work schedules prevent them from attending all their children's special activities such as sports games, school plays, or parent-teacher conferences. SAHMs, who may feel good about their situation overall, often feel guilty that they aren't "using" their college degrees or pulling their income-earning weight.

When our daughter was born, Doug and I made the decision that I would put my career in the freezer and stay home with her. I was happy to do this, not because I felt that all children need a mom at home (I believe that choice is personal), but because this is what we thought would be good for our family. Here I was sacrificing my career for a period of time to do what I thought we both wanted, but now I am feeling guilty. My husband works very long hours and has all of the responsibility of providing financially for our family. I wish we had devised a plan before making our decision. I think I might have done things differently. After all, had I been at work and wanted a new position, I would have submitted a proposal! I know my decision to stay at home would have remained the same, but talking about how this decision would change our family would have helped make the transition easier. I'm really surprised by how guilty I feel about no longer making a monetary contribution to our household every month. It causes problems in our marriage.

Work, like all life, is about balance and trade-offs. In another irony, while the workforce has never been more open to women, instead of feeling empowered by choice, many moms suffer a "grass is greener" guilt syndrome. If they work, they feel as if they should be staying home or vice versa. Many moms worry that they are being judged by other moms over their work situation. That may be so, but the Mommy Guilt-Free response is who cares what they think? To alter or not alter a career path is a personal decision. It may be based on choice or necessity, and it may certainly change over time.

After I gave birth to my second child, I eagerly left my job to stay home. I loved being a full-time mom! I loved the quiet, unexpected moments of joy and the free-flowing way I could teach my children about life as they experienced it. Money was tight, though. Still, every time my husband and I discussed my going back to work, we agreed I should continue to stay home. I felt guilty that I wasn't helping out financially and I felt guilty over spending money, too. Once, I bought my daughter Winnie-the-Pooh sheets instead of new shoes and felt alternately joyful about buying her something she loved, and guilty that I had spent our money so frivolously. Constantly worrying about money was not making me happy. When the baby was a year old, I started substitute teaching a few days a week to help out with cash, and discovered how much I desperately missed teaching, too. I decided to go back to teaching full-time. I've given up some time with my kids to go back to work, and I regret that, but my husband can work less now and gets to enjoy the kids more now, too.

It is also possible that a person can parent better to some ages than to others. Our society spoon-feeds us guilt by telling us that one way or the other way is "best." Keep in mind that what is best is what works for you and your family, and that the definition of best will change as you and your family age. For some moms, staying home when the kids are older—not younger—is the ideal circumstance.

I'm not what you would call a "baby person." I realize that sounds very shallow, but I am so much better with kids who can talk. I'm just not very patient and I felt very guilty for letting my son cry in his crib so much, but I just knew that if I held him any longer I would have probably shaken him. It was for his own safety that I put him back in the crib. When we had our second child, I decided not to stay at home. It made all the difference in the world. I was a much better mommy to my kids because I was not stressed out and impatient. I know that people say you should not let a stranger raise your kid, but had I stayed home with her, I would have been a stranger raising my kid. I no longer would have resembled myself anymore due to feeling so depressed and guilty. My plan is to work until they are at an age where I feel more comfortable with them.

Unhappy at work, unhappy at home

Many of us use work to define ourselves—we are doctors, engineers, full-time parents, lawyers, retail managers, teachers, and so on. If we are frustrated by work, or frustrated by the overall direction of our careers, only the saint-at-heart can keep such feelings from impacting how happy we are at home.

If work is such a huge misery that you have little energy left to enjoy your family life, the best advice we can offer to improve your parenting experience and your family's happiness is to take action to change your job—or to change your attitude about the job you have. (See the box "Getting More Out of the Job You Have.") You are not sentenced to suffer in work misery until the end of time, no matter the pay, location, or insurance situation. If you truly feel trapped, consider this feeling as a signal to research your options. From reading books on career changes to engaging career coaches—thousands of ideas on improving your situation are out there, right now, waiting for you to discover and engage them. As a matter of fact, many of the guidelines we are laying out for you to enjoy a happier home life are applicable to enjoying your job. (Try some of the behavior management techniques discussed in Chapter 6 on a problem coworker, for instance.)

I took a good job in the emergency services field. I've always been a hard worker and ES work is on twenty-four-hour shifts and demanding. I was soon working seventy-hour weeks. My husband, who was originally really happy with the pay, soon started to act angry all the time. My kids were upset with me, too. When I came home, my husband and kids wanted me to go out and do things with them. I tried to do that as much as I could but I also needed to rest—to read and sleep. To my credit, no matter how many hours I worked, I always made it to my kids' soccer games, which was good, but I knew it really wasn't good enough. I felt like I was missing my kids growing up. I had to make a change. I was offered another job that paid a lot less money but I took it. You know what? It's all working out, even on the financial side. We spend more time together as a family. We've gone on family vacations. Sure, I'd like to make more money, but I won't work like that again until my kids are grown.

This mom's demanding job taught her to appreciate Mommy Guilt-Free Principle No. 7 (Set aside time to have fun as a family).

Feeling guilty about time spent working isn't limited to those who work outside the home. SAHMs from the *Mommy Guilt* survey also expressed guilt that the hours they spent doing administrative tasks (cleaning, errands, etc.) was time taken away from their children.

I used to stress about having a clean house because all my friends seemed to be able to "do it all" and then I looked closely and saw things they were missing in terms of time spent with their kids. When I moved, I decided that playing with my kids was more important. I have stuck to it and am happy with it. I even have friends comment that I don't seem stressed about being a mom. This is all because of decisions I made not to be stressed out.

Prioritizing your own happiness, in addition to making sure you have time with your family, is tantamount in absolving your Mommy Guilt. It is perfectly okay to think about what *you* need. Focus on what works for *you* and your family. Think of it this way, happy moms make for happy households.

Getting More Out of the Job You Have

Sometimes minor tweaks lead to big changes. If you are frustrated with your job but not ready, willing, or able to change jobs, try adjusting your attitude toward your current job. Here are some tips to help in this effort:

➤ Concentrate on the work itself. No matter the job, there are always new aspects you can learn. Talk with someone about how you would be able to gain new skills. Managers typically love it when employees show this kind of initiative.

➤ Be your own cheerleader. If you feel underappreciated at work, gently tout your accomplishments to give your supervisor and co-workers a lot of reasons to believe in you.

➤ Study up on people management. If you are clashing with another personality or work style, take matters into your own hands and read some books that cover how to deal with difficult coworkers. Try to keep an open mind. Sometimes, it might be you who is the difficult person.

➤ Improve your time-management skills. Using your time effectively will do wonders for helping you feel less overworked. Books, on-line programs, and community college courses are all great re-sources for time-management training, and your company may even cover enrollment costs. (If you are thinking, "I don't have time to take a course!" then you *know* you need to manage your time better!)

➤ Develop a balance between work time and family time. If you have never consciously developed a set of work/family balance strate-gies, you may be headed for a crash. When work and home life are constantly colliding, guilt is the outcome. All sorts of tactics, training, and tools exist to help you balance work and family, some of them as simple as talking to your employer.

We realize there may be economic reasons as to why you will not be able to leave a job that is making you miserable, but ultimately at what cost are you keeping this job? Is any job worth sacrificing your mental health? What about the stress it causes on the people who live with you? You can find another job, even a temporary one, until you find something else more suitable. It may be a step down, it may not be in your chosen field, but sometimes anything is better than working where you feel stressed out and miserable. Weigh your options, write out a list of pros and cons for leaving/remaining at your job, explore whether you could make it on less money or could swing a longer commute. After weighing all your options, you may find out you can lighten your Mommy Guilt by making some small or large changes.

Transition time

Whether you are a WOHM or a SAHM, one of the secrets to enjoying your family life while juggling the demands of work lies in how well you handle the time just prior to and immediately after the workday. These transition times are universal rough spots for parents. The classic example of how transition times cause Mommy Guilt is the child who tantrums at exactly the moment when the mom is attempting to load the kids into the car in the morning to get to work or to an appointment. The mom has spent the morning getting ready to leave while helping the children get ready, too. Tension in the house is already high. The child senses the mom's stress and bursts. The mom loses her cool—sometimes in the driveway in front of the neighbors (always a plus, right?). There you have it, a failed transition!

While we can't promise that you will never experience another failed transition, we do have some surefire methods for coping with them in a more relaxed, Mommy Guilt-Free manner. The following transition tips apply whether your day is spent away from the house or not.

The first step is to take some time to observe how your children handle transitions. Some people (especially kids) feel confused during a transition time. Adults might scramble to find the car keys (when they were just, a moment ago, in the palm of the hand). Kids might get distracted with a task that doesn't even resemble grabbing their lunch box and getting into the car, or it may appear that they are not listening. While they may indeed be tuning you out, this may actually be a sign that they are trying to organize this chaotic moment in their heads. They may be attempting to transition from what was expected of them at the breakfast table to what will be expected of them at school. Few kids—and, in fact, few people—simply move robotically from one activity to another.

Consider the following as you make your observations about transition times. Does your child handle transitions easily, simply doing what he must do and moving on? Does your child's mood change during a transition? Can you always count on a tantrum, argument, or issue occurring the moment you try to get the kid in the car or go to your next stop? Some WOHMs view this turmoil as justification for their guilt. They interpret the tantrum to mean that their child is angry at them over leaving for work. Before jumping to this conclusion, observe more transition times. You may discover that your child isn't mad at you, but that she simply doesn't handle transitions easily.

Maybe your child is disorganized during a transition time—always looking for coats, shoes, or other stuff? Is your child talkative during a transition time—full of news to share and wanting to spill out all the information before she can move on to the next idea? You may find that your children cope with transitions exactly how you do—or perhaps, how their other parent does. When you understand how your child deals with transition times, you will be able to pinpoint the routines you need to smooth out your day.

My son was racing around the house looking for his homework folder, and I was freaking out about him being late to school. We got in the car and I began to lecture him about being responsible for his folder when, mid-lecture, I realized I did not have my car keys. I had to get out of the car and go look for my keys. When I found them and got back to the car, my son said, "You know mom, you never know where your keys are and now I am going to be even later to school. This happens all the time." He was right. I told him that after school I would put a nail in the wall near the garage door for my keys and from that point on I would only keep my keys on the nail. My son then said, "How about we put a shelf on the wall so we can keep your keys and my homework together."

Now we'll move on to a few suggestions on transition times specifically geared for WOHMs or SAHMs. But no matter your work situation, we encourage you to read both sections. Any of the following ideas might be workable for you.

Eight Tips for Smoother Mornings

1. Allow enough time for tasks to be completed at a relaxed pace. If an hour before the bus isn't enough, try an hour and fifteen minutes.
2. Limit tasks to only those things that truly need to be completed (dressing, washing, brushing teeth, eating breakfast, and packing lunch).
3. Give your children specific instructions as to what needs to be accomplished and when—that is, dress before coming downstairs; put shoes on before eating breakfast.
4. Your child should write down the list of instructions and post it where everyone can see it. Prereaders can draw pictures to

represent getting dressed and brushing teeth. When the child
makes the list, the child feels like a participant.

5. No TV until the to-do list is completed, or better still, not at
all in the mornings. Talk to each other if you have the extra
time. (Check the newspaper's weather report, the radio's traffic
updates.)

6. Allowing homework to be routinely finished in the morning is
asking for trouble. If the homework isn't completed at night,
then the natural consequence should follow; go to school without it being done.

7. Every evening prepare for the following day with a "getting
ready" routine. Have your children pick out clothes, find shoes,
pack show-and-tell, put homework folders in backpacks. This
helps put the burden of responsibility for getting ready on the
shoulders of your children, when time isn't at such a high premium. It also helps everyone get out of the door on time, less
stressed, and without you wallowing in guilt over lost homework, being late to work, the yelling fit you just had, and so
on.

8. To avoid yelling, think natural consequences (discussed in
Chapter 6) as this mom's story illustrates.

*Darla was a dawdler. She never liked mornings and would take forever
to get dressed. This made me late to work and her late to school. I finally
called the pediatrician because I felt so guilty about our miserable
mornings. Yelling at your kid to get ready every day is not a great way
to begin each morning. The pediatrician asked, "So, is it so terrible if she
goes to school in her pajamas?" That night I warned Darla that if she
chose to dawdle the next morning, she would go to school in her pajamas.
Darla looked at me as if to say "right mom." The next morning, I went
into my bedroom and quietly called Darla's school. I explained the issue
of my dawdling darling and the principal said it was okay to drop her
off in jammies but to make sure she had clothing to change into. I gave
Darla the five-minute warning. She was still in pajamas. After that, I
scooped her up and took her to the car. She was shocked! I dropped her
at school with her backpack. She never dawdled again.*

Evening transitions for work-outside-the-home moms

After a day of being on their best behavior for their teachers or daycare
providers, kids have often exhausted their store of good behavior. As soon

as Mom or Dad shows up, they can let down their guard and throw a nice, big tantrum. What a great release of tension! Wouldn't it be wonderful if you could join your kids and just flop on the floor, cry, and refuse to drive the car home?

While you may not be able to avoid the evening tantrum every day (nor join it)—you can learn to embrace it—or, at least, not let it derail any more of your enjoyable family time than necessary. Workable evening transition times for you and your kids are the solution. If you are dashing from your job to pick up the kids from daycare or after-school programs, then hurrying home to try and get dinner on the table while your kids are hanging on your knees or hollering for help with their homework, you'll have major stress.

A commute can be a stress-inducing time killer or, when viewed through Mommy Guilt-Free eyes, it can become your own personal transition time. Promise yourself you won't get anxious or angry over traffic, and make that promise easier to keep by playing a comedy tape, an audio book, a classical music CD—something you listen to only for the commute home. If you have a very short commute, try eating a few bites of your favorite candy bar or snack, keeping it special by having it only after work, alone in your car, during your transition time. In other words, do something special for yourself those few minutes after work—something you save for that time, that you do only in that time. You'll find yourself looking forward to the time, enjoying it, then setting off on your next set of requirements with a fresh attitude.

To orient yourself for a smooth and enjoyable transition time, apply the same methodology to yourself as you do to your child: mentally run through your expectations for the transition and how you will achieve them, then position yourself appropriately.

Once you arrive home with family in tow, whether the dad arrives home at roughly the same time or not, realize that you are in yet another transition time—you've transitioned from the commute to being at home. Another segue routine can work miracles. This mom discovered music to be her family's ideal evening transition routine:

I had a terrible commute. An hour and a half each way to work and by the time I got home, I was grumpy and tired. One day I was walking in the store and saw an under-the-counter CD player. I felt compelled to purchase it. I brought it home and put it in our kitchen. I noticed it had an alarm function where you could set the CD to play at a certain time. I began setting the alarm for the time I walked in the door to our house. When my kids were young I chose the

music, but as they got older, it was fun for them to pick the tunes.
When I walked in after a crummy commute, it was so much fun to
dance around the kitchen with my kids to whatever music came my
way.

Evening transitions for stay-at-home moms

At the end of a day at home, SAHMs often experience something called
"hurricane hour," because everything seems to be spinning out of control.
Try to set up a personal transition time for the few minutes *before* your
husband comes home. Think of taking a tiny segment of time to mentally
move from the end of the workday to the beginning of the evening and
family time. How about popping up to your bedroom for a rejuvenating
body spray or quick swish of mouthwash? Maybe you click on your favorite
music CD. Maybe you drink a special herbal tea blend, used only for this
end-of-day transition.

Remember, when Dad arrives in the door, he'll be undergoing his own
transition time. Some dads can jump right in so you can "go on break"
while others need a little more time to unwind on their own before joining
in on the family antics. Try to choose a whole-family transition activity that
allows your children to express themselves while you and your spouse can
participate in a relaxing way. Perhaps they could read you a story they
wrote at school while you rest your aching feet on the sofa.

Above all, make sure the first thing you do when your family gathers
together at the end of the day is to cheerfully greet one another. Before
any words exit your mouth use it to smile at your spouse when he returns,
and, if possible, kiss him as well. Ask that your children do the same. No
matter what happens after that, you know that you've prioritized your family's enjoyment, at least for a few moments.

CHAPTER 14

A SPORTING CASE OF MOMMY GUILT—OR STAGE FRIGHT?

The Mommy Guilt-Free Philosophy takes a broad view of extracurricular activities. We see numerous choices and ways to experience a positive competitive environment within and outside the scope of sports. Feelings of camaraderie and success among cast members of a play mirror those shared by teammates of a tournament-winning sports team. Likewise, the mom on the sidelines, the mom in the stage wings, and the one on the edge of her seat at the competitive chess match all experience similar joys and anxieties. Those anxieties can lead to intense bouts of Mommy Guilt, much of them due to some disturbing trends in the world of children's competitive activities.

In the adult world, if you want to get ahead, you work harder. You log longer hours and work when others rest. Adults have errantly applied this logic to childhood activities. They think that kids must start younger, practice more hours, and practice more often, with far more pressure to perform than ever before.

With soccer, hockey, gymnastics, skiing, and a slew of other sports, if your children aren't skilled by the time they are ten years old, they have likely missed the chance to play competitively. Just try to find a beginning soccer team for an eleven year old. The realization strikes guilt in the hearts of many a parent. Parents want their children to know the joys of being on the winning team and to have a lifelong love of sports and fitness.

Sports are not the only area where this skewed adult logic has run amok. We all know stories of stage moms who spend nights worrying if their children's performance resumes are good enough to get them the meaty auditions, or of Scout leaders who pressure their own children to become the superachievers of the troop.

When those enrollment forms come around, we suggest that subscribers to the Mommy Guilt-Free Philosophy remember Mommy Guilt-Free Principle No. 2 (Parenting is not a competitive sport). We suggest that you think about the experiences you want for your child (fun, friendship, self-discovery) rather than any performance-related goals (winning a championship, starring in the school musical). By this simple twist in focus, you can slice through years of activities-related stress and guilt. Let's examine this new focus in detail.

Running into sports guilt

When it comes to childhood sports, there's no denying that the pressure can be intense. Practices are long and frequent, and participants grow highly competitive at startlingly young ages (such as traveling teams for third graders). While a full-grown, emotionally mature adult can handle draining schedules, demanding this of a child, whose body and mind are still growing, is dicey.

The sad reality is that this adult "work harder" logic is making it tougher for our kids to experience and discover the benefits many activities have to offer. Children wind up being expected to commit to a single sport early on, when their young bodies are barely coordinated enough to hold a hockey stick, let alone execute slap shots like a pro. Past the early elementary years, demanding schedules may make it impossible for children to even try other sports. During the off-season, kids frequently attend sports camps to keep their skills sharp. The focus on competition and highly developed skill "weeds out" kids at ridiculously early ages. The awkward goalie at age nine could have been a star by age fifteen, but either won't get that chance or won't want it if he remains turned off by his earlier bad experience.

All of this leads to Mommy Guilt for many a mom. In fact, 41 percent of *Mommy Guilt* survey respondents with children old enough to participate in sports, named sports-related issues as an area that caused them guilt (although only 5 percent said it caused them to feel their highest levels of guilt).

Should you push your child to enter a sport? Mothers of boys worry that their children will take a hit in social status if they can't make a respectable showing on the field—and for good reason. In many parts of the country, the pressure on boys to excel at sports is enormous.

My son is made to feel very badly because he has chosen to be in the drama department instead of on the basketball team. He's 6 feet 3 inches and knows nothing about basketball, but he runs circles around anyone when it comes to memorizing his lines for Macbeth.

Mothers of girls know that girls, too, are facing increasing social pressure to be good at sports, or at least active participants. Plus, mothers worry that if they don't pressure girls into sports, they won't develop lifelong habits of fitness. Girls are under tremendous pressure to maintain their bodies' appearance.

My eleven-year-old is starting to get pudgy. She used to do soccer and swimming but now refuses to engage in any kind of organized sport and spends more time than I would like at the computer. I am feeling awfully guilty. Should I push her harder? She needs to learn to value fitness, and if she won't exercise on her own, as her parent, maybe I should make her do it.

Sidelining sports guilt

Even when your children have a burning desire for a sport, how much should their participation rule the family's world? How much should they be allowed to sacrifice other activities, time spent with family, or time spent on homework to concentrate on that sport? Where do you play in all of it? Call for a time-out! Then draft yourself a Mommy Guilt-Free playbook to childhood sports.

For mothers with a child already involved in sports, grab a hot dog, sit down on the bench, and give us a moment to address the beginners.

There may come a time when your child expresses an interest in beginning a sport. There may come a time when you express an interest in your child beginning a sport. There may come a time when you realize that you and your child are in separate end zones regarding this decision. There is rarely a middle ground when it comes to sports. Not only is being involved in a sport time-consuming, both for the parent (the schlepper) and the child (the schleppee), it can also be expensive. Some sports such as hockey, ski racing, and competitive gymnastics can really tap into your savings. Do yourself a favor and research the costs before filling out the enrollment forms. (See the box "Questions to Ask About Sports Programs" on page 151.) Look into fees, cost of gear, availability of rental or secondhand gear (and the market for selling your child's outgrown gear), potential for travel, and other associated costs. You may, without guilt, simply decide that the sport in question consumes too many family resources and that you can find an equally fulfilling, less draining alternative. Your child will probably be disappointed at first. But the lower stress level in the household without this sports commitment should ultimately leave both parents and kids happier.

My husband and I decided no hockey. In our area, hockey is intensely popular. It's also an expensive, time-consuming sport with lots of odd-hour practice sessions. I felt guilty about saying no when all of my kids' friends were into hockey and tried to convince my kids to take up ski racing instead, as several of my friends' kids were into that. It was also expensive, time consuming, and required volunteer time and traveling, but at least it allowed me to hit the slopes while the ski team practiced. The kids told me no. They didn't want to work that hard at an activity they thought of as fun. So I backed off, figuring why pay big fees and volunteer, only to wind up with kids who were hating the experience? Instead, I enrolled them in ski "clubs" which are noncompetitive but include a little training on timed slalom courses. The clubs were a big hit! The kids got training for the money I spent. I got to ski when they skied. Best of all, it lasted only a few Saturdays.

Popular sports will have a variety of leagues (sometimes also called clubs) from which to choose. Each will likely have differing attitudes toward competitiveness and win/loss records. Some leagues grow competitive breathtakingly fast. They'll have traveling teams for grade-schoolers that include daily practice. Other leagues will offer dual tracks of developmental teams alongside competitive teams. In theory, developmental teams don't require tryouts and have an emphasis on skill building and playing the game; score keeping is deemphasized. Competitive teams typically require tryouts and the win/loss record may be much more of a focal point. But no matter the label, competitiveness will also depend heavily on the coach's attitude, as the following two stories show:

I signed my seven-year-old up for baseball and she sat on the bench the entire season! I was shocked to find out that, depending on the coach, your kids might not ever get to play if they aren't shining stars right out of the gate.

* * * * *

I just enrolled my son on his first sports team. He's been loving it. The coach is teaching the kids about real baseball and everyone gets equal playing time. He still tries to make sure that the players with the most skills are challenged. Sure they sometimes lose, but they always have fun. I don't want our seven-year-old stressed out because he's been a benchwarmer. Plus, who wants to pay to have your child sit on a bench?

During your research, you'll also discover that various leagues may have various levels of social cachet. If you live in a community where being involved in sports borders on obsession, don't be surprised if parents describe the most competitive league as "better." Keep in mind that finding a league that is a good match for your child's eagerness and skill is really what makes a league better for your family. Children whose skill level has surpassed their teammates may grow frustrated with their playing experience. Children who are in the early stages of the sport's learning curve may lose face and feel inferior to more competitive, experienced players. Matching your child's level to the league, club, or team will help bench that Mommy Guilt.

Also, remember that scores of options exist for your children to do individual sports, and progress at their own speed while staying fit, meeting friends, and learning sports ethics. Some examples include indoor rock climbing, swimming, tennis, track and field, bicycling/mountain biking, golfing, and skating. (Did you know that roller hockey leagues are known to be more laid back than the iced variety?) So consider the best fit for your kid. When parenting is not a competitive sport, options abound as to how to help your child have a positive sports experience.

Questions to Ask About Sports Programs

1. What is the coach's philosophy about giving kids playing time?
2. What are you looking for in a coach and what do you consider to be unacceptable behavior?
3. What is the coach's experience level and training?
4. What does the coach consider to be unacceptable coaching behavior for this sport and age group?
5. How are the teams formed—by school attended, grade, age, or tryouts?
6. How is skill level or experience considered when forming teams?

7. How does your child submit a request to be on the same team
    as a specific friend?
8. How long is the season?
9. How many games/meets/races per week?
10. On what days/times are practices held?
11. Does the team play/practice on any religious holidays?
12. What are the costs for registration?
13. What other fees might be involved (purchasing team treats, an
    end-of-game party, a coach's gift)?
14. What are the costs of the equipment and what options do you
    have to sell, rent, buy used, or sell outgrown equipment?
15. How does the program deal with difficult parents or players
    who are unsportsmanlike?
16. What resources are available if your child struggles and needs
    extra help?

Knowing the show must go on

Being involved in extracurricular activities teaches sportsmanship, patience, time management, following directions, as well as the fact that life
is not always going to be played by the rules. This is the case for any activity
be it sports, the performing arts, Scouts, you name it. So, if you have a
child who sometimes needs a push, go ahead and push—enroll your child
in an activity that you are confident she will enjoy. But after that ask yourself, does she love it? Or does she want to quit? (Hey, you people with the
hot dogs! Time to start paying attention.) If your child wants to quit should
you let her? If so, will you be teaching your kid to be a quitter?

Here is what we suggest: With younger children (in second grade or
younger), do not overexplain what is going to happen. Sign them up, answer questions about the activity, buy, borrow, or rent the minimal equipment and show up. If you see your child having a hard time, then enlist
the help of the coach/adult leader and be your child's cheerleader. If the
adult in charge is inexperienced or oblivious, take the situation into your
own hands and walk your child through the difficulties. When problems
arise, ask open-ended questions and let your child come up with possible
solutions. If quitting is one of the solutions your child suggests, be open
to it, but before pulling the plug, brainstorm together about a possible
compromise and/or solution. You might want to discuss with your child
one or more of the following ideas:

- Play out the season/session until it ends and don't sign up for the next one.
- Have a more experienced kid help or practice with your child during the season/session to see if skills can be improved or a better understanding of the activity attained.
- Contact the coach/leader/director for input or ideas.
- Ask other parents how their children are doing with the adult in charge or activity in question. It may be that your child isn't the only one who is having some sort of issue.
- Have your child give you a list of pros and cons, and then you list your pros and cons. Together, you look at what you both are able to control and what is out of your control.

While you never want to take the option of quitting completely off the table, there may be circumstances when you will not agree to it. If your child was told beforehand that signing up for the play meant participating in the performance, or you researched the sports team in question and found its demands reasonable, then your child probably should see the activity through (assuming she isn't sick or absolutely miserable).

See if you can discover the reason your child has lost interest by attending a practice, rehearsal, or meeting. If your child is upset because she hasn't achieved her goal—scored points, earned a badge—remind her that she'll never get to her goal if she quits. Learning new skills is hard work and working through it can be a powerful lifelong lesson. It is one that can make a previously tentative child feel like a star.

My daughter, Alicia, played soccer all through elementary school. She was a hard worker, and always tried her best, but no natural athlete. She had a great coach though. During her fourth year playing, she told her coach that it was her goal this season to score—something she had never done before (when most of the other kids had). Her coach rotated Alicia into slots on the offense. Even though Alicia frequently lost the ball to the other team, her coach continued to give her a shot on offense during every game. Toward the end of the season, the coach put Alicia in as a forward and yelled instructions out to the other girls to pass her the ball. The best players took their cues and supported Alicia, passing her the ball for repeated shots on goal, and keeping the other team away from her. After many tries, Alicia scored! All of her teammates cheered, and so did I. Although Alicia was not the girl who had scored the most points in the game, afterward

all the girls fussed over her goal. On the way home, Alicia described
it as one of the best days of her life.

However, if the child's activity simply isn't working out despite everyone's best efforts and intentions, quitting is certainly a reasonable option. It can also be every bit as valuable a learning experience as sticking it out.

My son auditioned for the school musical and was cast in the chorus.
Halfway though the rehearsal schedule he no longer wanted to be in
the show. I spoke to the music director because I thought I should let
him know that my son would no longer be coming to rehearsals. The
director said, "Mom, it's nice that you are letting me know, but why
isn't your son telling me this?" He caught me off guard with that. I
thought, "Gee, why am I the one here and not my son?" The director
then suggested I tell my son that it was fine for him to quit, but it
would be my son's responsibility to inform the director. I did as the
director suggested and instead of my son reacting with the anger and
fear I had expected, he said, "Can I call him now?"

Certainly there will be times when your kids will want to, or have to, bow out of things, so teach them how to do it gracefully and responsibly. Release yourself from feeling guilty about allowing your child to quit. Sometimes, only experience proves what in life is or isn't a good fit.

Handling audience participation

Youth activities can be stressful for both children and parents. Numerous childhood sports programs actually require parents to attend workshops on proper audience behavior and sign behavior contracts promising to refrain from name-calling, yelling at the officials, teasing and/or taunting, and so forth. This lousy adult behavior isn't limited to sports—as ballet mothers, music mothers, drama mothers, and chess mothers all know.

Restraining your behavior doesn't mean you have to be silent in the stands or in the audience. Cheer your kids on, loudly while on the sidelines or with rousing applause from the theater seats. Give them empathetic support when they miss their shot or flub their lines. Stay within these boundaries and guilt-free spectatorship is yours. But unless you are wearing a coach's uniform, sitting in the director's chair, or holding the conductor's baton, keep instructions and criticism to yourself. Let's put it to you this way—no parent ever got "eighty-sixed" for supportive comments. How guilty would you feel if you embarrassed yourself and your kid by saying something offensive in the heat of the moment—to your kid, another child, or to other adults? How would you feel if that comment resulted in your dismissal from watching your child perform? This is clearly a case of preventable Mommy Guilt.

If you want to coach or direct, then sign up to be an official adult leader. Most children's activities are in chronic need of knowledgeable coaches, and many organizations will happily train the less-than-knowledgeable, free of charge. This experience could be a highlight of your parenting career. If this is something you are considering, make sure your little player is enthusiastic about this action. While many children love the idea—particularly in early elementary school—some are reluctant to play for their parent's teams. If your idea to be a leader is not met with resounding enthusiasm, offer to be your child's practice partner. If you are refused for this, too, take it in stride.

If you do take on a leadership role, and your practice sessions end with your kid in frustration or tears, pay attention and back off. Parents mean well but sometimes our efforts at teaching can be unintentionally heavy-handed. Practice is just that, zeroing in on a specific task, and then repeating it. If you are working with your children on catching pop-up fly balls, for instance, then hit the pop-ups and avoid an ongoing corrective monologue. The same applies to reading lines in a play, calling out instructions in the Scouting patch or badge book, or being the spotter during multiple pirouettes. By staying quiet and watching your children for cues as to when they need a dash of your wisdom while practicing, you will ensure you are helping, not dominating.

Avoiding attendance trouble

Missing your children's game or performance can feel like missing the world. Sometimes, moving the world to be at a game is what we need to do.

My husband is now retired, but when our kids were little, he was an executive who traveled constantly. He was rarely around for any of the kids' games. However, he will forever be known for flying in one afternoon, renting a limo at the airport, driving to the field where our son's big playoff game was being held, watching his son play, then getting back in the limo and going to the airport to catch another plane.

Still, no regulation exists that says a parent who doesn't attend every game and performance will be traded to another family. Attending these activities is fun, and if you have an entertaining group of parents that you've gotten to know, it adds to your enjoyment. Still, if circumstances keep you from being able to come out and support your kid each and every time, focus on gleaning the highlights from your child after the fact. When your schedule won't allow you to play spectator at many of your child's events in a particular time frame—or your children have conflicting schedules so you must divide your support among them, try thinking outside the attendance box. Can you go to practices or rehearsals to observe and support your child that way? Can you have a friend or relative go and videotape the event for you? Your child would surely enjoy watching the replay action with you when you are able.

Sometimes, being able to get to the action yourself becomes possible with a little creativity, too. Perhaps you could make an arrangement with a coworker who would also like to attend more of her children's events. You cover for her while she ducks out for a few hours to attend her kids' activities; she covers for you in return. As soon as the season/session begins, plug the event schedule into your calendar and see where some schedule maneuvering might be possible. Perhaps you can delay a trip for a few hours or a day so you can be among the spectators. Maybe you can cash in some of your time off or call in some baby-sitting favors so you can be free to attend the activity's big days. Or, with your schedule spread in front of you, you might see that you can complete another commitment early to free up some time. If attendance relies on childcare arrangements for your younger children, try arranging for a primary and a backup sitter. If one falls through, you can count on the other.

If all fails and the event goes on without you, know that your feelings of disappointment and guilt are natural reactions to missing out on any of your child's big days. Let your child know that you feel badly and can understand his disappointment. It may lessen your feelings of guilt to share your feelings with your child and to tell him the steps you took to try to make it work out. Some scheduling conflicts just can't be resolved and it is important for your child to see that adults sometimes have other commitments that may take precedence.

CHAPTER 15

AN EXTRAORDINARY GUILT

Every parent dreams of a healthy baby. "Boy or girl, it doesn't matter as long as it's healthy," rings in our ears. So when a child is diagnosed with health issues, the mother may be swept away by Mommy Guilt, feeling like she somehow failed her child. This is a natural response, but being a failure is *not* what she is!

When you receive the news that your child is different from what society says is "normal," "healthy," or "looks right," whether the child has a severe allergy, a lifelong medical condition, or a genetic anomaly, the information is a shock to your parental system. For many mothers of children with extraordinary needs this shock, and the guilt that accompanies it, can feel monumental and completely insurmountable. In other chapters, we have encouraged moms to let go of their guilt, and in this chapter we will do so as well, but we will also pay attention to the special brand of Mommy Guilt reserved for moms with a child who needs special care.

Handling postdiagnosis emotion

A variety of emotions, negative and positive, will surface once you receive information of your child's extraordinary need. Whether your child's condition is recognized prior to birth or diagnosed later on in life, you will need some time to be able to fully absorb the news. Put your life on hold if you can for a few days: take some time off work, get a baby-sitter for your other children or explore respite care options, or call on your friends and family to take over the routine tasks of your daily life while you allow yourself to feel the wide range of emotions that will accompany the diagnosis. Seek out and ask for help at this time, even if you don't think you need it. Others who would be glad to support you may be unaware of the turmoil your family is experiencing, and may not know how to approach you to offer their assistance.

Realize that the Mommy Guilt that comes with parenting a child with extraordinary needs is part of a grief process. While it may never go away entirely, it will likely lessen over time. Instead of focusing on what you think went wrong, or why this happened, or what could have been done to prevent it, try to turn your sights toward Mommy Guilt-Free Principle No.4 (Focus on the here and now). Getting a handle on the situation for your child and your family is one of the ways to cope with what is going on right now. Taking the time you need to regroup is essential. When a mom is emotionally depleted, she may find it difficult to see any light at the end of the tunnel. But there is, most definitely, light. It may not be a steady stream, it may start as a strobe, but once a mom believes that she will experience enjoyment from bringing this child into the world, her Mommy Guilt will ease up, and the world will seem brighter.

When our first daughter was born, we were shocked to find out that she had a rare chromosomal disorder. We weren't even remotely prepared to be thrown into the world of therapies, doctors, hospitals, and a future of so many unknowns. Would she ever walk? (She does.) Would she ever talk? (She doesn't.) Would we ever be able to look past her disability and enjoy our daughter? (We do.) In the early days, I felt as if our daughter might somehow be less cute or less lovable than other children. I thought that her disabilities might make people less likely to connect with her, and I admit that I felt guilty about it. Although on a cognitive level I knew that I had done everything right, and my daughter's chromosomes were "different" by chance alone, I still felt incredibly guilty on an emotional level.

The first couple years of her life, I went overboard trying to help other people accept her. I realize now that I was actually trying to accept my own daughter. We never left the house without an outfit that included matching bows, socks, and shoes. She had more clothes than any little girl could dream of having. My husband thought I was nuts, but he went along with it because he knew I was grieving and doing the best that I could.

People noticed my little girl. They stopped me to tell me how adorable she was. They made comments about how tiny she was (less than 5 pounds birth, and about 14 pounds on her first birthday). I realize now that her clothes don't make her adorable and special. She's adorable and special no matter what she wears.

Finding support and support groups

One of the most effective ways to begin your healing process is to learn as much as you can about the extraordinary need your child has and find knowledgeable support for your family. This may come in the form of books, Internet research, or finding physicians you trust with your child's care. Gather all the information you need to feel more comfortable. It might also mean joining a support group of other parents who have a similar situation in their family. Listening to other people's experiences reassures you that you are not alone, and these people can be a great resource for you as you learn the ropes. Educate yourself but do not allow the information to consume you. As you venture out you are likely to encounter people with the urge to tell you every experience related to their child's condition. You may come across horror stories that cause you needless worry or tales of other children's accomplishments that seem beyond the scope of your child at this stage. Rather than compare your child to others with the same diagnosis, institute Mommy Guilt-Free Principle No. 2 (Parenting is not a competitive sport) and be sure to keep the particular needs of your child and your family at the forefront.

Finally, keep in mind that your child is learning right along with you. Support and encouragement are beneficial to both of you as you work your way through these educational stages.

Our daughter was diagnosed with celiac sprue when she was four years old. We luckily stumbled across her condition before it caused her much suffering. Celiac affects the small intestines. While there is no cure for it, it can be controlled with a strict gluten-free diet for life, but because its symptoms are so varied, and mimic so many other digestive tract or skin problems, many celiacs suffer for years misdiagnosed. Caring for a four-year-old who had a condition that I had never heard of before, needing to avoid a substance that I had never heard of before (and that seemed to be an ingredient in everything), caused me a lot of stress! I had enormous bouts of guilt when I made a mistake with her food, and she ate gluten and suffered. I bought books, joined an online support group, read everything I could. I quickly became an expert gluten-free cook and although, even today, my daughter may be exposed to gluten from time-to-time, I no longer wallow in guilt over it. Now that she's older, I've tried to teach her about her diet and I engage her in the decisions on whether she wants to try a food when I believe it is safe for her, but am not wholly positive. In this way, she feels more in control of her condition, and I feel I am her partner.

Educating the masses on your child's needs

I am a mom of two-year-old twins, both born with cerebral palsy. Why can't people just accept my kids for who they are? Why can't they just see them as kids, who just want to be played with and have fun? I know they can be difficult sometimes and that's scary for people, but they're just kids. It breaks my heart to see them shunned.

Every mom wants to be able to give her children the best life has to offer. When you have a child with extraordinary needs, you may find yourself feeling as if you have somehow let everyone down, especially your own child. While you will need to inform your school, your camp, and other critical care people about your child's condition, try not to consider the condition to be the defining element in your child's life. Encourage your child to participate in all activities.

My daughter has severe food allergies, but I have never restricted her from any activity that we can work around. I work with teachers when cooking or food is involved in the day's lesson. I've even sent her to overnight camp, packing all of her food along with her clothes and sleeping bag.

Caretakers can become excessively worried about caring for a child with an extraordinary need. Any way you can help get them past the label and focus on the kid as a *kid* will serve everyone well. Write a form letter that you can hand to teachers, camp counselors, and others that explains your child's condition, his extraordinary needs, any information related to dangers to consider, and any doctor-prescribed medical information. Stick to the facts and remember that this person is not an expert and they don't need a lot of technical stuff. Have informational brochures on hand from support groups and doctors' offices; that way you have the technical stuff if someone asks you for it.

Encourage others to think outside the box. If your child has a food allergy, suggest food-free alternatives to teachers or Scout leaders. Instead of a pizza party for reaching a goal, why not a paper airplane–making party? Children will be equally happy with either—it is a reward, after all! Most people are happy to cooperate. If they seem reluctant to deviate from the planned reward routine, it could be that they think it will mean more work for them or infringe upon their already tight schedule. When you encounter this, roll up your sleeves and offer to head up the project or party. Volunteering to be the top planner will guarantee a more inclusive party/project for your child, and it can be a blast. You'll get to laugh and spend time with your child (Mommy Guilt-Free Principles No. 6 and 7) while you blow that left-out-child Mommy Guilt out of the water.

Engaging your child as a full partner

Even preschoolers can learn about their own extraordinary needs and help you to help them. A child with a peanut allergy, for instance, can be taught not to eat anything at all except the food that his mom has sent with him. An older child can be shown videos of what a full-blown asthma attack looks like in order to bring home the point that asthma can be serious business. Role-play situations with your child so they can think of ways to handle questions or stares from other people who notice their extraordinary need. Think of some funny responses or situations too, because adding humor only helps. Mommy Guilt-Free Principle No. 6 (Laugh with your child) can be worked in here, so do it! Be open to your child's questions and encourage her to participate in her own care by asking questions of the doctors themselves at appointments. Seek out ways for your child to succeed, get others involved with their successes, and be at the sidelines cheering your kid on. This is, after all, how you parent any child.

Seeing past the differences

You are a role model for your child. A big positive for your relationship with your child is that you are adept at dealing with the child's extraordinary need. In fact, you and the dad are probably the only ones doing the inside job of caring for your child. This means that you are also an integral part of how other people will learn about children with extraordinary needs. In many cases, your attitude toward your child's needs will be the one that others in her life adopt toward her, too.

My daughter has a severe peanut allergy. I had to work past a stage when I was overanxious and didn't let her engage in any activity where I thought a possibility of exposure could occur. One day, I took a deep breath and told myself that she was going to have to learn to function in the world. The teacher always did an annual project that used nuts. With my consent, the teacher discussed the situation with my daughter and my daughter said she didn't mind if the teacher did the lesson, and that she would go to the library during that time. I was so proud of her for making that choice! But that's not all. After the lesson, one of my daughter's friends asked the teacher if they should scrub all the tables and chairs first before my daughter returned to the classroom. The whole class scrubbed the room to make it safe for my child. Her friends are amazingly considerate when planning snacks during play dates, too. They don't think of her as different. They just want to protect her.

Recognize that the Mommy Guilt you feel is a natural reaction that will ebb and flow over time. By studying up, finding support, and educating other people about your child's extraordinary need, you will grow empowered. While you don't have to become the ambassador of extraordinary needs, it is helpful if you are willing to give people a tour of your unique little country. The goal is to enjoy your child and feel good about the parent you are to your extraordinary little person. Remind yourself of this often and you will feel Mommy Guilt recede.

We are in the military so we move a lot. Our daughter is autistic and I recently ran into her former pediatrician at our new military installation. The doctor asked how my daughter was doing and I told her that she was doing much better than anyone ever expected. The pediatrician beamed a huge smile and said, "I am so happy to hear that. Are you enjoying your daughter?" I thought about it for a moment and then answered, "Yes, I am enjoying her. It took a while, but now I am definitely enjoying her." The doctor smiled again and said, "Good, because when you first had her in your life, I could see you struggling. Your guilt was so strong. My prayer for your family was that you would eventually be able to enjoy your daughter."

Realize that with guidance, support, and a little time, even this extraordinary type of Mommy Guilt can be pushed aside and replaced with the enjoyment of a special child.

CHAPTER 16

OTHER ISSUES THAT CAUSE GUILT

Before we designate you an official Mommy Guilt-Free philosopher, we've got a few more guilt-inducing issues to cover: solo parenting, blended families, toilet learning, sharing and other play date plights, the use of television and other "techno baby-sitters," and common illnesses and injuries.

Solo parenting

Most of us will be responsible for solo parenting at some point during our parenting careers. This is as true for the married mom as it is for the full-time single mom. Regardless of the cause, you are responsible for the workload yourself, and you need support.

If you are flying solo because you've recently been anointed a full-time single mom (divorce, widowhood, a choice to have a baby or adopt on your own), you are likely to encounter a lot of emotional turmoil. Solo parenting is tough to do! But even if solo parenting is just your temp job, the negative feelings such as resentment, anger, frustration, and guilt typically stem from the same source: dwelling on "What got me here?" and "Am I doing a good enough job being everything to everyone?" It's worth noting, too, that solo parenting can also generate the positive message that independence can be learned and your entire family can take pride in its ability to work as a differently structured unit.

Moms who can quickly move past the why-am-I-here stage will find themselves getting to the acceptance stage more quickly. Once a mom accepts her situation, she'll find competence is only a small leap away. With another hop or two, she will arrive at success. So when you find yourself solo parenting, remember that by gliding past any initial negative feelings as quickly as possible, you'll recapture the energy you need to focus on yourself and your kids.

Did we say to focus on yourself? Why yes, we did!

The first rule of successful solo parenting is to take care of you. Think of yourself as the advance team. The advance team anticipates the needs of the president while traveling. They arrive ahead and set everything up so that when the president arrives, all is ready. The beauty of the advance team is that it plans for the situation, yet allows deviations from the plan due to unexpected circumstances.

Pick and choose

When you first find out that you will be solo parenting, put yourself in advance-team mode and make a list of everything going on with you and your family during the time you will be flying solo. If you are heading out into permanent solo parenting, ask yourself how long of an adjustment period feels comfortable for you. Just take a guess, you can always revise it later. At what point down the road do you anticipate that you'll be feeling like daily life has a normal routine? Three months? A school year? A calendar year? By getting your arms around how long your stint as a solo parent will last, or how long your solo-parenting adjustment period will last, you will be ready to organize your life and lessen your anxiety. You'll regain your sense of control.

Grab your list and take a look. If it helps, grab a pencil (or a crayon, even that lipstick will do) and make some notes for yourself. Ask yourself the following questions:

1. Why did I put this item on the list? Who is affected by this item? What is meaningful about this item? What are my feelings toward this item?
2. What will happen if this doesn't get done? (Walk yourself through all the foreseeable consequences.)
3. Is there another time I can get this done? (Consider your time. Consider available resources. Consider the logistics. If your answer is yes, then remove this puppy from your list and free yourself from it.)
4. What do I need from anyone else in order to get this done? (This includes your children.) How and when should I contact them?
5. How will this affect me? Don't forget about me!

Give No. 5 a real thinking-through. Ultimately, everything is going to funnel down to you, the one in charge. This is your list. You control it. Make it work for you and your family. Think in terms of how you can accomplish what you need to accomplish while expending the least amount of energy. Focus your energy on what you can control and only what you can control.

If you decide to nix an item from the list because you feel it won't be easy for you to accomplish, flip up the lever on Mommy Guilt-Free Principle No. 1 (Let it go, guilt-free). Don't get caught in a tailspin by thinking that prioritizing yourself, your needs, your stress level, or your time is selfish. Think of yourself as your family's parachute! You must use a parachute while you are flying solo. If you frame it this way, you will succeed as you head into survival mode. In survival mode, you are meeting the basic needs of you and your family and forgoing everything else.

By thinking of solo parenting as if it were a solo flight, the previous list of questions can help you determine your flight plan. Every successful pilot needs a flight plan! Your plan will assist you in keeping your feelings in perspective, scheduling your time effectively, and determining realistic objectives and goals. We realize that there are those of you who may say, "I don't have time for this nonsense. I have way too many things I need to get done." We are telling you that if you spend time preparing a flight plan, then you will not only be able to fly through this solo parenting period but soar with flying colors. Check your Mommy Guilt baggage at the gate. Remember, you are the advance team. Your role is to identify obstacles and remove as many as possible. This does not mean other obstacles will not appear, because they will, and when they do you will be in a better place to deal with them.

Blended families: a special blend of guilt

While most women wouldn't mind if their lives resembled a fairy tale, complete with "happily ever after" and a SUV-producing fairy godmother, some tales depict rather frightening families: unhappy stepchildren and wicked stepparents. No wonder moms worry about how life will change when new characters—a stepparent and stepchildren—are added to their story.

My daughter and I had been on our own for five years when I remarried. In addition to my daughter having to get used to a new man in the family, my new husband and I decided to have a child together. I always made sure I said, "have a child together," instead of saying "having a child of our own." I was afraid it would make my first daughter feel like an outsider in her own family. I also worried how the baby would grow up to view my daughter. I realized I was double-dipping into my feelings of guilt.

"Happily ever after" is work, hard work. This is why 27 percent of Mommy Guilt survey respondents with blended families report feelings of guilt associated with their home lives. When that work gets tough, guilt can creep in and take over on issues such as who does the discipline; conflicts among custodial, noncustodial, and stepparents; or even seemingly obvious issues like sleep arrangements for all family members. By keeping in mind that all members of a blended family have their own histories, you can avoid falling into a deep well of guilt. Forming a new family is not easy. Feeling overwhelmed is normal and to be expected, particularly if the adults are already parents. But the Mommy Guilt-Free Philosophy can help you with this hot topic (all seven principles, but particularly Mommy Guilt-Free Principle No. 3—Look toward the future and at the big picture). The following ideas may help you put those "evil stepchildren" and "wicked stepparent" thoughts back in the storybooks where they belong:

➤ Talk about how parenting decisions will be made and who will make them.
➤ Discuss discipline techniques, who will use them and under what circumstances.
➤ Consider the sleeping arrangements at your home and that of any other home where your children will be living and if there are any privacy issues that need to be addressed.
➤ Include custodial and noncustodial parents in as many decisions as possible to create consistency in parenting choices and to aid your children in feeling loved and supported.
➤ Develop a flexible attitude and good communication practices. Sometimes this will be easy, other times difficult. Being flexible whenever possible and reasonable will help things along.

Members of blended families do not share a history but will be sharing a future. Respect each other's past while anticipating what will come next. This allows all members to learn to enjoy their new experiences as a family.

Once upon a time, you may have felt guilty about getting remarried and what that meant for your children. Use these suggestions, as well as educating yourself through other books, lectures, parenting classes, or support groups, to help you kiss that frog of a guilty feeling good-bye.

Toilet learning

When another mom tells you that all her children were potty trained at eighteen months, she is either lying or just recalling the days when she trained herself to bring her kids to the toilet at regular intervals. In either case, rest assured that it is highly unlikely that the little ones were fully trained prior to twenty-four months of age. For most children at that age, the brain and body have not made all the necessary connections to be able to control these functions.

Some moms feel terrible when their kid is the last one in the play group wearing diapers or when their six-year-old wets the bed at night. But the Mommy Guilt-Free Philosophy says that it's not such a big deal, so try not to sweat it. Truly, it's normal! Remember Mommy Guilt-Free Principle No. 2 (Parenting is not a competitive sport). As one of our survey respondents aptly said: *"None of them ever starts kindergarten in diapers. Potty training happens when it happens and despite what anyone will tell you pushing them won't help."*

Just as it is your job to provide nourishing food and their job to eat it; it is your job to give them the basics for toilet use and their job to use it. You can aid the process along by bringing them into the bathroom with you or with other children and encouraging everyone to go at the same time (potty parties). You can make sure they have a little potty chair of their very own or a child's potty insert for the big toilet so they don't have to worry about falling in. You can encourage them, without nagging or pressuring, to start thinking about their bathroom needs by suggesting trips to the potty at regular intervals (in the morning, an hour after eating, and so forth). You can remind them that the bathroom is available when they tell you about a "funny feeling" they have in their tummies (especially when you see the potty dance starting). Keep focused on praising and rewarding bathroom success whenever it happens.

Even if you are working on toilet learning in order to enroll your child in a preschool that requires its completion prior to admittance, your child may not need to meet as high a standard as you think. Honestly, preschools realize that their students will have accidents and are not looking for perfection in potty use. They may need to require toilet learning due to state laws or school guidelines, but their definition of trained may be fairly flexible. Don't assume. Ask. If you feel that their requirements cannot be met by your child, pick another school or daycare facility. This one can wait a year. If you do enroll your child, let him know the expectation in a matter-of-fact, no pressure way. Often when moms feel pressured for their child to perform, their child feels the pressure, too. Children who feel pressured to toilet learn before they are ready may hold their bowel movements or refuse to urinate. This can lead to urinary tract infections or digestive problems. If you suspect your child might be going down the holding-onto-it road, please bring this concern to your pediatrician's attention.

You cannot, however, force them to urinate or have a bowel movement on demand, so why stress over it? Like many of the issues surrounding child rearing, many parents tend to make a big deal out of things that will happen on their own in due time.

Here are some tips to help flush away the Mommy Guilt:

> Have all the equipment for your child available before he is ready to use it. This way you won't miss the opportunity when it arises. If your child shows an interest, let him choose what type of potty seat, which toilet paper, which themed underwear, and so on.

> When your child expresses an interest in using the toilet, go for it—no matter what his age may be. Keep in mind, however, that any child will use the potty around two years old and then may completely forget about it for a while. You can always try again, right?

> If your child shows no concern over being wet or having a dirty diaper, you may want to lay low on the toilet learning until she does.

> Instead of pull-on diapers, buy plastic-backed cotton training pants or the new "feel wet" style of pull-ons. These actually feel wet when they get wet.

> If you are dealing with "accidents" in training pants every day, go back to diapers. Continuing with training pants will only frustrate you. Do not make a big issue about it. Keep your emotions out of it. It is important that your child see that this is a natural conse- quence and not a punishment. Ditch the guilt. Setbacks happen. Put the diapers on the kid and get on with your lives.

> If your child is walking the line between diapers and training pants, let her decide what she wants to wear that day. If she picks diapers, she is letting you know that she is not ready for the responsibility— honor her request and be glad you won't have to clean messy un- derpants. If she picks training pants, praise her for her decision and let her know that the two of you can reevaluate the decision as the day progresses, if needed.

All children develop this skill at different times and in different ways. Every story that you hear people tell you about toilet learning probably has some truth in it so rip off the sheets you need and leave the rest on the roll.

Play date plights: sharing and ignoring

Asking toddlers to share their toys is like asking adults to share their under- wear. It just doesn't seem right. *Share* is one of those words that we should try to eliminate from our conversations with our young children. It is a complicated concept to learn. When we "share" food, we don't get it back, but we want them to share their stuffed animals. No wonder our kids are confused!

We often feel tremendously embarrassed and guilty when we invite other children over to play and our child spends the whole time grabbing toys out of the other child's hands. We feel the need to jump in, chastise, and demand that our child share. But when you think about it, adults aren't all that great at sharing our toys either. If you were to buy a new RV, would you just let your neighbors take it out and play with it? When was the last time you handed over your car to your friends because they stood on your driveway and demanded that you share? Have an awesome husband? Odds are you aren't sharing with your friend, even if she says, "Please." Really, we all have certain things that we absolutely will not share, no matter what. Our children feel that way about their possessions, too, and they need to be allowed to feel that way.

When we jump in and yell "share!" they look at us like we're insane and do everything they can to hold onto their possession. Chances are pretty good that if we would stay out of it, they would check out each other's stuff for a little while and then drop it and move on—or even return it. If they don't figure this out on their own, then we can encourage them to trade. It is not sneaky or tricky; it is the earliest form of bartering. Children can understand that trading means we give up something in order to get something else—even temporarily.

Being prepared for play dates is one way to encourage successful sharing. Avoid conflicts during play dates by telling your kids that their special things must be put away before their friends arrive. This is also an opportunity to remind your child that the toys left out are for everyone's enjoyment. Another great tactic is to bring out a carton of toys that are different from the ones your child is used to playing with. You may either keep a set of toys that are used only for play dates or take some of the little-used toys out of the playroom and put them in a "play date" box that you normally keep out of sight. If your children are preschool age or older, they may even want to help you select the toys for the play date box. Just be sure that you never place a favorite toy into the play date box—even if it hasn't been your child's favorite for a long time. We think that the old adage "better safe than sorry" is enough said. When going to someone else's house to play, special loveys can be left in the car.

Also remember that to a child, toys are objects to be used, not simply looked at. If you want to protect that porcelain doll your grandmother gave you, don't put it out in your five-year-old's line of sight, and certainly don't hand it to her to play with. Consider that even if your child is careful with special toys, her friends may not be as careful or aware of the toy's elevated status.

Maybe your toddler isn't going around hoarding all the toys. Maybe your child is sitting in a corner, playing by herself just as if she were home alone. This kind of behavior also causes mothers a lot of unnecessary guilt and worry. They wonder about their child's socialization skills. They worry that it's because they haven't created enough opportunities for their children to play with other kids. Or they wonder if they have somehow created a selfish, self-centered child. They may feel guilty inviting another child over to play, only to see their child snub the other child's attempt to interact. The mother wonders why her child doesn't like others.

No need to assign blame here. Until kids are about four years old they engage in what is commonly called parallel play. They sit in the same area and have a good time doing their own thing. They have limited interest in interacting with other children; they are more interested in exploring what they can accomplish on their own. During a play date, a child may momentarily take a brief interest in what a playmate is doing, and more specifically in what toys are being used by that playmate. Often this interest is accompanied by the action of trying to take those toys away. As children grow, their social skills mature, and with very little help from you, they will learn the ropes on how to interact, play, and share. If problems between older kids arise, review Chapters 10 and 12 for guidance on dealing with them the Mommy Guilt-Free way.

Techno baby-sitters

Town meetings gave way to televisions. Telegraphs gave way to telephones and then e-mail and instant messaging. As technology has shouldered the increasing burden of communication, we are rapidly losing our social protocol—the rules of conduct for polite communication, the interpersonal skills that teach us how to behave, face-to-face, in all sorts of situations.

We define this as "dehumanization," meaning that as technology increases, our interest in and ability to interact with other humans decreases. Think about this: Our technological advancements now make it possible to get a newborn baby from the house to the store and back home again without ever having been touched by human hands. Pediatricians are finding that they need to ask parents to take babies out of their infant seats and hold them during checkups.

As if VCR and DVD technology isn't enough, we can now stop live television to grab a quick bite to eat before returning to a favorite show. People eat in front of TVs and not in front of each other. It is our belief, and we know we aren't going to win a popularity contest with this one, that children are plugged in too much and for too long. We say cut the power cord!

Loving Touches

One of the saddest things happening in our world today is a decrease in physical contact. Part of this is because we have gadgets to take the place of carrying our children, part of it is due to the dehumanizing effect of technology in our culture. But regardless of the reasons, the line between acceptable and unacceptable touching has blurred. As such, people are often opting to simply avoid touching the children in their lives at all. Teachers are afraid to hug their students for fear of it being perceived the wrong way; long-time family friends refrain from giving their friend's toddlers a kiss on the cheek. Lack of interaction, though, is creating a society immune to the glorious feeling of physical affection. Some children are hugged so infrequently that on the rare occasion when an adult does give them a well-meaning, great big hug, they don't know how to react.

One of the most exquisite ways to enjoy your experience of parenthood is to hold your children, hug and kiss them, every day, year-after-year as they grow. We're not talking about smothering them with kisses to their embarrassed horror while they play with their friends (though, that is fun!). We are talking about frequent, daily contact integrated naturally into their lives. A rub of the back as you walk by. A stop-what-you-are-doing-just-to-hug hug. The security it brings them will make a tremendous difference in the way they behave around others.

My eleven-year-old son, who once loved me to hold him as a part of our bedtime routine, started to rebuff my nightly hug. I wasn't sure what to do about it. I didn't know if he had outgrown my hug or what. After we took him to see The Lion King, *that night I grabbed onto him and started singing Simba and Nala's love theme in my terrible tone-deaf way. My son began to laugh and stated dramatically, "I feel the love, I feel the love!" That became our new hug. Every night I go into his room, we read a book and then I hug him tight and say, "Can you feel the love? Are you feeling it?" and he jokes back, "Yes. Now go!" I'm not sure how long he will let me do this, but for now it's working for us.*

While you're at it, go ahead and be gently affectionate with the other children in your lives whom you care about, if they don't mind. Your best friend's preschooler? You baby-sat him, changed his diapers, rocked and soothed him when he was an infant. Go on and ask him to give you a hug. Your preteen niece? Throw your arm around her shoulders and ask her if she wants to learn the cancan. If nothing else, you will surely illicit a smile from her.

Screen time and alternatives

The sentiments of our survey respondent sums up how most of us at one time or another feel about television:

The amount of television my children watch causes me to feel guilty. As a stay-at-home mom, I find myself turning the television on for them so I can complete household chores, and while I am working I think constantly about how I should be reading to them or playing with them. Current studies released by the media regarding ADD/ learning problems and the amount of television children are watching make me feel extremely guilty. Is my battle for clean floors, clean clothes, and clean toilets worth my child's ability to learn in school? I watched Sesame Street *and* Electric Company *as a child. Did I not go to Harvard because of it? Or not finish my postgraduate degree because I loved* Scooby Doo? *Are my kids doomed to a lifetime of learning issues because I wanted to eat my lunch and read the paper undisturbed? Am I politically incorrect to admit I use the television to "sedate and contain" my children? The guilt is amazing.*

Using television entertainment as a form of quiet time is perfectly appropriate—this is one role TV is meant to fill in our lives. TV can be an engrossing distraction for your children while you accomplish a task. Mommy Guilt will lessen if you are in tune with what your children are watching on TV and how much time they are tuned in.

Young children can be very affected by visual images. Cartoons that feature babies and toddlers constantly breaking the rules and being nasty to each other do not exactly model the behavior you want your kids to be studying. Because we are big fans of legalizing and regulating though, one suggestion is to compromise. Try allowing your children to occasionally watch a show that borders on acceptable to you even though it depicts some behavior you find to be inappropriate. However, the moment any of the unacceptable behavior spills out of the TV into real life, the show is history.

Generally speaking, your children should be limited to no more than two hours total daily "screen time" and possibly less for school-age children during weekdays. This includes TV, computer, video games, handheld electronics, etc. When they clamor for more, it's time to encourage them to engage in something more mentally or physical challenging. Look for alternatives that require more brain cells than photo cells—offer books, word puzzles, craft projects, or a deck of cards. Instead of killing time in front of the TV or computer, turn on some music and ask them to prepare a dance show to perform for you after dinner. Then there's always the tried-and-true, going outside to play. Go out there with them for a few minutes. When you get moving, your kids will too.

Limiting screen time to within reasonable amounts may be wise for your children's social development, too. Screens have no human, nonverbal communication—computers don't shrug if they don't know an answer—and so children who spend too much time with screens can grow rusty with their nonverbal communication skills.

Feel free to get creative in how you structure your TV viewing. Some families require that one month out of every summer vacation be TV-free, as this mom describes:

At first, I felt like I was punishing myself because I expected my kids to whine and complain about being bored. A couple of days later my decision was reinforced as my kids began discovering toys they had long abandoned, books they had not read, and games they never knew existed. We all had fun learning to play.

Limiting TV by providing alterative quiet-time activities will help you feel empowered that you are requiring your kids to engage their minds without electricity. When a power failure happens, your kids will be prepared! All this technology is not a "need." The more you can help your kids learn other ways to entertain and enjoy themselves, the less you'll find yourself having to encroach upon the two-hour guideline to keep them amused while you do something else. By declaring TV, computers, and other screen time as a privilege, you will all feel better when they can't, or shouldn't, have it. Guilt will not overtake you for denying them a privilege.

The time of day your child watches TV should also be considered. If your children have trouble getting ready for school on time each morning, don't let them turn on the TV in the mornings at all—it can be the biggest distraction in the house. If you customarily turn it on, change that custom and try grabbing the weather forecast from the daily paper and the traffic report from the radio instead.

The habit of turning on the TV at home the minute anyone walks in the door is another area where you need to remain wary. Transition time between school life and family life, and focusing in on reconnecting with family can't happen if the TV is the first thing that gets everyone's attention when arriving back home. Carefully consider what will work for your family. At one of the authors' houses, kids are required to do their homework before they can turn on the TV. When the kids have a lot of homework, they may not watch TV at all that day. If only a little time remains before bedtime after all the homework is completed, they'll spend it talking with the family, and they are perfectly content to do so. In another author's house, her son needs some time to unwind after school and is allowed to watch a half hour of TV prior to beginning homework with the understanding that this is a privilege and not a necessity in his life. Should her son abuse this privilege, away it goes!

Certainly, TV can be a useful parenting tool. Its content can have educational value. Its hypnotic ability can help quiet a wound-up child. It isn't evil. TV shows are something that kids discuss with each other at school, too, so please be aware that if your children don't watch any TV there may be times when they feel left out of their peer group's discussions. Still you can avoid this guilt when you treat screens as limited-use luxuries, not household necessities.

Illness and injury

Accidents happen. Illnesses happen. Parenting always seems to require a strong dose of first aid and an awesome bedside manner. When we don't know how to fix the boo-boo or we second-guess ourselves as to how we could have protected our child, boy do we work ourselves over with the guilt! While having an ill or injured child is scary, the Mommy Guilt-Free Philosophy suggests that you look for the silver lining. It's wonderful to know that a kiss from Mommy can make the pain go away.

Despite our best efforts to keep our kids healthy and safe, they will get sick and they will take a tumble. It's okay if your kids get hurt on occasion. It is a required part of growing up. If your kids never get scrapes on their knees, they probably aren't getting enough exercise. If your ten-year-old daughter falls off the monkey bars on the playground and winds up in a cast, don't beat yourself up over not being there to catch her fall. It is a waste of your emotional energy, and it will only prevent you from focusing on living in the here-and-now moment of comforting her (Mommy Guilt-Free Principle No. 4). Focus on giving your child what she needs now, which may be a mom who can joke about what color her cast will be. Children heal. With healing comes experience, learning, and wisdom, too.

You and the Doctor

Parents sometimes worry about calling the doctor too frequently. If you had a series of plumbing problems, would you think twice about calling the plumber repeatedly to fix a clogged sink, a dribbling showerhead, or a leaky pipe? Heck no! You'd just pick up the phone and dial. Same goes for medical care. If you need it, get it.

When taking your sick or injured child to see the doctor, remember your role is to be the child's advocate. Doctors increasingly expect and encourage that role from parents. When reporting the reasons for your visit, don't underplay your child's symptoms in a misguided or guilt-driven attempt to appear blameless. Don't overplay them either. Simply explain the situation as calmly and matter-of-factly as you can manage.

Feel free to ask the doctor to explain all tests, diagnostic procedures, and so forth. If the doctor is being too technical, ask her to reword things so you understand what she is talking about. If you don't understand the doctor's explanation, keep asking questions until you do. While you probably want to wait until after the doctor has completed the examination before dashing off your questions, after that pipe up. Write down a list of questions in advance of the visit, if that helps you remember to bring up all your concerns.

Doctors are highly educated people, but they are still people, no more or less perfect than other people. A lot of them are parents, too. By playing consumer of the medical services they provide, you'll be better able to find a physician who is a good match for your family care needs. If you find the doctor unwilling to treat you as an equal and explain medical information in terms you can understand, find another doctor.

I was walking with my son and boom! He fell. When I realized that his shoelace was untied, I told myself what a terrible mother I was for not tying his shoe properly. We dashed to the emergency room. I blamed myself for his stitches and for the scar he would have for the rest of his life. I felt like I had ruined his face, a face I helped create. At the emergency room, I told the doctor about the accident and how it was all my fault. The doctor looked me straight in the eye and said, "Ma'am, they are called 'accidents' not 'on purposes.' It wasn't your fault."

Even when your child gets a nasty cold from the neighbor because you saw an opportunity for an uninterrupted bath while he played at their house, you are not to blame! Human immune systems need practice to stay strong. Your garden-variety head cold helps give it a workout. Parental responsibility is not defined by being able to keep any possible harmful experience away from your child. A responsible parent is one who helps her child learn to cope with the unexpected pitfalls just as she teaches him how to relish the good stuff. Being a Mommy Guilt-Free parent means learning how to get the joy out of every experience, even the not-so-good ones. In the case of illness and injury, there is hidden joy in nurturing, being the hero with the magic healing kiss, teaching that the misery of a head cold ends, and that being healthy is something to be cherished.

➤ PART 3 ◀

Building on Your Mommy Guilt-Free Foundation

CHAPTER 17

TIME: HOW TO MAKE IT, HOW TO TAKE IT, AND HOW TO SPEND IT, GUILT-FREE

The Mommy Guilt-Free Philosophy helps you keep the parenthood portion of your life bubbling away as if it were a stream, not the Nile River. Permitting the daily tasks of life to completely overflow our banks results in drowning out some of the best of what we have to offer ourselves and our children. Swimming in Mommy Guilt is also not particularly good for us or our children.

After a couple years of parenting, you may start to think, "I'm sure I used to exercise regularly, go to the theater, go dancing, read books, or treat myself to one evening a week at the bookstore with just a cup of coffee and a few magazines. Didn't I?" Then you think, "Who has the time? Right now I've got to shop for dinner, go to the dry cleaners, fill out these school forms, type up a memo, fold a load of laundry, return some phone calls . . ." Parenting has flooded out your "me" time.

How can I stop the flow of endless responsibilities that take me all day to complete? I can't just turn twenty-four hours into twenty-five, now can I? I'm pooped! Who has time or energy to engage in a hobby?

If you feel like life is an endless stream of chores then you are spending far too many hours of your day-to-day life doing activities you dislike. To change that, pinpoint how you are spending your time and which of those time-consuming tasks you despise the most. Then look for alternatives to getting those beastly things done, if they truly need to be done at all.

It isn't mission impossible! We're going to walk you through a few exercises to help you figure it all out. Then we'll help you examine the toll your children's schedules may be taking on your time, and move on to how to keep interruptions from derailing you. A word of warning, however, your parenting life is overflowing its banks because you haven't built any dams. You let it run wild because of a complex societal viewpoint that pressures parents (particularly mothers) into believing that if they aren't elevating all things related to their families to numero uno, then they are selfish and undeserving people. *Self* is not a bad word, it has just been given a bad connotation. If you act with your self in mind, you are self*ish*. If you consider your own feelings when making decisions, you are self-*centered*. So let's try out some new words—self-aware? Does that sound so bad?

Making your "self" aware

If becoming a bundle of resentment is your goal, by all means, continue to spend most of your hours on chores. But if you dream of more time for yourself and your family, you must prioritize making time for you. Remember who you were before you became a mother? How has that person— this you—changed during the course of parenting? Be aware that your children will eventually leave the nest and when they do, you will still be left with you. If you've lost yourself along the way, then where will you be?

As your children age, parenting moves from being a very physical job to being a primarily intellectual and emotional job. Once they can feed themselves, then bathe themselves, then drive themselves to school, you have some choices. You can fill those hours up doing things for yourself, including tending to your other relationships. Or you can fill those hours up doing ever more things for them.

An old friend of mine called the other day, wanting me to go with her to New Mexico to take a two-day writing workshop. Some famous writer was going to be teaching—my friend made it sound like a once-in-a-lifetime deal. I am so frustrated that I had to say no. My daughter is moving this weekend from one apartment to another and I know if I don't go help her clean her apartment—which really means clean it for her—she won't get her rental deposit back. The moms of her roommates will be there, too. Plus, she doesn't have a car and I promised to drive her grocery shopping so she can stock up for her new place. She doesn't have another time to do it with her heavy class schedule at college. They say that when your kids move out, you get your life back. What a joke! My kid has been out of the house for two years now at college and I'm still cleaning, shopping, and turning down once-in-a-lifetime chances. But what am I supposed to do? She needs the money and she's got to eat. I'd feel so guilty if I left her stranded like that.

If you begin to take back the time that becomes available as your children grow and spend it on yourself, you will discover amazing, empowering things about yourself, your world, and even your children.

Giving to your "self"

Maybe you are thinking, "Ah ha! This is one area that I do not feel guilty about! I *do* make time for myself. Last month, I went shopping. Two months before that, I had a massage. At least once a week, I take a candle-lit bath." Yes, pampering yourself is a step in the right direction, but only a step. How many hours this week have you spent doing an activity that you absolutely love, outside of mothering? How about yesterday? Today? Taking time for yourself is more than slipping away for a few simple indulgences. You are entitled to be clothed, which requires shopping. You are entitled to get the knots worked out of your back. You are most certainly entitled to bathe, especially in a relaxing way. But what have you done for yourself lately that you find enriching—an activity that left you feeling passionate and alive? Yes, we're talking hobbies and interests. Prioritizing these is vital! The hours that you spend on these enriching activities prevents the banks of your parenting river from accidentally eroding the shores of your life.

Let's try out another word: giving. Oh, wow, do we moms give! We give time, comfort, support, money, and even part of our physical selves to our family. We give with little hesitation. Why, then, do we come to a screeching halt when we need to give to ourselves? Could it be that Mommy Guilt makes us believe that time spent on ourselves is time taken away from another family member? But hey, aren't we also members of our families?

Mommy Guilt will dry up when you remember that sensible parenting includes taking care of yourself in all the ways your "self" needs caring for. By doing so, you are modeling for your children that when the time comes to raise their own families, their favorite parts of themselves needn't evaporate for them to be good parents. When you look at the future and at the big picture—and are not overly hung up on the here and now (Mommy Guilt-Free Principle No. 3)—do you see your adult children living happy, fulfilled lives? Or do you see them as stressed-out parents, bogged down with responsibilities, dreaming of relief, and hardly remembering themselves as the carefree children to whom you gave (and gave up for) so much? If you don't demonstrate the path to adult happiness with your own life, and teach them how to become the delighted, delightful people you envision, who will? So go on, prioritize enjoying your life, guilt-free. It is one of the best parenting decisions you can make. And who knows, you may also be introducing your children to activities that will become great passions in their lives, too, as one of the authors, Aviva Pflock, found out.

When my kids were two and four, my family moved to a new community where I discovered a musical performing group. I joined it and was thrilled to be on stage again, something I hadn't done since starting a family. I hadn't even realized I missed it so much. Leaving my family every Tuesday night for rehearsals was difficult, though, and the week prior to opening night was the worst. I was out every night until midnight or later. The first season, I often pulled out of the driveway to the sight of a crying child or two and a husband wondering why he had agreed to support me in doing this. By the time I got to the theater, though, I was filled with a new energy that made me feel so complete, I knew I was doing the right thing. The children got used to the schedule and my husband got to regularly run solo as a parent—an accomplishment he, too, was proud of. I was careful to keep perspective; I limited the impact on my family by limiting myself to two productions a year.

After a few years, my husband joined a soccer league on Tuesday nights, something he had done growing up but had also sacrificed in recent years. We hired a baby-sitter for Tuesday nights. When our third child was born, we continued our hobbies. I brought my newborn to rehearsals but when he hit the three-month mark, left him at home so his dad could enjoy some evenings with him. During dress-rehearsal week, my husband brought the baby to the theater for feedings as needed. The baby is now a singing and dancing preschooler who has even won his first dance contest. My two daughters have also caught the performing bug and are regulars in children's regional theater.

Self-fulfillment nourishes a weary mom. When you feel full and personally satisfied, you will discover you have no room left to feel guilty! Don't let Mommy Guilt make you fear that engaging in your hobby will create insurmountable scheduling conflicts with your children's needs or activities. Will they grow up hating you for missing a few soccer games or leaving them once a week with a baby-sitter? Nah! You won't be missing the really big stuff, like plays, tournaments, spelling bee finals—because attending those events will always be a priority in your life, which you will want to share and enjoy with them. They know this and will continue to know it as they see you prioritize such events, even as they see you spend some hours attending to your own needs. More important, your children will benefit from seeing you as a whole person, not simply their mom, chauffeur, maid, and cook. Give them the chance to cheer *you* on for a change, an experience they will savor. They will see *you* glow with pride when you achieve something *you* have worked hard for and they will learn how adults must balance work, self, and family to live happier lives.

So, right now, we want you to go find some paper and a pen. The next section will walk you through some worksheets designed to help you become more self-aware.

EXERCISE: Activities I Love

Write down a list of at least fifty activities in your life that you love. Keep parenting-related items to fewer than half your list, but other than that, activities can be anything from things you do daily to those you've done only once in your life. Be specific. Describe in detail why you love this activity. If you love making crafts write, "taking a basic design and using my own creativity to transform that into something beautiful and completely my own." Got it? Don't stop until you reach fifty. If you find that you can easily come up with fifty, keep on adding. If you start to peter out before you hit fifty, take a break, think about it, then come back to the list. It is important that you keep going until you feel the only way to add another item would be to repeat yourself.

Now, examine the list for patterns. Group the activities according to the patterns you see, then prioritize them according to things you would like to do, can do, and dream about doing. Commit yourself to trying to engage in at least one activity on that list this month, even a small step toward it. For instance, if you love reading, writing, poetry, and all things word-related, can you join or even start a book club/ writer's club that meets once a month? Even the busiest of parents can typically manage a few hours per month. Even that step of prioritizing yourself for a once-a-month activity will help you learn how to include yourself in all the things you balance. Soon, you'll be tackling the next item on your list.

EXERCISE: Imagine a Freer You

Set a timer for fifteen minutes. On the top of a blank piece of paper, write the words: "I've always thought it would be fun to . . ."

Now, come up with as many answers to that question as you possibly can. Don't think. Don't question. Don't ponder. Just scribble.

You can also use the words "I've always wanted to . . ." or "I've always dreamed of . . ."

Now take each item and visualize yourself getting it done. This can be done while washing the dishes or doing some other mechanical activity. Think about what it feels like to do these things. Let yourself smile while you think about it.

EXERCISE: Remember Your Own Goals

Write out the answers to the following questions:

1. Before you became a parent, what kinds of accomplishments did you dream of experiencing?

2. If time and money were not issues, how might you go about experiencing some of the items from the previous list?

For example, you wanted to be an actor? Maybe you could try out for a local play and your friend would watch your kids while you went to the audition. If you got the part, you could cross the bridge of child care when you got to it. Many people who perform in regional theater are parents. They will be full of suggestions on how to juggle rehearsals with dinnertimes.

Finding time

Now that you have revisited yourself as a happy, unencumbered adult, and have identified at least one hobby that you would like to engage in, it is time to take the time. Next up, we offer you some worksheets to help you identify which things in your life you really don't like and how you might minimize or offload them entirely.

EXERCISE: Activities I Would Love to Live Without

This is the same exercise as "Fifty Activities I Love," but this time, concentrate on items that you do not enjoy. Again, be specific about the exact part of the activity that you dislike. For instance, rather than writing "the laundry" write "the fifteen minutes it takes me to gather everyone's dirty clothes from all over the house because they couldn't be bothered to use the hamper."

This list can be from any area of your life: housework, phone calls from high-maintenance friends, tasks at the office, or volunteer jobs, to name a few. The feeling you have for the items can range from an absolute dread (making phone calls for committee work) to a softer feeling of dislike (pulling weeds).

Again, examine the list for patterns. Chances are you'll find certain types of chores or whole categories repeated. What areas of your life are the most troublesome to you? Do you always seem to agree to work that you hate? Are you spending hours supporting a needy friend who seems to jump from one crisis to another, dragging you along? Is daily upkeep—the dishes and the driving, the laundry and the lunch packing—your point of pain? The patterns indicate the major areas that you need to limit in your life. With these areas identified, start thinking up ways to shed these yucky tasks. Can you simply stop doing them—resign from a committee, say no to the next one? Can you hire help, a maid service, or a neighborhood child as a mother's helper?

Ask your friends to help you come up with alternatives. If you have trouble finding the patterns, ask your friends to read the list with you and help you find them—they *are* there. Brainstorm! Don't automatically reject every possible solution. Vow to try one! Sometimes, the simplest solutions are the ones we have the most difficulty coming up with on our own. Be willing to do whatever is necessary to change things whenever possible. If you adopt this attitude, how can things not be different?

EXERCISE: Where Has the Time Gone?

List the activities for a typical day and the time at which you do them. Then rate how you feel about each activity. A rating of 1 means that you get little personal enjoyment from the activity and a 5 means you receive a high level of personal fulfillment from it. Use more than one worksheet if your daily grind varies significantly from day to day.

Time	Activity	Enjoyment rating
	Wake up	1 2 3 4 5
		1 2 3 4 5
		1 2 3 4 5
		1 2 3 4 5
		1 2 3 4 5
		1 2 3 4 5
		1 2 3 4 5
		1 2 3 4 5
		1 2 3 4 5
		1 2 3 4 5
		1 2 3 4 5
		1 2 3 4 5
		1 2 3 4 5
		1 2 3 4 5
	Sleep	1 2 3 4 5

Look over your worksheet. Which of the lowest-rated items can be done by others (including your children) or simply abandoned completely? Which are the ones you and absolutely only you must do? When looking at those "musts," what might be done to help you move an item up on the enjoyment rating scale? Can you reduce its frequency, duration, or somehow make it more pleasant? Can you do the task with your kids while listening to fun music or swapping jokes? Can you put on headphones and do the task while listening to a comedy tape or audio book? Dropping dreaded tasks and thinking up ways to make the ones you can't drop more pleasant is a critical Mommy Guilt-Free Philosophy skill. The more you learn to focus on doing activities that you enjoy, the more enjoyment you will experience in your daily life and the more enriched your family life will become. Happy people attract happiness. Pesky things in your life will get done but they shouldn't become the focus of your life, or a self-sacrifice. Once you become self-aware, you will be aware of the positive changes that happen as a result of your positive attitude.

Managing your kids' schedules

Any discussion on balancing parenting needs with personal time must include a look at your children's schedules. The overscheduled school-age child is a well-documented phenomenon. If your every possible free moment is spent schlepping your children to one activity after another, how can you possibly achieve balance—for you or for them?

We're going to set a simple bar as to what we feel is a reasonable childhood schedule. Ideally, a child should be engaged in no more than two activities outside of school. This includes Sunday school or other religious school activities (youth groups, Catechism, Hebrew school, and so forth). We did say "ideally" because we know that some sports require several nights a week for practice and a couple of nights a week for games. Limiting your child to one sport per season is what we recommend. (Review Chapter 14 for more information.) For now, we'll offer this benchmark: if, among homework, school, sports, and other extracurricular activities, your child cannot get at least ten hours of sleep per night, six nights a week, your child has too much going on. Many school-age children continue to need about twelve hours per night. Your children may be used to operating with less sleep, but that doesn't mean they should. Even teenagers often need ten to twelve hours of sleep. Their bodies are still growing, their lives are often stressful, and their minds need to rest. (See "Helpful Hint: Ideas for Unscheduled Playtime" on the next page.)

So, if you've got children who rise by 7 A.M. for school, run around after school for activities, eat dinner, and then do as little as an hour of homework a night, you've got kids with twelve-hour days. Think about how tired an adult feels when regularly working twelve-hour days at the office. Think about how crabby a tired person—adult or child—can be. Now visualize all of you in the car *together*. The choice on how many extracurricular activities your children should have will become clear.

Hesitant about limiting your child's activities? Feeling some Mommy Guilt because you may be preventing them from doing what they want to do? In limiting activities for our children, we are teaching them to prioritize those things they enjoy and truly want to have in their lives over things that they think they want to do just because their best friends do them. What a wonderful step toward self-fulfillment and independence. The added bonus is that you aren't spending all your time being a mobile mommy who neglects her own hobbies and feels guilty to boot.

HELPFUL HINT

Ideas for Unscheduled Playtime

Children of all ages need unstructured time in their lives. This is extremely important from a developmental standpoint. Unstructured playtime allows children to absorb all the new things constantly thrown at them. From a life-skill approach, it teaches kids how to self-entertain and prioritize personal time. When they are with friends, unstructured playtime allows the group to learn and practice their social skills. Even a newborn baby needs time alone to ponder the amazement of his little fingers and toes. It is how we learn to move in our own space in this world. The Mommy Guilt-Free Philosophy recognizes that when your children can entertain themselves, you will be free to engage in your own playtime or get your task list done. Give some of these methods a try for encouraging unscheduled playtime at different ages while avoiding the "I'm bored" syndrome.

AGE	ACTIVITY
newborn	Back and tummy time to gaze at a baby gym or colorful board book.
1–3 years	A special kitchen cupboard or drawer accessible to your toddler with lots of plastic containers and wooden utensils.
4–6 years	An activity mat (flannel-backed plastic tablecloth) thrown on any floor so your children can color, paint, use play dough, or even practice scissor skills (child-safe, of course) without your help.
7–11 years	Crafts! From beading projects to messier paints and glues in a cleanable environment. By requiring them to clean before quitting, they practice their cleaning skills, too.
12 years or older	Books, magazines, puzzles. Keep a good selection around the house. Also just hanging out with friends or listening to music, or both.
All ages	Computer games can be a great source of activities for children as long as you limit the time they spend on them and ensure that important files or inappropriate materials are inaccessible.

Stopping interruption insanity

All right, you've coordinated your children's schedule with your own and you're ready to—hang on a minute . . . I hear a child crying downstairs. . . . Okay, so you're ready to—wait just another second, got to change a dirty diaper—start doing more fun things. But no sooner do you start—hang on, again . . . what? You need me to get you a glass of juice? Be right there—than you have to stop. Where were you? What were you about to do? Finish a task? Heck, you never finish a thought anymore! The children have developed busy-mom radar. As soon as you are on the phone or absorbed in any kind of activity, they scramble from all corners of the house for a tête-à-tête.

Sadly, there is no magic wand to wave over your home and stop interruptions entirely. They are part of the same parenting protocol as the 2 A.M. trip to the slumber party to pick up a kid who wants to come home. We just can't ignore a baby with a leaky diaper or a toddler standing on top of the refrigerator. Now reducing the number and frequency of interruptions is possible and we will explain how.

Reducing interruptions requires action on your part. Forewarn your family that interruptions are appropriate when a need is *urgent*, then define urgent. What is urgent to your children may not be urgent to you. Explain to your children your expectation that they wait next to you, patiently, while you are on the phone, absorbed in a task, or speaking to another person. Let them know that you will eventually give them your full attention. Do your part by acknowledging your child immediately but briefly (the old hang-on-a-minute index finger ought to do) and then do not keep your child waiting too long before attending to her—two minutes seems like an eternity to a young child. For older kids, this second, longer acknowledgement may simply be a brief explanation of how long you will be busy and that you are aware they want you. Tell them you will get to them when you are done. The kicker is that you will have to remember what they wanted and make sure you follow through on it.

But what if your children don't wait? Well, then you don't have to respond. You can walk out of the room, put them out of the room, or ignore them altogether until they get with the prescribed program. If you follow the plan, then your children may still interrupt you, but they will do so politely—after you finish your task, thought, or sentence.

Once you have taught them how to politely grab your attention, you can begin to teach them alternatives to interrupting you altogether. As discussed in Chapter 8 and elsewhere, your ultimate goal is for them to learn how to take care of themselves. To achieve it, you must teach them how to take on an increasing share of the responsibilities.

I had a to-do list a mile long and, as I had some fun plans for Sunday, I had dedicated Saturday to get through the list so I could enjoy the rest of my weekend. My kids each had their cleaning tasks, too. My oldest blazed through her tasks and then stormed into the kitchen, asking me if we could go do something fun with the rest of the day, like see a movie. I told her no. I explained my day to her and I saw the fight brewing. She did her chores! Why couldn't we have fun now? So, I turned the tables. Instead of fighting or letting her interrupt me all day long with her whining, or being interrupted to drive to and from her friends' houses, I laid out my long to-do list for her. I told her if she and her sister could come up with a plan that completed the list in time for us to go see a movie, we would follow their plan and see the movie. They accepted the challenge, and drafted a plan in which the two of them did far more chores than I had originally assigned to them, so they could get through the list more quickly. They felt empowered while also learning, firsthand, my reasons for resisting their interruptions.

Having other roles, other priorities

We leave this chapter with one more tip on avoiding a river of chores run amok. You are more than just a parent. You are also a friend, a child to your own parent, perhaps a sibling or a cousin. These relationships should be ones that nurture and support you. If a relationship with another adult has become nothing but another chore to deal with, it's time to rethink how you are spending your time.

The Mommy Guilt-Free Philosophy gives you permission to prioritize yourself by putting limits on activities or people that cause you stress. If you have only a limited amount of time to give to yourself and others, there is no crime in making sure it is time well spent. Just because someone says he is entitled to your time doesn't mean he is deserving of it at the sacrifice of you or your family. Those who follow the Mommy Guilt-Free Philosophy limit the time they spend on relationships that pump them dry.

CHAPTER 18

GUILT-FREE PLEASURE— TIME WITH YOUR SPOUSE

We promised in Chapter 1 that we would help you prioritize your to-do list and we have been faithfully keeping our word. Here we go again. If you are married, it's time to think about how your spouse fits into your new Mommy Guilt-Free Philosophy. A strong relationship with your spouse should come second only to taking care of yourself. When your marriage is in trouble, your entire family is on the line.

A major source of guilt

Figuring out how, when, and where to find time for your marriage is tough. Over half of our survey participants named finding time to spend with their spouses as an issue that caused them guilt. One-third went so far as to name it as the issue that causes them their highest level of guilt.

The situation is understandable. Couples become families in a matter of hours. The first months are exhausting and they learn to use what little energy they have left enjoying their new child or tending to household or work-related responsibilities. That is fine, and a period of adjustment is definitely in order. The danger is when that adjustment period becomes a permanent habit. The basic principles that apply to being Mommy Guilt-Free similarly apply to being Wife Guilt-Free.

> **The Seven Principles of the Wife Guilt-Free Philosophy**
>
> 1. Learn when to let go and when to let it all hang out.
>
> 2. Marriage may not be a competitive sport, but dating sure was.

3. Look toward the future—until death do us part is a long time.

4. Live in the moment, be spontaneous.

5. Say yes, yes, oh, yes!

6. Laugh a lot, there will be less time to fight.

7. Make sure you set aside time to be alone together as a couple.

Wife Guilt-Free Principle No. 1: Learn when to let go and when to let it all hang out

We have talked a great deal about letting things go in this book. Yet, we caution you that "letting go" does not equate with not caring. Just because our families love us no matter what, it does not mean that we should no longer give them the best of ourselves. This is especially true when we are talking about our spouses. From our daily attitude to our daily appearance, by giving the best of what you've got to your spouse, the whole family is elevated to a higher standard. Go to your closet, no really, go! Is it filled with T-shirts and sweats? Does everything have a spit-up stain on the shoulder? A missing button or loose threads? Looking good helps us feel good about ourselves and it also moves us giant leaps toward boosting our relationships with our spouses. No need to buy a whole new wardrobe, just dust the shoulders off those outfits you save for special occasions (that seemed to vanish after the kids were born). No, we're not insisting that you greet your husband at the door with a glass of wine every night wearing a beautiful dress and string of pearls—maybe once a month isn't a bad idea though. Dress up, let him be dazzled by you again, and relish in his response. It can make an old mom feel like a new woman!

Wife Guilt-Free Principle No. 2: Marriage may not be a competitive sport, but dating sure was

Remember your other lifetime? You know the one, that era commonly referred to as BK—before kids. A time in your life when you went overboard to look good, danced the night away, flirted, and caught the eye of many a man. Okay, maybe this was BE, before engagement. Whenever it was, it was fun! You felt great about who you were and loved the attention. Who wouldn't? You can feel that way again with your husband and your marriage. Truly, you can get that satisfaction from him again!

Married women, especially moms, miss the passion and desire that filled those BK days. Wives have countless opportunities to mingle with men other than their husbands. Business meetings, Internet connections, business trips, even going to the grocery store all present opportunity, and so women who value their marriages might have to work a little harder these days if the urge to stray creeps up. Why not gather all those tricks and trades from dating years gone by and apply them to your husband? Certainly, making yourself appear desirable is part of the process, but desiring your man is also part of it. Show a sincere interest in his life. Listen to him talk about his day at work, be his cheerleader at softball, soccer, or golf games. Flatter him again like you did before he was all yours and you may find that he begins to flatter you more often. The mutual interest in each other's lives is what helps to keep the flame alive. Once couples get settled in a comfortable relationship, they can easily forget that their mates have special attributes that made them attractive in the first place. Make the effort to be amazed by him again.

Wife Guilt-Free Principle No. 3: Look toward the future—until death do us part is a long time

Some moms equate spending time with their spouse as expending energy by taking care of yet another human being. Did you vow to love, feed, and clean up after? Probably not. We know the demands of running a household are always on your mind, so we caution you not to confuse marital commitment with the one you made when you became a mom. Feeding and dressing your children are surefire ways to love and nurture them. When you're in the mood to nurture hubby, though, you'll score bigger points by offering a backrub than by offering to cut up his food. Then there's the fact that your children will eventually grow up and move out. Your husband won't.

All relationships evolve over time. Some require big efforts up front that get easier over time (with your children), others are quickly ended (with your old boss), and one must be constantly refueled in order to last (with your spouse). The refueling is not solely your responsibility though. A relationship requires that you work together so don't be afraid to ask your husband to contribute.

I had spent days arranging child care, carpools, hotel reservations, and theater tickets for a two-night getaway with my husband. Then it hit—my three-year-old came home from preschool covered in spots. Three kids, all with chicken pox, one right after another. The family was sequestered for nearly six weeks. The epidemic meant we had to cancel the weekend we so desperately wanted. When the kids were finally back in school, I told my husband that I was too exhausted to think about going anywhere but to bed, alone. If he wanted to do the arranging for us to get away, I would go. So he did! He took the kids to a friend's house for the weekend and we left town. The first day, I slept in, read a book, and relaxed while he went sailing. The next day we went antique shopping together. I had forgotten how great it felt to be a couple—and those precious hours alone were glorious.

Wife Guilt-Free Principle No. 4: Live in the moment, be spontaneous

Grab every little chance you can to reconnect. Tuck a love note in his briefcase. Sneak a sexy nightgown into his car before he leaves for work to put a smile on his face all day long. Little things make the difference. Find a quiet moment every evening to ask him about his day. If the evening rush hour is too hectic, try a daily phone call. It can be a quick one just to say you love him. Have more time? Turn that call into phone sex. Not only might you surprise him, but you are sure to brighten up his day and a happy spouse is a happy parent. He'll come home in a mood to get in on the action of getting the kids fed and quickly tucked in so the two of you can be alone.

After fifteen years of marriage, we still talk to each other on the phone every day. We've learned over the years that mornings are never good, evenings are unreliable—we can both be tired and crabby by then— but that midday is the perfect time for a refreshing little "I love you." Thanks to phones and cell phones, we can act on this urge whenever it strikes and it strikes every day.

Wife Guilt-Free Principle No. 5: Say yes, yes, oh, yes!

Unless a doctor has told you otherwise, just do it! Not in the mood? So what? Sex is vital to a healthy marriage. Find time to have sex: afternoons; a shower together while the baby sits in her bouncy seat in your bedroom; a middle-of-the night rendezvous courtesy of your alarm clock. See how quiet and creative you can be!

If you find that you routinely go more than a week without having sex with your spouse, you better figure out a way to change that. You may think the phrase, "Gentlemen, start your engines!" does not apply in your bedroom, but it really does. The more often you rev up your engines, the stronger and longer your drive will go.

Outside of procreating, sex has one purpose—pleasure! This is pleasure that you and your spouse are entitled to have and the resulting feeling of intimacy is yours to keep. You both work hard at your jobs, your family, your very existence. Give yourself the gift of sex on a regular basis. How often? Let's just say that you should get used to saying yes and be able to defend your no with more than just, "I'm too tired." Making love can be a great way to unwind from an exhausting day and be able to get a wonderful night of sleep.

Wife Guilt-Free Principle No. 6: Laugh a lot, there will be less time to fight

As parents, we have lots of serious business to deal with every day. A little extra effort may be required to laugh together. Smile at your husband. Sometimes laughter begins that simply. If you need to jumpstart your laughter with a little more juice, make reservations at a comedy club or watch a funny movie together. Buy a book of jokes and take turns reading it to each other. Be on the lookout for one funny event each day—something the kids did, something you saw at the store—and recount those stories to your husband in the evenings or over coffee on Sunday mornings.

At the same time, don't infringe on fun time with household business. Set aside specific time each day or week for a "business" discussion when you can talk about the bills, the dentist visit, appliance repair, and so on. In this way, you won't have your precious smile time engulfed by an abundance of annoying, yet routine, household business.

If you find that squabbles routinely take away from smile time together then put an end to them. Don't think it's possible? Try this one out:

Sharon, a mother of twin boy toddlers and a new baby girl, and her husband have designated Wednesday as fight day. Whenever Sharon hears a trivial fight coming on she simply reminds her husband that they both have their hands full with the kids and work so the fight will have to wait until Wednesday. The best part is that by then, the entire incident has often become a nonissue.

Wife Guilt-Free Principle No. 7: Make sure you set aside time to be alone together as a couple

In Chapter 11, we offered numerous suggestions on how to let Dad be a dad. Here, we want to nudge you not to confuse a dad with a husband. The easiest way to keep the two straight is to remember what it was like when you were husband and wife, before you were mom and dad, and set aside specific time to be together as these two people. Sex is one way, sure, but just because you are grown up, you don't always have to do grown-up things or go to grown-up places. Spend a day with your husband at the park without your kids. Climb, swing, picnic, nap under a big tree, and soak up the sun together.

Try taking up a new hobby, sport, or activity together. One great way to add laughter into your marriage and time together is to be beginners at something exciting and new. Relive those courting days, too. Go hiking or camping together. Rent a movie and stay up late. Cook and enjoy a gourmet meal together. (See the exercise "Prioritizing Your Marriage.")

EXERCISE: Prioritizing Your Marriage

Get your pencil ready again. We recommend that you review your answers to the last chapter's exercises before proceeding to this one. The purpose of this exercise is to help you recognize how to prioritize your marriage. We encourage you to do this exercise on your own, have your spouse do it, and then share your answers. Try to be as specific as possible in your answers. Rather than "going to the beach" write "body surfing, picnicking, and laying in the sun at the beach." Rather than "we would cook together" write "we would look through cookbooks to pick out a meal, shop together, and then cook."

Step 1: Remembering

On a blank sheet of paper, complete the following phrases.

1. My spouse and I never laughed so hard as the time we . . .

2. Before we were married, we would spend a typical date . . .

3. My favorite activities with my spouse before we had kids were . . .

Step 2: Imagining

1. If time and money were no object, and we knew that the kids were well cared for, this is how I would spend an ideal romantic weekend with my spouse . . .

2. My spouse and I have always talked about doing the following things together . . .

3. I wish my spouse and I would spend more time doing the following fun things together . . .

Step 3: Reality check

1. Since we had the baby (or children), the most fun activity we do together alone is . . .

2. The last time we spent three hours or more alone and awake together was . . . . The time before that was . . . the time before that was . . .

3. Based on the previous question, we tend to spend time together about this frequently: _____

4. If we were to engage in an activity from Statement 1 together, how much time would we need to develop this new activity as a regular hobby?

5. What are the items that presently limit us from engaging in our old hobbies or starting new ones (finances, child care, work schedules, etc.)?

6. What could we do to work with or alter items from the previous list—at least one time?

Be creative in your answers to No. 6. Don't worry about feasibility, just toss some ideas out. For instance, if money is an issue, is there a way to do a similar activity on a smaller scale? Rather than buying a sailboat, maybe a single dinner cruise on a nearby lake would suffice. Rather than an evening at a five-star restaurant, check out a book of gourmet recipes from the library and make dinner together at home.

Your children should mean the world to you, but if you center your universe around them and drift away from your spouse, your marriage may end up in a black hole. If you become concerned that your marriage has drifted toward that blackness, you may want to ask yourself some questions. The answers might be waiting for you in a marriage counselor's office. Go if you need to go! Marriage is hard work and sometimes we run out of tools to fix the holes when we find them.

The Mommy Guilt-Free Philosophy encourages moms to take one small step toward your man and one giant leap for your relationship. Whether you pick up a tennis racket or a garter belt, making your marriage a happy one is what matters most.

➤ PART 4 ◀

Appendices

APPENDIX A

TAKE THE *MOMMY GUILT* SURVEY

More than 1,300 parents participated in the *Mommy Guilt* survey prior to publication. You can participate, too. Take the survey now, and then compare your answers with the charts published at the end of the survey. Better yet, head online and contribute directly to this important research. Visit www.mommy-guilt.com and follow the instructions. Updated survey results are available to you immediately after taking the survey.

Please tell us a little about yourself by filling in or circling the appropriate answer:

Question 1: Are you a mother or a father?

Mother
Father

Question 2: How old are you?

18–24
25–29
30–34
35–39
40–44
45–49
50–55
Over 55

Question 3: What is your marital status?

Married/common-law married
Divorced
Separated

Single (never married)
Widowed

Question 4: What is your work situation?

I am a full-time stay-at-home parent.
I have a full-time job outside the home.
I work full-time from a home office (as a telecommuter, self-
    employed, etc.).
I have a part-time job outside the home (or in a home office).

Question 5: How many kids do you have (including
stepchildren)? _____

Question 6: At what stages are your kids (including stepchildren)?
(Circle all answers that apply.)

Infant
Toddler
Preschooler
School age
Middle-school age
High-school age
College age or older

Question 7: How many stepchildren do you have? _____

Question 8: What genders are your kids?

All boys
All girls
Boy(s) and girl(s)

Question 9: Generally, how happy are you with your life?

Very happy
Mostly happy
Neither happy nor unhappy
Mostly unhappy (or disappointed or frustrated, etc.)
Very unhappy (or disappointed or frustrated, etc.)

Question 10: If you have feelings of guilt, please tell us about them. (If you don't, please circle the *last answer*.) Which of the following parenting related issues has caused you guilt? (Circle all answers that apply.)

Working/sending my child/kids to daycare instead of staying home.

Setting aside my college degree or career to stay home with the children.

Spending too much time at work.

Neglecting my job/leaving work early to deal with childcare issues.

Yelling at my child/kids.

My child's/kids' sleep habits (sleeping in your bed, allowing to cry before going to sleep, etc.).

My child's/kids' eating habits (allowing junk food for dinner; lack of veggies in the diet; eating too much or not enough, etc.).

Keeping up with housework/living in a messy house.

Finding enough time, after taking care of the child/kids, to spend with my spouse.

Fairly dividing my time, chores, financial resources, and so forth among my children.

Balancing a blended family that includes my children and my step-children.

School-related issues (selecting a school, selecting academic programs, finding time to volunteer, etc.).

Sports-related issues (finding time to attend matches or volunteer, "pushing"/"not pushing" child, etc.).

Parenting issues, other than the ones listed here.

Not applicable. I've never felt guilty over parenting.

Question 11: On a scale of 1 to 5, (with 1 representing *no* guilt and 5 representing *severe* guilt), what is the *maximum level* of guilt you regularly feel?

1   2   3   4   5

Question 12: How often do you feel this guilty?

Constantly

Hourly

Daily

Weekly

Monthly
Less then once a month
Not applicable. I never feel guilty.

Question 13: Which situations cause you to experience your highest level of guilt? (Circle all answers that apply. If you never feel guilty, circle the *last answer.*)

Finding time to spend with your spouse
Fairly sharing resources and time among your children
Your work/stay-at-home choice
Demands of an outside job interfering with family life
Demands of family life interfering with your job
Yelling at your child/kids
Child's/kids' sleep habits
Child's/kids' eating habits
Living in a messy house
Finding time to attend sports matches or to volunteer for sports
Finding time for your child's/kids' school activities (volunteering
    or helping with homework, etc.)
Decisions regarding where your child/kids attend(s) school or
    which programs they participate in
Pushing (or not pushing) your child to excel at sports
Other parenting issues (Please tell us about them by visiting www
    .mommy-guilt.com.)
Not applicable. I never feel guilty.

Question 14: As your kid(s) age, do you feel an increase in the intensity/frequency of guilt surrounding parenting? (If you never feel guilty, circle the *last answer.*)

Yes, I feel an increase.
No, I feel a decrease.
No, I feel the same.

Question 15: Thinking over your parenting experience to date, at what point was the guilt most frequent or severe? (If you never feel guilty, circle the *last answer.*)

Pregnancy
Infant year
Toddler years

Preschool years
Grade-school years
High-school years
College years
Not applicable. I've never felt guilty over parenting.

Question 16: In what ways has parenting more than one child affected your feelings of guilt?

Increased it
Decreased it
Had no effect on it (If you have never felt guilty over parenting, please select this.)
I only have one child

Question 17: Please tell us about yourself as a parent. How much help with parenting tasks do you receive from you child's/children's other parent on a daily basis?

Practically none
A tiny bit
Not half, but a sturdy contribution
He/she does half
He/she does most to all of it
None, the other parent doesn't (or can't) actively participate in my child's/kids' daily life/lives

Question 18: How many hours *weekly* do you typically spend doing childcare-related tasks including routine housework (driving kids, help with homework, cooking meals, laundry, shopping, etc.)?

0–6 hours (less than an hour a day)
7–13 hours (at least an hour but less than two hours a day)
14–20 hours (at least two hours but less than three hours a day)
21–27 (at least three hours but less than four hours a day)
28 hours or more (half or more of my day is spent on child care)

Question 19: When considering both childcare tasks (meals, baths, help with homework) and fun time (talking, playing, watching the child's sports matches), about how many hours *weekly* do you typically spend interacting with your child/kids?

0–6 hours (about an hour a day or less)
7–13 hours (at least an hour but less than two hours a day)

14–20 hours (at least two hours but less than three hours a day)
21–27 (at least three hours but less than four hours a day)
28 hours or more (half or more of my day is spent interacting)

Question 20: Do you travel with your children alone (without your spouse or another adult)?

No, never
Yes, but rarely
Yes, frequently
Yes, always

Question 21: How often do you and your kid(s) laugh together?

Daily
A few times a week
Almost never

Question 22: How often do you and your kid(s) fight with each other?

Daily
A few times a week
Almost never

Question 23: Please tell us a little bit more about you. If you live in the United States, please indicate in what region you live, then type in the two-letter abbreviation of your state.

Question 24: What is the highest level of education you have completed?

Now compare your answers with the general survey results.

Mommy Guilt survey results

The Mommy Guilt survey asked 1,306 respondents to name the areas that caused them guilt as it related to their roles as parents. It also asked them to quantify those feelings of guilt, to share insight into important quality-of-life factors. Here are the full results.

QUESTION	% OF RESPONDENTS	NOTES
1. Are you a mother or a father?		
Mother	94%	
Father	6%	
2. How old are you?		
18–24	7%	
25–29	17%	
30–34	27%	
35–39	22%	
40–44	13%	
45–49	6%	
50–55	4%	
Over 55	4%	
3. What is your marital status?		
Married/common-law married	86%	
Divorced	6%	
Single (never married)	5%	
Separated	2%	
Widowed	1%	
4. What is your work situation?		
I am a full-time stay-at-home parent.	44%	
I have a full-time job outside the home.	29%	
I have a part-time job outside the home (or in a home office).	21%	
I work full-time from a home	6%	

QUESTION	% OF RESPONDENTS	NOTES
office (as a telecommuter, self-employed, etc.).		
5. How many kids do you have (including stepchildren)?		
1	30%	
2	42%	
3	17%	
4	7%	
5	2%	
6 or more	2%	
6. At what stages are your kids (including stepchildren)?		
Infant	13%	
Toddler	22%	
Preschooler	20%	
School age	22%	
Middle-school age	8%	
High-school age	7%	
College age or older	8%	
7. How many stepchildren do you have?		
0	89%	
1	5%	
2	4%	
3	1%	
4	1%	
5	0%	
6 or more	0%	
8. What genders are your kids?		
Boy(s) and girl(s)	44%	
All girls	29%	
All boys	27%	
9. Generally, about how happy are you with your life?		

QUESTION	% OF RESPONDENTS	NOTES
Mostly happy	60%	
Very happy	22%	
Neither happy nor unhappy	9%	
Mostly unhappy (or disappointed or frustrated, etc.)	8%	
Very unhappy (or disappointed or frustrated, etc.)	1%	
10. If you have feelings of guilt, please tell us about them. (If you don't, please select the LAST ANSWER.) Which of the following parenting related issues has caused you guilt?		
Yelling at my child/kids	60%	
Keeping up with housework/ living in a messy house	59%	
Spending too much time at work	51%	excludes SAHMs*
Finding enough time, after taking care of the child/ kids, to spend with my spouse	57%	adjusted to reflect married parents only
Sports-related issues (finding time to attend matches or volunteer, "pushing"/"not pushing" child, etc.)	41%	adjusted to exclude infants and toddlers
Working/sending my child/ kids to day care instead of staying home	38%	excludes SAHMs
My child's/kids' eating habits (allowing junk food for dinner; lack of veggies in the diet; eating too much or not enough, etc.)	35%	
Setting aside my college degree or career in order to stay home	35%	includes SAHMs only
Fairly dividing time, chores,	35%	

QUESTION	% OF RESPONDENTS	NOTES
financial resources, and so forth among my children		
School-related issues (selecting a school, selecting academic programs, finding time to volunteer, etc.)	31%	adjusted to exclude parents of infants and toddlers
Neglecting my job/leaving work early to deal with childcare issues	29%	excludes SAHMs
Balancing a blended family that includes my children and my stepchildren.	27%	blended families only
My child's/kids' sleep habits (such as sleeping in your bed or allowing to cry before going to sleep)	22%	
Parenting issues, other than the ones listed here. (Please tell us about them at the end of the survey.)	16%	
NOT APPLICABLE. I've never felt guilty over parenting.	6%	
11. On a scale of 1 to 5, (with 1 representing NO guilt and 5 representing SEVERE guilt), what is the MAXIMUM LEVEL of guilt you regularly feel?		
1	7%	
2	31%	
3	43%	
4	16%	
5	3%	
12. How often do you feel this guilty?		
Constantly	5%	
Hourly	1%	
Daily	27%	
Weekly	40%	
Monthly	13%	

QUESTION	% OF RESPONDENTS	NOTES
Less then once a month	9%	
NOT APPLICABLE. I never feel guilty.	5%	
13. Which situations cause you to experience your highest level of guilt? (If you never feel guilty, please select the LAST ANSWER.)		
Demands of an outside job interfering with family life	51%	excludes SAHMs
Yelling at your child/kids	47%	
Living in a messy house	34%	
Finding time to spend with your spouse	30%	married resp. only
Finding time for your child's/ kids' school activities (volunteering or helping with homework, etc.)	18%	adjusted to exclude parents of infants and toddlers
Your work/stay-at-home choice	16%	
Child's/kids' eating habits	14%	
Demands of family life interfering with your job	14%	excludes SAHMs
Fairly sharing resources among your children	14%	
Other parenting issues (please tell us about them at the end of the survey)	14%	
Child's/kids' sleep habits	9%	
Pushing (or not pushing) your child to excel at sports	5%	adjusted to exclude infants and toddlers
NOT APPLICABLE. I never feel guilty	5%	
14. As your kid(s) age, do you feel an increase in the intensity/ frequency of guilt surrounding parenting? (If you never feel guilty, please select the LAST ANSWER.)		

QUESTION	% OF RESPONDENTS	NOTES
Yes, I feel an increase. No, I feel a decrease. No, I feel the same.	40% 21% 39%	
15. Thinking over your parenting experience to date, at what point was the guilt most frequent or severe? (If you never feel guilty, please select the LAST ANSWER.)		
Pregnancy Infant year Toddler years Preschool years Grade-school years High-school years College years NOT APPLICABLE. I've never felt guilty over parenting.	2% 21% 27% 17% 21% 5% 1% 6%	
16. In what ways has parenting more than one child affected your feelings of guilt?		adjusted to include only parents of two or more children
Increased it Decreased it Had no effect on it	70% 9% 21%	
17. Please tell us about yourself as a parent. How much help with parenting tasks do you receive from your child's/children's other parent on a daily basis?		
Not half, but a sturdy contribution A tiny bit He/she does half Practically none	42% 21% 18% 9%	

QUESTION	% OF RESPONDENTS	NOTES
None, the other parent doesn't (or can't) actively participate in my child's/ kids' daily life/lives.	7%	
He/she does most to all of it	3%	
18. How many hours WEEKLY do you typically spend doing childcare-related tasks including routine housework (driving kids, help with homework, cooking meals, laundry, shopping, etc.)?		
28 hours or more (half or more of my day is spent on child care)	46%	
21–27 (at least three hours but less than four hours a day)	21%	
14–20 hours (at least two hours but less than three hours a day)	17%	
7–13 hours (at least an hour but less than two hours a day)	10%	
0–6 hours (less than an hour a day)	6%	
19. When considering both childcare tasks (meals, baths, help with homework) and fun time (talking, playing, watching the child's sports matches), about how many hours WEEKLY do you typically spend interacting with your child/kids?		
28 hours or more (half or more of my day is spent interacting)	51%	
21–27 (at least three hours but less than four hours a day)	20%	

QUESTION	% OF RESPONDENTS	NOTES
14–20 hours (at least two hours but less than three hours a day)	13%	
7–13 hours (at least an hour but less than two hours a day)	10%	
0–6 hours (about an hour a day or less)	6%	
20. Do you travel with your children alone (without your spouse or another adult)?		
Yes, but rarely	46%	
Yes, frequently	32%	
No, never	16%	
Yes, always	6%	
21. How often do you and your kid(s) laugh together?		
Daily	83%	
A few times a week	15%	
Almost never	2%	
22. How often do you and your kid(s) fight with each other?		
Daily	28%	
A few times a week	38%	
Almost never	34%	
23. Please tell us a little bit more about you. If you live in the United States, please indicate in what region you live, then type in the two-letter abbreviation of your state below.		
Midwest (OH, MI, IN, WI, IL, MN, IA, MO, ND, SD, NE, KS)	26%	

QUESTION	% OF RESPONDENTS	NOTES
South Atlantic (WV, VA, NC, SC, GA, FL)	14%	
Mid-Atlantic (NY, PA, MD, NJ, DE, D.C.)	13%	
South (KY, TN, AL, MS, AR, LA, OK, TX)	12%	
Mountain (MT, WY, ID, CO, UT)	10%	
Pacific (WA, OR, CA, AK, HI)	10%	
New England (CT, ME, MA, NH, RI, VT)	7%	
Southwest (NM, AZ, NV)	3%	
I don't live in the United States. I've typed in the name of my country below.	5%	
24. What is the highest level of education you have completed?		
High-school diploma/GED	30%	
Currently in college for an undergraduate degree	5%	
BA/BS	23%	
AA/AS	9%	
Some postgraduate studies	11%	
One or more postgraduate degrees	20%	
None of the above; I didn't complete high school and haven't gotten my GED yet.	2%	

Source: The *Mommy Guilt* survey.
*Stay-at-home moms (SAHMs)

Insights from the *Mommy Guilt* survey respondents

This book was ten years in development. When we decided to write *Mommy Guilt,* we were young moms ourselves and in the throes of our own Mommy Guilt. So, we knew the issues that were causing moms stress and pain. These were areas where we had struggled personally.

We know that a primary source of guilt is a feeling of "wrongness" and that this feeling is nearly universally accompanied by a feeling of isolation. The *Mommy Guilt* survey, which spanned 18 months and 1,306 people, was embarked upon to show moms that they are not alone in their feelings of guilt. As the preceding pages illustrate, no matter the parenting pain, there are others out there who worry about the things you worry about, and feel guilt over their decisions, mistakes, and lives. Every single parenting issue we asked about in our survey was named as a source of guilt by about one-quarter of respondents, or more. Plus, 16 percent told us that they felt guilty over additional areas of parenting not asked about on the survey. A mere 6 percent report no feelings of Mommy Guilt whatsoever, and of those guilt-free respondents, two-thirds were men.

But we went further in our survey than simply asking people to indicate and quantify their feelings of guilt. We asked them to share their wisdom, their struggles, and their triumphs. We were profoundly moved by the outpouring of stories—more than seven hundred of them. When possible, many of these anecdotes were slipped into the pages of specific chapters. Because of the large volume of anecdotes, however, most could not be included in the chapters. So, we've compiled a short selection of the remaining stories. Among these tales are sure to be more gems that will speak to you and help you refine your own Mommy Guilt-Free Philosophy.

Tricks of the trade: parents share their best wisdom and advice

On behavior

Rest and reasonableness. I do best if I make sure I am well rested. I also try to look for the "why" of the behavior before I react to the behavior. When I am able to address the why, the overall situation is much less likely to escalate.

Prearranged consequences. Emotionally remove yourself from discipline and children wanting an argument by having a chore menu. When a child breaks a rule, simply say, "Uh-oh. Please choose a five-minute chore from the menu (or ten minutes or fifteen minutes, depending on severity of offense)." It removes explanations that lead to arguing, disagreements about appropriate consequences, etc. I have a child who thrives on arguing, and this is a lifesaver!

Expectations and experiences. I expect that things will go smoothly and do not worry about the what-ifs. We take our daughter everywhere and she has learned to manage many experiences well—from dining at fine restaurants to going on long car trips. We are always well prepared with snacks and activities when we go out on excursions.

The laughter tool. I have found that the most frequent and common trick that works is to get them laughing and smiling. My daughter can have the worst day ever, be completely uncooperative, and within ten minutes, I can have her laughing and within fifteen minutes working with us to get things done. Plus, trying to make someone else laugh will invariably improve your mood.

Gotta dance. I use humor and/or music to help break through some tough moments such as sibling bickering, bad moods, etc. Being silly with them always helps, or turning on some music that they love to dance to.

Sing a song. Sing. Out loud, and often with your child. They don't care if you can't carry a tune. It's a great diversion in the car, and also for doing chores together. Sort of the "whistle while you work" idea.

Hang out together. A few nights a week, I read with my ten-year-old daughter, alternating reading pages aloud. I read books the same way with her older sister, when she was younger. It's a great way to stay connected as they become more independent.

The Waving Game. My kids would always hang onto me and refuse to let go when I had to leave the house without them, so I invented the Waving Game. After kissing them good-bye, I'd remind them that we would play the Waving Game, and they learned to run to the window that faces the driveway. I'd leave the house and get into my car and we'd wave to each other and throw kisses. I started this eight years ago when my oldest was about two years old, and we're still playing. It makes departures so much easier on everyone.

Turn misbehavior around. Discipline is to teach. It is not about creating a negative experience. For example, if my stepson did something that upset me he had to do something that made me feel better, such as washing my car.

It takes two to stop fighting. When my daughter turned fourteen, our relationship nearly fell apart. She was going through her puberty stuff and I had my own life stressors. We clashed hourly. One time, I smacked her for "smarting off." That was the breaking point. We realized we needed to draw near each other rather than antagonize one another. We worked on our relationship, building understanding again, and today we have a fun, healthy, happy bond.

On housework

Breakfast for dinner. Try not to worry about having a great dinner every night—sometimes cereal is fine.

Cleaning tip. Hire a cleaning lady! It's the *best* thing I ever did!

Crack a smile. Kids pitch in cheerfully if you let them.

No time like tomorrow. When I am stressed, I remind myself that the housework will be here after they move out. I can perfect it then!

On marriage

Cuddle and coo. Don't forget your husband! Be just as cuddly with him as you are with your baby.

Start your day. Now that the kids are gone from the house, my husband and I frequently go out for breakfast on the weekend. I wish we had done that when the kids were younger. It would have been a cheaper date and would have given us a leisurely chance to talk. It's a good alternative to a night out.

Love thy wife. I have always put my wife first, then our child. If the relationship between my wife and me isn't working, how are we to communicate well as a united front to our child, and provide the same amount of love to our child?

On taking care of yourself

A dose a day. Make sure to take at least one moment of time per day to do something that you enjoy, whether that is taking a hot bath at the end of the day or drinking coffee and reading a book in the quiet of the morning. You can't give something to the children if you are totally empty yourself. Work on your spiritual side. Ask for help when you need it.

Five or more minutes. A good novel, a candle, and a pot of very good tea can make a huge difference in my day, even if I spend only five minutes with them.

You are the teacup. I find that you need time to spend on yourself to remain able to give to your children. I once heard that you are like a cup, and if you don't fill yourself up then you'll have nothing to give away. You also must remember that you can't possibly do everything. You need to choose what is important to you and your family. Try your hardest to be happy and have fun as a family.

You're a mom, not a toy. I used to feel guilty that I wasn't playing with my kids all day long. I never had any alone time while they were awake and still felt like I was not doing everything I should. Then I realized that siblings, mine are one and three years old, are perfectly happy playing with one another and I am not neglectful in expecting them to spend time with one another while I tend to other things.

Secure the oxygen mask. Really, the best thing you can do for your child is to lead by example and make sure to take good care of yourself. You know that little speech that they give you on an airplane about putting your oxygen mask on before you put your child's mask on? This is because you won't be able to help them without having oxygen first. I take this to heart and remember that I have to take care of myself so that I can take care of my kids. Without me, their world will be a lot worse.

On having a second child

Two to love. I was feeling guilty about the diminished attention my second child received from me as compared with my first child, but as time has gone on, I realize she has the great experience of having a brother to love and give her attention! That realization has greatly eased my guilt over attention shared!

On solo parenting

Exercise together. I'm a single parent. In order for me to get exercise I must do it with my son, so my son is developing a great lifetime health habit. Plus, nothing seems to break up bad moods like both of us getting out and getting some fresh air.

Love thy solo flight plan. Being married to a workaholic (my husband travels for work very frequently), my advice is to plan, plan, plan! When I know in advance that he will be gone, I plan something almost every day he is away: a trip to the park, a lunch or dinner out, window-shopping at a toy store. Anything to keep the kids busy and to keep my sanity!

Take off the black hat. I'm often faced with parenting alone because my wonderful hardworking husband works a tremendous amount of time each week. It can be hard to be the bad guy all the time. I call my husband Santa Claus because when he comes home, it's all fun and games. I'm left to be the bad guy who says it's time for homework or bed. Try to have a discussion ahead of time with your spouse to balance this out, otherwise, you will become resentful and he'll have no idea why. Also, make sure you get out of the house and let him be the single parent sometimes!

Choose enjoyment. Parenting alone can be stressful, hard, and lonely but every day I tell myself that I have a choice. I can be overwhelmed by the situation or I can have fun. I can play with my child, enjoy and cherish every moment because when it's all said and done, this day will pass just like all the rest of them and I'll only have the memories. I'd much rather have a bag full of good memories than one filled with unhappiness and stress.

On special-needs parenting

A new day. With three children, I sometimes feel guilty that I do not spend enough time with each one. I am currently home with a preschooler and an eight-year-old who is homebound due to illness. The seven-year-old goes to school and it feels like I spend the least amount of time with him. My feeling though, is that I can only do the best job I can and each day is a new day so I greet it as a new beginning.

On sports

Team up. For sports, it's helpful if you can get on a team with the child of a close friend or coworker. One of my coworker's daughters and my daughter play on the same team, so when one of us has to be at work the other can get them to practice.

Doctor your schedule. I am a high-level manager (and have been for years) with little administrative support. But I treat my child's sports events like doctor appointments—I don't miss them! And it's fun.

Miss the practice, not the family. We encourage sports but I won't let it affect our family time too much. If it does, then they just have to miss practice once in a while.

On handling stress

Slow down. I think what helps the most is a calm, easygoing attitude. When I got pregnant, I had a new rule—no rushing. So, even if we're late, grumpy, or whatever, we still don't rush. We can't always dawdle, but we don't rush. When we rush, we just forget things and become more stressed out.

Do the routine. Kids love a routine; it makes them feel safe and secure. If they know what to expect next, there is little stress. Bedtime should be consistent with a routine for the process. It makes life much easier! Same with a steady dinner routine.

Your two-letter friend. Learn to say *no*. Whether it's to volunteering at school, hosting a party, or having the in-laws over for dinner. If you can't do it, just say no!

The longest shortcut. My father always says, "Sometimes the longest way around is the shortest way around," and I have found that this is so with parenting. Sometimes I want to run screaming from the stress of a demanding child but find that a little extra time spent with her makes her less unbearable, sometimes downright pleasurable!

On traveling with kids

Hike out alone. Don't fail to take family vacations because one of the parents is hardly available.

Pack a surprise. When traveling, always have some new toys or books or activities planned and bring plenty of snacks. Don't ever expect a small child to sit still for long trips—surprise them with fun things to do.

On work

Dad at work. As the working spouse with a stay-at-home dad, I know that educating the world that men are parents too is important, and hard. Teach doctors and others that moms are not the only ones who know how to parent and understand kids.

Choose your attitude. I keep my stress level down by constantly reminding myself that I always have choices. For example, I choose to work to maintain a modest standard of living and to prepare for retirement and college for the kids. My husband and I could choose different financial goals and work less. I also can't overestimate the value of a supportive workplace and a flexible schedule. I am lucky to be able to take off when I need/want to focus on being a mom.

Talk to the boss. The source of 99 percent of my guilt is the demands of my job. Although I *am* the boss (I'm a consultant) and manage my own hours/schedule, I still feel very conflicted about the time pulled away from my kids. If I won the lottery, I'd shred the business cards and never look back.

Aim for balance. When people realize I work thirty hours a week and have two-year-old twins and a five-year-old, they ask me, "How do you do it all?" My reply is, "I don't." You can't do it all, and indeed, shouldn't. There are always sacrifices in life, but the key is to recognize how much of a sacrifice you are willing to make. For me, working outside the home is necessary primarily for my own peace of mind. I know that my kids don't get what other kids do when they stay home, but they get other experiences at day care and other activities that balance things out. In order to deal with my guilt over not being at home with them every day, I have made very conscious choices about what day cares I choose, about how I spend my time with my kids when we are home, and the type of job I am in. I have chosen a job that allows me a great deal of flexibility. If it didn't, I wouldn't have been able to make that choice. It's all about balance.

On all sorts of other things

Your assumptions. Always explain everything, over and over again if necessary. Never get impatient. The child is not trying to frustrate you. Always assume that everyone is doing his or her best.

Listen while you drive. As your kids get older, make sure to be the carpool driver. You'll learn about their lives.

The common advice. Before you have kids, everyone tells you to let common sense be your guide. After you have kids, you're suddenly inundated with advice that contradicts the common sense mantra. It took me until the second child to get back to common sense parenting, and it's made a huge difference in my life.

Know their day. Get involved in their school activities, even if only to ask them at the end of each day to share one special memory from the day, or one interesting fact that they learned.

Yes they can. Always encourage them to be the best person they can be. I have made them a poster that reads, "You CAN do it but the question is WILL you?" It's so important that they know that you are behind them 110 percent about anything they feel, anything they accomplish, anything they want to be, etc. I have often found that if you expect the very best from your children, you often get it.

Give yourself a break . . . away. Guilt that surrounds parenting teens looks really different. It's about balancing your desire to get them on their way with having to let go a little at a time.

Keep up your parenting vocational training. I read a lot and ask questions of pediatricians. I also try to communicate with my spouse on parenting issues to share and make sure we are on the same page, or to solicit specific help when it is needed.

Blurry hindsight vision. I think most parents—in *all* situations—do what they think is best for their child at that given moment. And then it's in retrospect that we look back and say, "Damn, that was a crappy way of dealing with that." Be easy on yourself. This parenting gig is a tough job—the most humbling I've found to date.

Hear this. Listen more than you talk.

You are not alone

If you worry that no one else out there feels the same guilt you do, think again. Here are some stories to let you know just how much we are all in this parenting gig together.

Even as a stay-at-home mom, I have guilt over some *bad habits* I haven't been able to break in my son. He is a very picky eater and I wish I hadn't been such a short-order cook when he was young. I'm sure I contributed to his pickiness, and now that he's school age, it is too entrenched a habit to break.

At this stage, the most difficult thing for me is *being exhausted* with working all day and then coming home to all the house and cooking chores, running kids to dance class or swimming, and trying to have patience to help with homework questions and projects. The homework volume of research projects has increased dramatically on top of the rest of homework, and many days I don't feel I have the energy to deal with all of it, so I end up feeling inadequate.

I have a kid with *learning disabilities* and making time to help him, and worrying about whether we should have caught some things earlier has certainly created guilt.

As an older parent, I feel I've been able (luckily!) to see how fleeting this time is. My husband is gone for months at a time, and is not an active participant in the kids' daily lives. I worry about whether *my parenting* will give my kids what they need to be happy, responsible, and respectful people.

Dealing with a *temperamentally challenging* child has been a major source of guilt for me. Am I giving her what she needs? Am I repeating my parents' mistakes that inadvertently caused me emotional harm? Will I be able to help her develop the tools to be happy?

For me I have felt much more in control and able to handle my feelings of guilt and my ability to get things done since I have been on antidepressants, which I started taking for the *baby blues* after my second child. I feel much better about myself and more relaxed about everything. I even have less Mommy Guilt.

When the *grandparents step over boundaries* and try to act like they are the parent and think they know my child better than I do, I feel frustrated. Also, the grandparents overspend on material things, giving my child every single thing she desires. I feel guilty if I take no action and guilty if I do.

I feel guilty about not saving *enough money* for my children's education. I feel guilty about not having enough income to enroll my children in many extracurricular activities.

I always worried that *my eating habits* were not good during my first pregnancy and could possibly be the cause of some potential health problems in my child's adulthood. When I shared this long-standing concern with my firstborn, she replied with such grace and acceptance, both recognizing my guilt and immediately forgiving me. When I thanked her, she replied that she learned it from me.

I am *a guilt-driven person.* I am not saying I like it like that, but that is me. I am a firm believer that a certain degree of guilt can be helpful. And in certain areas, it can make you better at what you do. I am also a registered nurse and nursing is a guilt-driven profession. It has helped me to be a better nurse and a better mommy. Guilt helps raise your awareness and makes you more conscientious, *but* there is a fine line between healthy guilt and destructive guilt. I sometimes have a hard time seeing it.

I am a forty-one-year-old single mom to a six-year-old son who will *probably never have siblings.* He asks often about it and even tries to think of ways to play matchmaker for me so I can give him a sibling. I try to keep him involved in extracurricular activities and athletic teams so that he has a sense of belonging with other children. We also have a closely knit neighborhood in which he can feel like a sibling, but I know it isn't enough for him.

I don't feel like I do *holidays* well enough. I have such idyllic memories of childhood Christmases and Easters. Sometimes I don't get around to decorating the house until two days before Easter, and then only because my mother is coming for dinner. I'm a little better for Christmas—my tree always looks great and makes it up at least two weeks before, but the rest of the house is pretty barren. My girls probably don't even notice it, but when we go to my parents' home, it looks like Santa's workshop exploded in my mother's living room, I do feel those pangs of inadequacy coming on. After all, she did it with four kids and I only have two. What's my problem?

I experience more guilt and stress related to *finding time for myself* and for exercise than anything else.

I feel guilt about wanting to go *back to work.*

I feel guilty sometimes because my partner and I are gay and my son keeps wanting to know *why we aren't married* and all his friends' parents are.

I feel guilty that I don't *spend enough time* with my older kids—the younger ones demand more of my attention. Taking four kids to a movie or dinner is sometimes chaotic! Every once in a while, I get a babysitter for the younger kids and I take the older ones out somewhere. I never have enough time for one-on-one attention for each child. My husband and I struggle to find time for us, too. There are not enough hours in the day.

Although I love my son, I hate changing diapers. I hate giving baths. I hate messy meal times. Then *I hate myself for hating* these things.

I feel guilty when I ask my mom or my mother-in-law to watch my daughter. There are just days I want to be alone. But I feel like a bad parent because *I want to be alone.*

I feel guilty when my son gets into arguments with other kids in the neighborhood and doesn't deal with it well. I have to remind myself that he's only six years old and we are working on *his conflict resolution skills* (using appropriate words and not getting physical).

I hate dentist appointments. My son's teeth don't form enamel, and we're always having surgeries, and it's a nightmare. But one time, I finally got it—I'm not a bad mom for *putting him through this.* The choice isn't pain or no pain. It's pain now or pain later—and later might mean uncontrollable pain in the middle of the night and widespread damage to his system. So, controlled and scheduled pain every few months is the most compassionate, most responsible choice I have.

I have a son who began speech therapy at the age of two. We have now nearly conquered the battle, with three years of flashcards and daily mouth exercises. We are now embarking on the new challenge, a short-term memory problem with symbols, letters, and numbers. He is five years old. He has no apparent disabilities and he is extremely social. However, the guilt I feel for having *a child that is behind the curve* is intense. I feel that it is somehow my fault, something I did or did not do during pregnancy that caused his situation to be such a challenge each day. There are no speech problems to date; however, we are now beginning our next battle and I'm scared and feel guilty. Did I not do things with him I should have done when he was an infant? I'm just always so tired and trying my best each day and still I feel guilty, which takes away from the joy I could be feeling right now, that I have the luxury of staying home with my kids.

I have always spent a lot of time with my children. I almost feel that I may have *been there too much* for them. However, I feel guilty sometimes when

I back off. I guess I feel that when I don't play dolls that one time, it may be the last time they want to play because they grow up so fast. I want to be there too much because they are only little once, but I know it is not good to always play with them. Yet, I feel anxious and a bit guilty when I don't. I have learned the importance of time with my husband. I think I lost it during my children's infant and toddler years. I am glad I understand now. He has been patient with me.

I have major guilt on *quitting nursing* before my kids were a year old.

I feel guilty because I have to deal with helping my kids cope with *a second divorce.*

I often feel that I don't spend enough time with them. Whether it's playing (I'm not good at make believe and other games) or reading (I can't seem to read aloud for more than about ten minutes). I guess *I'm just not good at being a kid.*

I refer to myself as a recovering perfectionist. I have worked hard to learn how to relax and enjoy life, and not spend all my time cleaning, doing chores, or just being busy. Now that I have a six-month-old and a three-year-old, it is hard to stay on top of *all of the household stuff,* while spending lots of quality time with my kids. I know that I have not been doing much for myself because there are always so many things to get done. I battle the subconscious need to be superwoman. It is hard to accept that you cannot do it all.

I struggle when my daughter is crying in public. I get hot and flustered and feel that everyone is looking at me. I feel guilty that I've not timed the day to suit my child's needs and created a situation that has upset her. Sometimes, in this situation, I *lose my cool* and shout, "Will you just shut up!" knowing that it isn't my daughter's fault that she's crying and knowing that my shouting will only exacerbate the situation. But sometimes the heat of the moment is overwhelming. Moments later I find myself in tears, saying I'm sorry. Sleep deprivation is the biggest cause of me losing my cool.

I teach theater and I try to perform one or two times a year. I always feel guilty about *spending those nights away from my boys.* This year, my husband and I were both doing shows that overlapped and we needed to use a babysitter for an entire week. It was a new sitter, so I was feeling incredibly guilty. After three nights, the boys refused to stay with her. After hearing why, I agreed and said I would call in and miss rehearsal. They told me they would come and sit in the dressing room and play quietly. They are five and eight, so I said we would try, but I didn't think it would work. They came, they watched some of the rehearsal, and played fairly quietly. Several weeks later, I was going to turn down a role because I thought it would be too much time away again. My eight-year-old said to do it because "it makes you happy mom, you deserve to have fun." I guess you never know what they are capable of until you try.

I think that guilt can also be felt when parents are *mourning a loved one* and don't know how to show joy for what their children are doing while also grieving. If the kids are old enough, you can talk about it but if they aren't old enough—then there is some guilt you feel in experiencing happiness during a sorrowful time.

It makes me feel resentful to hear *"I want my daddy"* when my daughter is in trouble and my husband is at work. I need a good comeback for that one! I usually say, "Me too!"

My three oldest children are adopted. My three youngest are biological. I sometimes feel like I have *not met the needs of the adopted children*, but as we all get older I realize we have had better success than most. All six children have become responsible adults. The three adopted ones have more difficulty making lasting relationships. All three have been married more than once while the two biological children who are married have been married to the same person for nine or ten years.

My biggest problem that causes me the most guilt is that I do not feel as *close to my stepchild* as my other two. I do love him, and care for him to the best of my abilities, but there just is not the same bond there. Even when he calls me Momma and hugs me, I can not feel the same as when my other children hug me.

My daughter had major surgery for an otherwise fatal condition this year. My three-year-old son was traumatized by having his life turned upside down. His grief caused a major amount of guilt and stress. In addition, I missed five weeks of work, causing me to fall behind, which is another source of stress and guilt in my life.

My guilt comes from the impaired relationship I have with their father, and them having to deal with *a disabled parent*. When my husband became ill, I was pregnant with my youngest child and chose to remain married. Since then, I have virtually been a single parent. I fear my children will have a very unhealthy view of adult relationships and will have difficulty breaking the cycle of dysfunction in which they have grown up.

My guilt is more with regard to the person I now am. Between work and being a parent, I barely have time to breathe some days. I worry that my daughter won't realize that I'm someone who really enjoys life. I just think for now that providing for her and taking care of her are more important than finding free time for myself and hope that by the time I'm able to start relaxing again (less job stress, my daughter able to do more for herself) *I haven't permanently lost my sense of fun.*

My main source of Mommy Guilt relates to dealing with my daughter. No matter how much time I spend with her, *it is never "enough" for her.* She never seems to reach a point where she is satisfied with the amount of attention or time together. I tend to be a person who is a little less social and I crave more time alone, so this is a constant struggle in our relationship. I have tried setting aside a certain amount of time together uninterrupted each day, which some days helps, but it still is difficult. My husband and I are both psychotherapists (although I'm not currently practicing), and so maybe I'm overanalyzing the situation, but I do worry about my daughter feeling like I don't want to spend the amount of time with her that she would like. I spend at least part of each day feeling like I am trying to escape from her for at least a little bit, and don't want her to pick up on that!

My older son has *some mental health issues.* I often wonder if I'm doing enough for him. Also, because these issues (anxiety and depression) are hereditary and on both sides of his family, I sometimes feel guilty.

My spouse always buys our son gifts when I know we need the money for bills. So I hold back. But I would love to be the one to spoil him with gifts.

One area of guilt is that it seems like the more time I spend away from my kids, *the more time I want to spend away.* Suddenly, that two-and-a-half-hour break at the gym isn't enough. I want all day!

One parenting issue that causes me guilt is *fighting with my spouse* in front of the kids.

The issue of discipline. Am I using the right forms? Am I too harsh? Will my methods pay off or be a big disaster?

The reason grandchildren are routinely spoiled rotten by their grand-parents (assuming they can do so) is because we are attempting to obtain absolution from *our "failures" as parents* by showering everything on our grandkids that we, probably mistakenly, wish we could have given to our kids.

The thing that causes me the most guilt is that we're pretty sure we are *only going to have one child.* Before I had my son, I had always planned on having two, but I really don't think that I have the time, patience, or energy for another, and my husband is content with just one. I feel guilty that I am depriving my son of having a sibling.

Adding to guilt over a lack of parenting time was *time spent with elderly parents,* when my children were young. That caused a lot of stress. But we didn't regret spending that time with them, and my children were richer for the experience.

We are relatively young parents. I am twenty-three and my husband just turned twenty-four. We are providing our children with everything they need, but I often feel guilty that *we are not wealthy* and because I stay home, outsiders are constantly making me feel selfish for not going out and making more money. I feel guilty that we cannot provide our children with the endless luxuries that many of the other children in our area re-ceive.

We have a daughter who is two years old and a son who is five. *Our daugh-ter has profound special needs* and needs total care. So, my guilt is pretty much based around feeling like I don't have enough time for our five-year-old son. That I have to *give-give-give* to her, and he needs that too, even though he seems less fragile and needy. But in reality, he needs it just as much, but for different reasons. I've really struggled with feeling as if I am neglecting him. I *know* she needs me to help with all aspects of her life, but he needs the same love and attention, too. It's so easy to overlook that need when he appears so able compared with her. Finding the balance has been tough. I'm still struggling, but it's improving little by little as I find my place in this very different life than I ever anticipated. Life *is* good though—I have the best kids in the world. My issues are all mine with regard to the guilt!

When my daughter was thirteen months old, she had a cold. It lingered on and on and I treated her with cold medicine when necessary. I finally took her to the doctor after two weeks of the sniffles—and she had pneumonia. I felt like a failure. *I didn't even know she was that sick.*

When my son was born with a bilateral club foot, I felt so much guilt over what I had done wrong. Even though doctors told me there was nothing that I did wrong, *I always felt like it was my fault.* His foot has been corrected now and the feelings have subsided some, but it was an extremely horrible feeling.

FOOD STAPLES TO KEEP IN YOUR HOUSE

One way to diminish dinnertime Mommy Guilt is to plan to cook no more than three full-fledged recipes per week. Leave the other nights available for leftovers, take out, or a quick frozen or prepared item. By recipes, we mean dinners that use mainly unprocessed foods—vegetables, meat, and whole grains without a lot of added food chemicals, preservatives, salt, or sugar. We're talking homemade here (chicken soup: chicken, salt, onion, carrots, celery, water) versus canned (modified food starch, sodium erythorbate, and that oh-so-mysterious "natural flavor"). Recipes allow your family to try out new dishes and to eat a variety of foods. Home-cooked meals also help to limit the fat, sugar, and especially sodium that your family ingests. Once your children are old enough to read, buy them their own cookbook or let them search online for new recipes to try.

But unprocessed food doesn't stay fresh long and buying too much at once could also land you on the guilt highway. You'll wind up throwing out spoiled food because you didn't have time to cook it. Since you don't want to be wasteful but you have to be ready to feed your family each night, always keep a list of staples on hand from which you can quickly create many meals. We call this framework cooking. Rather than needing ingredients on hand to create a specific recipe, you create recipes out of the ingredients you have on hand. For instance, if you look around your kitchen at 5 P.M. and find only a frozen sirloin steak, a can of pineapples, a bottle of soy sauce, and your complement of spices, would you have to run out to the store? Not with framework cooking. Thanks to the microwave's defrost button, and a little know-how, you'd have delicious marinated steak on the table within the hour.

Framework cooks learn over time what their particular staples are, but we've constructed a list to start you off.

For marinades and glazes: great taste in little time

Marinades require something acidic to penetrate and tenderize the meat. Balance that with oil and spices. With this approach and fifteen minutes, even a cheap, barely defrosted cut of beef can be made delicious (though some cuts require more time to tenderize). Glazes are sugary coatings applied to meat that seal in juices. Be careful not to let the glazed meats get too hot because the glaze will burn.

Staples: Balsamic vinegar (balsamic vinegar gets sweet when cooked), lemons or refrigerated lemon juice, canned pineapple juice, mustard (both yellow and spicy), frozen limeade or lemonade, olive oil, frozen or canned orange juice, vinegar (preferably flavored, like red wine), honey, and soy sauce.

Examples of marinades: Combine equal parts of pineapple juice and soy sauce to one-third part olive oil. Sprinkle in 1 teaspoon each, garlic, onion powder, and ginger plus a pinch of cayenne pepper.

Mix balsamic vinegar with dry mustard and honey. Brush on vegetables like eggplant, zucchini, red onion, or bell peppers. Grill or sauté. Vary proportions until you get a flavor you like.

Example of a glaze: Brush chicken with thawed limeade concentrate diluted with a squeeze of fresh lime, onion powder or other seasonings to taste, and chopped fresh cilantro. Marinate up to fifteen minutes. Bake, broil, or grill on the barbeque.

Dried herbs and spices: the easiest way to add flavor without sodium

Staples: garlic powder (not garlic salt), onion powder, cumin, coriander, cinnamon, ginger, curry powder, cayenne pepper, saffron, rosemary, chili powder, thyme, oregano, black pepper, basil, white pepper, dried parsley, bullion cubes (beef, chicken, and vegetable).

Examples of spice use: For a south-of-the-border flavor, use cumin, coriander, and chili powder. For Italian foods, use oregano, basil, and thyme. Add a dash of cinnamon to meats for a Greek-food flavor. Add ginger to soy sauce as a base for an Asian-style marinade.

Pack the pantry: keep these foods on the shelf

Beans for meals (kidney, pinto), add to soups, stews, or use for chili. **Garbanzo beans**, add to salads, blend with roasted sesame seeds (sauté raw seeds in a dry pan) and spices for quick tahini dipping sauce. **Tomato paste,**

use as the base for soups, stews, and spaghetti sauce. **Quick-cooking rice** can be a quick side dish, tossed into soups, or made with cheese, milk, spices, and chopped veggies. **Pasta in long form** (spaghetti, angel hair, etc.) can be the basis for many meals. **Pasta in noodle form** (shells, macaroni, etc.) can be used for cold pasta dishes or to add to soups, stews, etc. **Canned vegetables** (green beans, peas, corn), fresh is best, but these will add fiber and some nutrition when your veggie bin is bare. A variety of **nuts** (cashews, almonds, dry roasted peanuts), easy quick snacks, but toss them into Asian-food recipes and salads to boost nutrition and fiber. Chop and rub onto meat prior to cooking. **Favorite canned soups** (tomato, lentil, etc.), an easy meal poured over rice or pasta, with microwaved shrimp or leftover meat, add a side salad. **Hot cereal and quick-cooking oatmeal**, an easy, quick dinner (yes, dinner!) that's nutrition packed. **Quinoa**, a great alternative to rice; cooks in minutes. **Dried tortellini**, toss into soups or use with Alfredo sauce, premade or homemade. **Jarred pizza sauce**, doubles as a pasta sauce, but without all the chunky veggies that many kids dislike. **Canned chili**, pour over noodles, rice, or potatoes or add water, bouillon, and veggies for a "quickie" minestrone-type soup. **Canned tuna, salmon, and chicken** (think beyond tuna fish sandwiches), for restaurant-style salmon cakes combine canned salmon (or other meat) with an egg, some diced fresh green onions, and 2 tablespoons of parmesan cheese. Create four patties and fry in hot oil until crispy on each side. **Taco shells/tostada shells**, get creative with how you stuff them. **Tortilla chips**, a relatively healthy chip and homemade nachos topped with chili can be a quick meal.

Stock the freezer: many frozen meats and fish can be microwaved without defrosting

Ground beef and **turkey; cheese** (blocks or grated, including Parmesan, mozzarella, and cheddar, but not cream-based cheeses, like cream cheese or ricotta); **frozen white fish** (tilapia, cod, or flounder), **hamburger patties, frozen shrimp, chuck roast** (for Crock-Pots), **frozen scallops** (from frozen to cooked in one minute—toss into soups, or eat as a main dish); thin **pork chops** (they cook fast); **chicken breast, chicken tenders** (smaller portions of breast meat—expensive but fast cooking).

In the refrigerator: these items have longer shelf lives (unless noted)

Eggs and **milk** (perishable). **Yellow onions**, for all your basic onion needs. **Red onions**, give a garlicky flavor that's great. **Potatoes**, try different varieties such as new, red, Yukon, sweet, etc. (If they will be used in a relatively short period of time, potatoes and onions should ideally be stored in a cool, dark place outside of the refrigerator.) **Lettuce**, washed and ready (get a salad-spinning device) or bags of lettuce (more expensive and sometimes contain food additives). **Zucchini,** toss into all kinds of dishes; slice and top with chicken salad; cut lengthwise, scoop out the seeds, stuff with ricotta cheese topped with tomato sauce and bake. **Green onions,** when you want a lighter oniony taste. **Bell peppers**, any color but buy red and yellow in season to roast, chop, stuff with hamburger/rice mixture, or skewer for shish kebobs. **Whole baby carrots,** pricier than large ones but far tastier and require minimal prep work to use for snacks or toss in salads, soups, or stews. **Cilantro** (highly perishable), it won't last longer than a week, but is inexpensive enough to keep around to add a quick zesty flavor to soups, stews, sandwiches, marinades, Mexican dishes, Asian dishes, and more. **Whole-wheat bread** and **pita bread,** from dinner (pizza bread: top toast with pizza sauce, mozzarella cheese) to snacking, bread can't be beat. **Cheese,** particularly **cheddar, mozzarella,** and **Parmesan,** shredded or whole—if you don't mind shredding cheese in your blender, the chunk cheeses have fewer additives, and cost less. But nothing beats the convenience of preshredded cheese. **Tortillas,** from sandwich wraps to enchiladas, the most versatile bread ever invented. **Premade alfredo sauce,** more expensive than the jarred, and high in fat, but tastier—pour over tortellini, microwave some frozen shrimp and you've got a meal.

EMERGENCY GUILT-RELIEF GUIDE

TOPIC	QUICK TIP	REFERENCE CHAPTER	MOMMY GUILT-FREE PRINCIPLE NO.
Backtalking	Teach children that everyone deserves to be treated with respect. Give them the ground rules and help them learn by demonstrating politeness and by having them restate their rude comments in a polite manner.	Chapter 7	3
Blended families	Communication with all parties is critical, as is a flexible attitude.	Chapter 16	1, 5, 6, 7
Bottle-feeding	Bottles and formula were not invented just for you and your baby.	Chapter 4	2
Children's chronic illnesses and conditions	After diagnosis, give yourself time to gain your balance. Seek support from loved ones, from support groups, from healthcare professionals.	Chapter 15	1, 2, 4
Daddy time	If you want Dad to help, you must be willing to let him help his way. Do not treat him as a baby-sitter; he is the parent just as you are.	Chapter 11	1, 2, 5
Dinnertime	See Appendix B for suggestions about foods to keep on hand. Dinnertime can be great family time. Enjoy each other's	Chapter 9	1, 7

TOPIC	QUICK TIP	REFERENCE CHAPTER	MOMMY GUILT-FREE PRINCIPLE NO.
	company more and worry about what is being eaten less. Let the kids help with the cooking. (See "Teaching Your Children to Cook.")		
Discipline	Calm, consistent, and caring. When you lose control of your own behavior, you are not in a position to teach your child the behavior you want to see your child use.	Chapter 6	all
Draining relationships	Your friends and relatives should be people who sustain and nurture you over the long haul. If a relationship is almost always a burden, think through solutions, including limiting the time you give to it.	Chapter 17	1
Extracurricular activities, pushing kids	Think experience instead of performance. What kinds of experiences are you hoping your child will have with the activity? Talk with other kids and parents to find one that sparks the child's interest and if you must push, push, but leave quitting on the table.	Chapter 14	2, 3
Fairness	Fair does not mean equal. Every child is an individual and should be treated as such. What is right for one person at one time may not be right for another person (or even the same person) at another time.	Chapter 10	1, 2, 3
Homework battles	Homework is 100 percent the child's responsibility. Its purpose is to teach children responsibility and to allow them	Chapter 12	1, 3

TOPIC	QUICK TIP	REFERENCE CHAPTER	MOMMY GUILT-FREE PRINCIPLE NO.
	to practice new skills. Limit how much you help with homework. If your child grows intensely frustrated, contact the teacher to discuss the homework or get assistance with the academic subject.		
Housekeeping	As long as your home is not a health hazard, prioritize playing with your child over cleaning your house. Review the box "Sanity Keepers for Household Dirtiness Run Amok" and the chart "Kids Love to Help: A Household Responsibility Guide" in Chapter 8. Engage your children in housekeeping duties—they are members of the household and should be expected to contribute to its upkeep.	Chapter 4, Chapter 8	1, 4, 7
"How-to" calls from dad	Politely tell the dad that you know he will make a great decision and then turn your cell phone off. For anything urgent, he can call 911. For anything else, he can handle it.	Chapter 11	1
Interruption insanity	Teach your child how to politely get your attention. Use the same tools to get your child's attention. Your days will feel far less chaotic when you are free to finish your tasks, sentences, and thoughts.	Chapter 17	3
Job stress hurting home life	Improve your situation by changing something in your life like your job, your attitude, or how you divvy up your family time. You can do it!	Chapter 13	1, 3, 4, 7

TOPIC	QUICK TIP	REFERENCE CHAPTER	MOMMY GUILT-FREE PRINCIPLE NO.
Managing kids' schedules	The most important item on your child's schedule should be getting enough sleep. Prioritize that and creating reasonable schedules for your children and yourself will automatically follow.	Chapter 17	1, 2, 3
Me time	No ifs, ands, or buts. The happiest parents are the ones who are enjoying their lives. Women who engage in fulfilling hobbies are making one of the best parenting decisions they can.	Chapter 17	3, 4, 6
Minor illness and injury	A silver-lining attitude works wonders. Concentrate on how good it feels to nurture your child and remember that growing up requires a few skinned knees.	Chapter 16	3, 4, 6
Missing performances and sports matches	Truthfully, 100 percent attendance is not required. Think creatively on how to be supportive of your child when you can't attend in person. If you think you can *never* attend in person, work on ways to try a few times—you'll be surprised at how much fun it is, how good you feel, and just how possible it is to find the time, at least sometimes.	Chapter 14	1, 5, 6, 7
Mommy exhaustion	Sleeping is not avoiding your responsibilities, it is making the responsible decision to take care of yourself in order to take better care of your family. If you already have children and you are pregnant, expect to be tired	Chapter 4	1, 3

TOPIC	QUICK TIP	REFERENCE CHAPTER	MOMMY GUILT-FREE PRINCIPLE NO.
	and, if possible, get help with caring for your other children.		
Not listening	This is often selective hearing rather than misbehavior. Children have trouble focusing on more than one thing at a time. Make sure you have their complete attention. If the problem seems severe, check with your doctor.	Chapter 7	4
Oral habits: thumb, bottle, pacifier	Any habit you can break by age twelve months will be much easier to break. Bottles can be put away as soon as your child is able to drink from a sippy cup. Pacifiers should be discarded when a child starts to talk. Distractions may work well to discourage an older child from thumb sucking.	Chapter 5	3
Parallel play	Babies, toddlers, and very young children typically do not interact with others when they play. If you are concerned, talk with your pediatrician.	Chapter 16	1, 2
Parent as spectator	If you can't resist offering instructions while being a spectator, sign up to coach or direct! Otherwise, develop supportive statements you can use as a spectator that do not correct or criticize your kid or anyone else.	Chapter 14	1, 6
Picky eater	Continue to offer new foods alongside familiar ones. Don't label the child as being picky. Don't be a personal chef for your child.	Chapter 5	3

TOPIC	QUICK TIP	REFERENCE CHAPTER	MOMMY GUILT-FREE PRINCIPLE NO.
Postpartum depression	It is a medical condition. Seek help to get relief.	Chapter 4	3, 4, 6
Public behavior	Avoid situations made for disaster like bringing tired, hungry kids out in public. Let your child know what to expect. Do not expect your child to behave like an adult in public. Bring along boredom busters. Don't be too proud to politely leave a cartful of groceries in the store if your child truly needs to get out. Remember, everyone was a child before they grew up!	Chapter 7	1, 3, 4
Quitting extracurricular activities	Never take quitting off the table if a child is truly miserable. Try many alternatives to solve the problem before quitting. If quitting is the best option, teach the child how to quit gracefully by telling the adult leader him-/ herself.	Chapter 14	1, 2, 5
Resources for developmental screenings	*Ages & Stages Questionnaires* (see Appendix D under "Parenting and child development"), County Health and Human Development Department, school district Child Find programs.	Chapter 3	2
SAHM* guilt	Working mothers and stay-at-home mothers actually stress and feel guilty over many of the same issues, including the feeling that time spent working decreases time spent with children. Don't assume that you must do it all and do it all	Chapter 13	1, 2

TOPIC	QUICK TIP	REFERENCE CHAPTER	MOMMY GUILT-FREE PRINCIPLE NO.
	yourself. Ask for help with child care and housework.		
School days	You do not need to volunteer in the class on a regular basis to make an impact. Just be a familiar face around your child's school. It will keep you in touch with how your child's days are spent and with whom. It will also put you in prime position to intervene on your child's behalf when needed.	Chapter 12	all
School selection	Gather facts. Talk to other adults in the know in the area as well as kids; a good match for your child is more important than anything else, trust your gut reaction when visiting schools, too.	Chapter 12	2
Sharing	Children should be allowed to keep their special toys to themselves. If you must intervene during a play date, encourage bartering.	Chapter 16	3, 5
Sibling squabbles	Respect and kindness are the keys to resolving issues. Try to stay out of it (unless someone is in danger) and let your kids work through the problem. Make sure everyone knows the fair-fighting rules given in Chapter 10. Teaching good negotiating skills now will certainly help them deal with confrontations throughout their lives.	Chapter 10	3
Sleep problems	Make a conscious decision to put your child to sleep at the	Chapter 5	3

TOPIC	QUICK TIP	REFERENCE CHAPTER	MOMMY GUILT-FREE PRINCIPLE NO.
	same time each night. Establish a brief bedtime routine and stick to it. Avoid television right before bed. Make sure everyone in the household is aware of the plan.		
Social crisis	You created the family, let your child choose the friends. Be confident that you have enriched your child with the ability to make good choices. Remain involved in his life but let him come to you with problems, don't go seeking out problems and resolutions for him.	Chapter 12	1, 3, 5, 7
Solo parenting	Get past how you got here and concentrate on making life as smooth for yourself as you can while you are running solo. Have a plan!	Chapter 16	1, 3, 5, 6
Sports, pushing kids	Think experience instead of performance. What kinds of experiences are you hoping your child will have with sports? View a wider range of activities to get these experiences including non-sports-related teams (theater, for instance) and individual sports.	Chapter 14	2, 3
Sports, time, and cost	Evaluate your family's resources and make a judgment call as to how much of that should be used for sports. Untold alternatives exist for your child to play and learn sportsmanship.	Chapter 14	1, 2, 3

TOPIC	QUICK TIP	REFERENCE CHAPTER	MOMMY GUILT-FREE PRINCIPLE NO.
Techno baby-sitters	TV, computers, and other screens can be ideal quiet-time entertainment, but limit time spent on these activities and monitor content closely.	Chapter 16	3, 4, 5
Time with spouse	Stubbornly look for creative ways to nurture and give to this relationship. Approach the no-time problem together—between the two of you, you will find a way to enjoy each other. Treat alone time like car maintenance—never let yourself go too long or too far without regular alone-time tune-ups.	Chapter 18	All
Toilet learning	It will happen when the child is ready. There will be setbacks along the way. Be prepared with the equipment and take the whole experience in stride.	Chapter 16	1, 2, 3
Transition times	Observe how you and your family members deal with moving from one activity to the next. Create solutions that target your own and your child's transition time problems, from a place near the door for homework (and keys) to allowing extra time to avoid rushing and tantrums.	Chapter 13	3
WOHM** guilt	Working mothers and stay-at-home mothers actually stress and feel guilty over many of the same issues, including the feeling that time spent working decreases time spent with children. Do not concern yourself with other people's	Chapter 13	1, 2

TOPIC	QUICK TIP	REFERENCE CHAPTER	MOMMY GUILT-FREE PRINCIPLE NO.
	opinions on work choices. Many happy, well-adjusted children have two-parent income earners. A child's tantrum before or after you return from work may indicate difficulty with transitions, not anger at the parent.		

*Stay-at-home moms (SAHM)
**Work-outside-the-home moms (WOHM)

APPENDIX D

ADDITIONAL READING

Parenting and child development

Ames, Louise Bates, Frances L. Ilg, and Carol C. Haber. *Your One Year Old: The Fun-Loving, Fussy 12-to-24 Month Old*. New York: Dell Publishing Company, 1983.

Brazelton, T. Berry. *Touchpoints: Your Child's Emotional and Behavioral Development: Birth to 3*. Cambridge, Mass.: Perseus Publishing, 1994.

Brazelton, T. Berry, and Joshua D. Sparrow. *Touchpoints 3 to 6*. Cambridge, Mass.: Perseus Publishing, 2002.

Bricker, Diane, and Jane Squires, Linda Mounts, Lawanda Potter, Robert Nickel, Elizabeth Twombly, and Jane Farrell. *Ages & Stages Questionnaires: A Parent-Completed Child-Monitoring System*. Baltimore, Md.: Brookes Publishing Company, 1999.

Faber, Adele, and Elaine Mazlish. *Siblings Without Rivalry: How to Help Your Children Live Together So You Can Live Too*. New York: HarperCollins, 1998.

Phelan Ph.D., Thomas. *1-2-3 Magic: Effective Discipline for Children 2–12*. Glen Ellyn, Ill.: Parent Magic, Inc., 2003.

Turecki, Stanley, and Leslie Tonner. *The Difficult Child*. New York: Bantam Books, 2000.

Weissbluth, Marc. *Healthy Sleep Habits, Happy Child*. New York: Ballantine Books, 1999.

Household management

Cilley, Marla. *Sink Reflections*. New York: Bantam Books, 2002.

Kermel, Annabel. *Healthy Baby Meal Planner*. New York: Fireside, 1992.

Lansky, Vicki. *Feed Me! I'm Yours*. Minnetonka, Minn.: Meadowbrook Press, 1994.

Young, Pam. *Sidetracked Home Executives: From Pigpen to Paradise*. New York: Warner Books, 2001.

Personal development

Crittenden, Ann. *The Price of Motherhood: Why the Most Important Job in the World Is Still the Least Valued.* New York: Owl Books, 2002.

The Dalai Lama and Howard C. Cutler. *The Art of Happiness.* New York: Penguin Putnam, 1998.

Kirshenbaum, Mira. *The Gift of a Year: How to Give Yourself the Most Meaningful, Satisfying, and Pleasurable Year of Your Life.* New York: Plume Books, 2001.

Sher, Barbara, and Annie Gottlieb. *Wishcraft, How to Get What You Really Want.* New York: Ballantine Books, 2003.

Relationships

Brinkman, Rick, and Rick Kirschner. *Dealing with People You Can't Stand: How to Bring Out the Best in People at Their Worst.* New York: McGraw-Hill, 2002.

Corn, Laura. *101 Nights of Grrreat Romance.* Oklahoma City, Okla.: Park Avenue Publishers, 1996.

Fisher, Roger, William Ury, and Bruce Patton. *Getting to Yes: Negotiating Agreement Without Giving In.* New York: Penguin Books, 1991.

Weiner-Davis, Michele. *A Woman's Guide to Changing Her Man Without His Even Knowing It.* New York: Golden Books Publishing Company, 1998.

INDEX

abuse, verbal, 59–60
academic programs, selecting,
    126–127
adoption, 32–33
affection, showing, 171–172
age of children, and staying at home,
    138–139
allergies, food, 91, 160
American Pediatric Association, 31
anger, 101
apologizing to your children, 64
avoidance
    of age-inappropriate experiences, 68
    of public humiliation, 72

baby blues, 38, 224
baby(-ies)
    bathing your, 41
    and birth plan, 30–31
    bonding with, 34–35
    decision to have a, 3, 4
    at family dinner, 90
    and fights, 6
    and guilt in parents, 9
    "honeymoon" following birth of, 4
    and housework, 41–43
    nursing, 31–35
    and second-child guilt, 97–98, 219
    unscheduled playtime with, 188
babysitting, 115, 116
backtalk, 73
bad habits, breaking, 54
bathrooms, cleaning, 79
bedtime rituals, 51–52

behavior modification, 60–64
big picture, looking at the, 22–23
bins (for clutter), 79
birth plan, 30–31
blaming, 135
blended families, 165–166
bonding
    by father and child, 32–33
    between mother and child, 34–35
books, picking up, 81
boredom-busting activities, 102–103
bottle, stopping the, 52–53
brainstorming, 131–132, 134
breastfeeding, see nursing
breast milk, 32, 34
breathing, 73
bulletin boards, 129
bullying, 132–133

calm, remaining, 65, 66
caring, 65, 66
cheerleader, being your own, 141
chief household officer (CHO), 77–78
clean, keeping, 39, 41
cleaning, see housekeeping
clutter, 79
coaching, 155
cocktail hour, kiddie, 88–89
code words, 99–100
consequences, natural, 62
consistent, being, 65, 66
cooking, 88–92
    food staples for, 233–236
    getting children's help with, 89

cooking (*continued*)
  and "personal chef syndrome,"
    90–92
counseling, 107, 133
crying
  by baby, 39, 40
  by mother, 36

dads, *see* father(s)
defending your child's behavior, 135
dehumanization, 170
depression, postpartum, 38
desserts, 48
developmental concerns, 20
diapers, 168
dictatorship, parenting, 113
dinner clubs, 93
disagreements, 99
disagreements, verbal, 101
discipline, 64, 217
dishes, washing the, 79
disorganization, 142–143
doctors, 175–176

eating
  and desserts, 48
  and going to restaurants, 68
  and moderation, 48–49
  and "no thank-you-bite," 47–48
eating habits, 45–49, 87, 225
emergency guilt-relief guide, 237–246
emotions
  and fighting, 101
  following diagnosis of extraordinary
    condition, 101
enjoying children, 5
enjoying your child, 38
environment
  providing a safe, 102
  for studying, 129
equality, fairness vs., 105–106
evening transitions, 144–146
excursions, "narrating," 68
exercise, 219
exhaustion, dealing with, 36–38

extended families, 109–110
extracurricular activity(-ies), 147–156
  attending, 155–156
  benefits of, 152
  deciding whether to quit, 153–154
  handling problems with, 152–154
  and making time to eat, 92–93
  parental participation in, 154–155
  signing up for, 147–148
  sports as, 147–152
extraordinary needs, children with,
    157–162, 220
  and being a role model, 161–162
  educating others about, 160–161
  and emotions following diagnosis,
    157–158
  and finding support, 158–159
  and partnering with your child, 161

fair-fighting rules, 99–100, 118
fairness, equality vs., 105–106
family(-ies)
  balancing time between work and,
    141
  extended, 109–110
  having fun as a, 28–29
family-oriented restaurants, 68
family responsibilities, 105–106
fast food, 95–96
father(s)
  delegation of childcare responsibili-
    ties to, 112
  frustration in, 117–119
  and giving space for father-child re-
    lationship, 113–116
  guilt in, 7, 116–117
  and nursing, 32–33
  presenting a united front with, 118
favoritism, 106–107
fighting, 98–103, 217–218
  and anger, 101
  arguing vs., 99
  and mediation, 101–102
  and the new baby, 6
  preventing, 102–103

and role of parent, 101
rules of fair, 99–100, 118
and sibling rivalry, 100–101
and 3Cs, 66
underlying causes of, 103
food allergies, 91, 160
food grinder, baby, 90
food staples, 233–236
formula, 33
freezing meals, 93–94
friendships, 130–132
frozen prepackaged foods, 96
frustration
and fighting, 101
with work, 139–141
fun, having, 28–29
future
looking forward to the, 22–23
not living in the, 23–25

"getting ready" routine, 144
grandparents, 108–109, 224
grocery shopping, 70, 233–236
guilt
definition of, 5
emergency relief of, 237–246
in fathers, 7, 116–117
sources of, 7
tuning in to, 9, 11–16
as valid emotion, 8
see also Mommy Guilt survey

habits, breaking bad, 54
happy, being, 23
hearing, selective, 74–76
here-and-now, living in the, 23–25
hobbies, 23
holidays, 225
home offices, 137
homework, 128–130
finishing, 144
and television, 174
honeymoon (following birth of
baby), 4
hormones, 36

housekeeping, 18–20, 77–86
children's role in, 80–84
creating a realistic schedule for,
79–80
fairness in, 105–106
getting help with, 42–43
interacting with children vs., 77–78
and newborns, 41–42
responsibility for, 77
tips for, 79, 218
and your management style, 84–86
humiliation, avoiding public, 72
humor, sense of, 27
husbands, see father(s)

illness, 103, 174–176
see also extraordinary needs, children with
incentives, 62–64
infants, see baby(-ies)
injuries, 174–176
interruptions, handling, 189–190
irritability, 103
"I" statements, 99

job, see work
joint activities, 104, 107
jokes, telling, 27
junk food, 70, 71

kiddie cocktail hour, 88–89

Lamaze, 73
laughing a lot, especially with your
children (Mommy Guilt-Free
Principle No. 6), 27–28, 195–196
and age-appropriate experiences, 68
and children with extraordinary
needs, 161
and positive reinforcement, 61–62
and spending time with your child,
107
and volunteering at school, 127
laughter, 217
leftovers, 93–94

letting go of things (Mommy Guilt-Free Principle No. 1), 17–20, 192
and housekeeping, 79, 81
and nursing, 33
and solo parenting, 165
linear thinking, multitask vs., 111–112
living in the moment and not in the future (Mommy Guilt-Free Principle No. 4), 23–25, 194
and children with extraordinary needs, 158
and cooking, 88
and injuries, 175
and rest, 36–37
and spending time with your child, 104, 107
looking toward the future and at the big picture (Mommy Guilt-Free Principle No. 3), 22–23, 193–194
and age-appropriate experiences, 68
and blended families, 166
and housekeeping, 84
and mediation of fights, 101
and positive reinforcement, 61
and taking care of yourself, 182
losing patience, 60

male lactation, 33
management style, evaluating your, 84–86
marathoners, 37
marriage, 218
mastitis, 32
meals, 46, 87–96
and extracurricular activities, 92–93
fast-food and take-out, 95–96
freezing leftover, 93–94
getting children's help with, 89, 92
and "personal chef syndrome," 90–92
prepackaged items at, 96
preparing, 88–89
quick, 94–95
snacks as, 95
mediation (of fights), 101–102

middle-school-age children
and cooking, 89
guilt in parents of, 10
and housekeeping, 83
unscheduled playtime for, 188
mistakes, making, 64
modeling behavior, 161–162, 181–182
moment, living in the, 23–25
Mommy Guilt-Free Principles, 17–29
No. 1, see letting go of things
No. 2, see parenting is not a competitive sport
No. 3, see looking toward the future and at the big picture
No. 4, see living in the moment and not in the future
No. 5, see saying yes more often and defending your no
No. 6, see laughing a lot, especially with your children
No. 7, see setting aside time to have fun as a family
Mommy Guilt survey, 201–231
insights from respondents to, 215–231
questions in, 201–206
results of, 207–215
money
and deciding whether to work, 138
spending, on each child, 105
morning transitions, 143–144
Mothers & More, 43
movies, going to the, 69
multitask thinking, linear vs., 111–112

name-calling, 99
"narrating," 68, 70
The National Association of Mother's Centers, 43
National Sleep Foundation (NSF), 49
natural consequences, 62
negative reinforcement, 64
newborns, see baby(-ies)
no, saying, 25–27, 221
non-parenting activities, engaging in, 22–23

"no-thank-you-bite," 47–48
NSF (National Sleep Foundation), 49
nursing, 6, 31–35
    and adoption, 32–33
    alternatives to, 33–34

open-enrollment laws, 121
oral habits, 52–54
overeating, 47

pacifiers, 53
pampering yourself, 181
parenting dictatorship, 113
parenting is not a competitive sport
        (Mommy Guilt-Free Principle
        No. 2), 20–22, 192–193
    and apologizing, 64
    and children with extraordinary
        needs, 159
    and enjoying your child, 38
    and extracurricular activities,
        147–148
    and toilet learning, 167
parent-teacher association (PTA), 127
peer problems, 131–135
personal chef syndrome, 90–92
physical contact, decrease in, 170–172
picky eaters, 90–91
play dates, 168–170
playground, child's behavior on, 132
playtime, unscheduled, 188
portion sizes, 47
positive reinforcement, 61–62
postpartum depression, 38
praise, 61–62, 74
preferential treatment, 106–107
prepackaged foods, 96
preschoolers
    and cooking, 89
    guilt in parents of, 10
    and housekeeping, 82
"preshopping narration," 70
pretending, 69
priorities, making, 18, 140, 190
private schools, 121

PTA (parent-teacher association), 127
public behavior, 67–73
public humiliation, avoiding, 72
pumping breast milk, 34
punishment (negative reinforcement),
        64
putting things away, 80–81, 83

quick-cooking dinners, 94–95
quiet-time activities, 173

reading with your child, 217
reinforcement
    negative, 64
    positive, 61–62
respect, showing, 65, 73–74
responsibility(-ies)
    delegation of childcare, 112
    family, 105–107
    for homework, 128–129
rest, need for, 36, 37, 216
restaurants, 68
rewards (reward systems), 54, 62–64
role model, being a, 161–162
role-playing, 134
rudeness, 73

safety, 18, 25
    and cleaning, 80
    and environment, 102
    and negative reinforcement, 64
SAHMs, see stay-at-home moms
sandwiches, freezing, 94
saying yes more often and defending
        your no (Mommy Guilt-Free
        Principle No. 5), 25–27, 95, 195
    and grocery shopping, 70
    and housekeeping, 84
    and nutritional choices, 95
    and spending time with your child,
        104
schedules, children's, 187
school
    choosing a, 120–126
    handling behavior problems at, 135

school (*continued*)
　and homework, 128–130
　selecting academic programs in,
　　126–127
　and social crises, 130–134
　volunteering at, 127
　see also extracurricular activity(-ies)
school-age children
　and cooking, 89
　guilt in parents of, 10
　and housekeeping, 82–83
　unscheduled playtime for, 188
school supplies, 129
screaming, *see* yelling
second-child guilt, 97–98, 219, 224
selective hearing, 74–76
self, 180
setting aside time to have fun as a fam-
　ily (Mommy Guilt-Free Principle
　No. 7), 28–29, 196–198
　and children with extraordinary
　　needs, 161
　and fighting, 98–99
　and work, 140
sharing, 168–169
showers, taking, 39, 41
sibling rivalry, 97–98, 100–101
siblings, 103–105, 225
sickness, *see* illness
silly, being, 217
singing, 217
sleep, getting enough, 35–38, 49, 103
sleeping habits, 45, 49–52
　and bedtime rituals, 51–52
　and parents' bed, 49–51
snacks, 70, 95
social crises, dealing with, 130–134
solo parenting, 163–165, 219–220
special-needs children, *see* extraordi-
　nary needs, children with
spoiling yourself, 5
sport(s), 147–152, 220–221
　beginning a, 149–150
　individual, 151
　signing your child up for, 148–149

sports camps, 148
sports leagues, 150–151
stay-at-home moms (SAHMs), 136
　and age of children, 138–139
　evening transitions for, 146
　guilt in, 137, 140
stepping-stone approach to age-appro-
　priate experiences, 68–69
stickers, 54, 63
stress, handling, 221
study style, 129
supermoms, 6
support groups, 158–159
"surface clean," 79, 80
survey, *see* Mommy Guilt survey
sweets, 48–49

take-out food, 95–96
taking care of yourself, 180–187,
　218–219
tantrums, in public places, 70–73
technology, 170
television, 144, 170, 172–174
"ten-minutes-first" rule, 79
3Cs, 64–66
thumb sucking, 53–54
time, 179–190, 226–227
　and children's schedules, 187
　with each of your children, 103–105
　for having fun as a family, 28–29
　for having meals, 92–93
　for housework, 78, 79
　and interruptions, 189–190
　"orchestrating" father-child,
　　113–114
　and other priorities, 190
　for taking care of yourself, 180–187,
　　218–219
　and 3Cs, 65–66
　unscheduled, 188
　with your spouse, 191–198
time-management skills, improving
　your, 141
toddlers
　and cooking, 89

guilt in parents of, 10
and housekeeping, 78, 82
and new baby, 98
play dates for, 168–170
portion sizes for, 47
and toilet learning, 166–168
unscheduled playtime with, 188
toilet learning, 166–168
toys
and play dates, 169–170
putting away, 80–81
training pants, 168
transition times, 142–146
evening, 144–146
morning, 143–144
observing your child's behavior during, 142–143
television during, 174
traveling with children, 221
tuning in to guilt, 9, 11–16

united front, presenting a, 118, 218
unscheduled playtime, 188
urgent situations, 189

vacuuming, 80
vacuum sealing, 93
venue, behavioral rules of, 69
verbal abuse, 59–60

verbal disagreements, 101
volunteering at school, 127

Waving Game, 217
weekends away, mother-child, 104
whistles, 76
Wife Guilt-Free Principles, 191–196
WOHMs, *see* work-outside-the-home
moms
work, 136–146
and age of children, 138–139
changing your attitude toward,
140–141
frustration with, 139–141
and nursing, 34
and quitting your job, 141
as source of guilt, 137–138
tips for dealing with, 221–222
and transition times, 142–146
work-outside-the-home moms
(WOHMs), 136
evening transitions for, 144–146
guilt in, 137

yelling, 59–60
as prime cause of guilt, 17–18
as punishment, 64
and selective hearing, 75
during transition times, 144
yes, saying, 25–27, 195

ABOUT THE AUTHORS

Julie Bort is an educator, journalist, and author who has published hundreds of articles and columns in a dozen countries and currently works as Executive Editor, Signature Series, for *Network World*, a national weekly news magazine for the computer industry.

Mommy Guilt is Bort's second book. In addition to writing, Bort is also an established speaker, seminar instructor, and teacher of online classes on a range of topics. She has appeared as a guest on live and taped radio, including National Public Radio and various talk-show programs.

As part of her duties for *Network World,* Bort frequently conducts nationwide editorial surveys, and she has put this expertise to use for *Mommy Guilt.* She has created and conducted original research in the form of a survey that examines guilt in association with parenting.

Bort's parenting experience includes caring for a child with the lifelong condition celiac disease. She is a happily married wife of fifteen years and the mother of two daughters, ages 12 and 10. Bort has a degree in English Education from Arizona State University, Tempe, Arizona.

For more information about Bort including a list of her upcoming seminars, please visit www.mommy-guilt.com.

Aviva Pflock founded the Berthoud/Loveland, Colorado, chapter of Parents As Teachers in 1998 (PAT is an international early childhood parent-education and family-support program.) Pflock has served PAT as a certified parent-education and child-development specialist, grant writer, and administrator.

Pflock received her Parent Educator certification from PAT in 1996. Since that time, she has provided home visits, facilitated playgroups, and spoken at PAT parent-education programs. She was a preschool teacher at Har Shalom Preschool in Ft. Collins, Colorado from its inception in 1997 until the birth of her third child in 2000. In this role, she helped establish the school's foundation as well as taught in the classroom. She has served on the board of the Loveland/Berthoud Early Childhood Interagency Network, of which she is still a member. She is also a member of the Larimer County Early Childhood Council and part of their Infant/Toddler focus group. She is invited to speak at local parenting seminars on a variety of early childhood topics.

Pflock has worked directly with families as a PAT "home visitor" specializing in the prenatal to five-year-old age group. She has also served as a PAT playgroup facilitator and a regular speaker representing PAT as well as speaking at PAT programs. Pflock has been featured in the *Reporter-Herald* on several occasions for her involvement with PAT as well as other early childhood programs in her community.

Pflock is also a trained presenter for Colorado Bright Beginnings: Maximizing Colorado's Brain Power, and Early Childhood Building Blocks to the Colorado Content Standards. Other speaking credits include conducting lectures at the Kid's Expo in Loveland, Colorado, as well as involvement as a scriptwriter, stage director, and performer with the Loveland Choral Society.

Pflock has a BA in Adolescent Behavior and Sexuality from the University of Colorado at Boulder. She currently lives in Loveland with her husband, Kurt, and their three children: two daughters, Lexi (age 12) and Arianna (age 10); and a son, Travis (age 4).

Devra Renner, MSW, is a master's level social worker with over a decade of experience helping parents, children, and families. She has worked as a clinical social worker in hospital, school, and summer camp settings. Renner completed social work internships in the Obstetrics and Pediatric units of Louisiana State University Medical Center and the Barksdale Air Force Base offices of the Family Advocacy Program and Mental Health Clinic. During the course of her internship, Renner facilitated a support group for parents of special needs children. After earning an MSW, Renner worked for the Bossier Parish School Board's INSITE Program providing individual, group, and family therapy in the school, home, and community settings to students ranging from prekindergarten to high school. Additionally, Renner worked in a physical rehabilitation hospital providing social work services to adult and pediatric patients and their families. Renner has also served as the Acting Director of Volunteer Services for Hospice Inc. in Wichita, Kansas. Renner volunteered her professional expertise for six years as a crisis counselor for the Kansas Children's Service League Parent Helpline, giving parenting advice and support to callers in crisis situations. Most recently Renner worked for the Jewish Community Center in St. Louis where she was the Assistant Director of the Saint Louis Council of the B'nai B'rith Youth Organization (BBYO), and for two summers Renner also served the Jewish Community Center of St. Louis as the social worker in residence at Camp Sabra, Lake of the Ozarks, where she provided training for camp staff in addition to providing social work services to staff, campers, and their families.

Renner is past President of the Wichita Kansas Chapter of Jewish Women International and a former coordinator of the chapter's Humor Cart Project, for which she was interviewed in print and television media. Renner currently serves as a Chapter Liaison for Jewish Women International and is a Life Member of that organization. Renner has served two terms on the board of directors for the Mid Kansas Jewish Federation and has also volunteered for the Federation as a case manager. Renner also volunteered her time to serve as a youth-group adviser for BBYO in Wichita, Kansas.

Renner's speaking credits include conducting parenting classes for the Bossier Parish School Board as well as for local chapters of Mothers & More in Kansas, Illinois, and Virginia. Renner, who is also a member of Mothers & More, has served on the National On-line Committee helping to connect chapter members nationally through the Internet. Renner has served on the chapter boards of Mothers & More in Kansas, Illinois, and Virginia. Renner has also been an online Chat Host for iVillage.com's Parent Soup, hosting parenting chats. Renner is a Life Member of Hadassah and is also a member of the National Association of Mothers' Centers as well as the National Association of Social Workers.

Renner earned a BA in Cultural Anthropology minoring in Sociology from the University of Arizona, Tucson, and a Masters Degree in Social Work with a concentration in Health and Mental Health from Grambling State University, Grambling, Louisiana. Renner lives in Virginia with her husband Pete and their sons Mitchell (age 9) and Joshua (age 4).